MW00651141

THE STATE OF
AMERICAN POLICING

THE STATE OF
AMERICAN POLICING

Psychology, Behavior, Problems, and Solutions

David J. Thomas, PhD, LMHC
Foreword by Jim Bueermann

Forensic Psychology
David J. Thomas, Series Editor

 PRAEGER™

An Imprint of ABC-CLIO, LLC
Santa Barbara, California • Denver, Colorado

Library of Congress Cataloging-in-Publication Data

Names: Thomas, David J. (David Jonathan), author.
Title: The state of American policing : psychology, behavior, problems, and
    solutions / David J. Thomas, PhD, LMHC ; foreword by Jim Bueermann.
Description: Santa Barbara, California : Praeger, [2019] | Series: Forensic
    psychology | Includes index.
Identifiers: LCCN 2018030307 (print) | LCCN 2018033312 (ebook) | ISBN
    9781440860072 (ebook) | ISBN 9781440860065 (print : alk. paper)
Subjects: LCSH: Police—United States. | Police administration—United States.
Classification: LCC HV8139 (ebook) | LCC HV8139 .T46 2019 (print) |
    DDC 363.201/9—dc23
LC record available at https://lccn.loc.gov/2018030307

ISBN: 978-1-4408-6006-5 (print)
       978-1-4408-6007-2 (ebook)

23 22 21 20 19   1 2 3 4 5

This book is also available as an eBook.

Praeger
An Imprint of ABC-CLIO, LLC

ABC-CLIO, LLC
130 Cremona Drive, P.O. Box 1911
Santa Barbara, California 93116-1911
www.abc-clio.com

This book is printed on acid-free paper ∞

Manufactured in the United States of America

This book is dedicated to the old timers at the Grand Rapids Police Department, Grand Rapids, Michigan, who taught me how to be the real police. My first training officers were White males, Jim Dingman and Dave Stephan who started their careers in 1958, when I was two years old. I started my career, when I was 22 years old with a degree in psychology. Dingman and Stephan had degrees in people and understood human nature, better than any psychologist. It was never about race; it was about people and their needs. Finally, I dedicate this book to the minority communities, my community, and those who have endured years of mistreatment by police. My hope is that both can find a common ground, stop the rhetoric, and learn to work together.

Contents

Series Foreword

I start every course that I teach in forensic psychology by asking my students to define the term forensic psychology. Technically forensic psychology is defined as the research and application of psychological knowledge to the legal system. Television depicts forensic psychologists as profilers working for the FBI and hunting serial offenders, pitting the profilers' knowledge against the wits of the criminal. The reality is that this opportunity is limited to a select few. However, when I examine the field, it is one that is truly diverse and includes specialties where clinicians offer their expertise in such areas as competency to stand trial, police psychology, criminal behavior, criminal responsibility, eyewitness testimony/credibility, victimology, trauma, terrorism, child custody, worker compensation cases, personal injury cases, and cases involving the handicap.

The aforementioned list is far from exhaustive; rather it is a fair representation of the diversity in the field and its many opportunities. It should also be clear that no one specialty is stand-alone, meaning that other fields interact and have an impact on the clinician's findings. One could not make a judgment of criminal behavior or insanity based on an interview and the administration of an assessment instrument. I would compare the role of a clinician to that of a criminal investigator. A criminal investigator must examine the totality of the circumstances before charges can be filed in court. In comparison a clinician must complete a thorough assessment of one's psychological, biological, and environmental histories, which is the totality of an offender/

client's mental health. There is one caveat when dealing with assessments and that is the clinician must be constantly aware of an offender/client's attempts to malinger and manipulate the outcomes to benefit themselves.

This is an exciting time in the field of forensic psychology because of its diversity and the state of the world. We struggle to understand acts of terrorism, school shootings, bullying, murder within families, and the aftermath of such incidents. As series editor, I challenge you to take what you learn from our series and use it as a catalyst for social change.

David J. Thomas, PhD, LMHC
Series Editor

Foreword

What is the role of police in American society? Dr. David Thomas poses this persistent question in the opening of this book. It has been defining for most practitioners, policymakers, and community members in the important discussions about controlling crime and disorder in America. Any talk of how to reduce crime invariably begins with policing—even though research has long proven that crime is best controlled through a holistic approach that incorporates prevention, intervention, *and* suppression strategies. It is clear that, as the primary actor in local government assigned with the responsibility of dealing with crime, the police have a role in controlling crime and the collateral consequences of doing so.

The perception of American policing has evolved, as policing itself has, over time. For much of its history, the police have been viewed by many as the strong-arm agents of the power elite, essentially corrupt and heavy-handed, ensuring the nonprivileged were kept in their place and the power dynamics maintained through the enforcement of the law. In the 20th century, in many communities—especially suburban or rural ones—people began viewing the police as the friendly enforcer of community norms and statutes. With the advent of "community policing" many saw them—as did the police themselves—as community "brokers" of peace and solutions to crime, disorder, and social ailments.

Where one stands largely determines what one sees. For many Americans, the police have not really evolved. They have simply changed the manner in which they abuse the underprivileged. People of color who have been abused by the police, know someone who has been abused, or witnessed police abuse—all in front of the historic backdrop of police involvement in civil rights violations—are likely to believe that the police do not treat them, or people like them, in a fair and equitable manner. This is irrespective of the fact that we are well into the allegedly "evolved and informed" 21st century. These feelings have been consistently reflected in polling, which highlights the differences in perceptions about the police held by varying ethnic groups.

Therefore, given the complicated environment in which policing is now carried out, what are the police, policymakers, and the community members the police are paid to protect supposed to do about the problematic issues they all confront? How are the police to carry out their duties when they are receiving the seemingly contradictory messages of their role in society—be proactive in your crime suppression activities versus engage the community, collaboratively solve problems, and de-escalate potentially violent situations.

Today, whether they like it or not, receive adequate training or not, or have adequate resources to do what they are asked to, the police find themselves at the center of a diverse and contentious set of discussions and debates about issues such as mental illness, homelessness, drug addiction, adolescent problem prevention, racial and class bias, privilege, and social and criminal justice. The abdication by elected officials of their responsibilities to solve these knotty social problems, coupled with policing's inherent bias for action, results in the police being the first responders to these issues irrespective of logic and common sense that dictate professionals with proper training and resources should handle these issues.

Policing is a complicated business. It is frequently messy, with no clear "one right way" of handling things. The process of "serving and protecting" America's communities requires police officers to jump from a guardian mentally to a warrior posture, and back again, with amazing alacrity. Our laws give police officers the distinction of being the only governmental employees who, without prior judicial review, have the authority to restrict the freedom and use justified force—including deadly force—against the same people they are paid to protect. At its best, policing is a noble undertaking, full of heroic instances of bravery and valor. At its most challenging moments, its leaders must respond to claims of abuse of power and an unbridled use of force.

In *The State of American Policing: Psychology, Behavior, Problems, and Solutions,* David Thomas has presented a comprehensive, and candid, view of the complicated nature of policing to help anyone interested in understanding modern-day policing to know how we arrived at today's police-community landscape.

Through his presentation of the history, culture, and psychology of policing, Thomas provides the reader with a framework within which contemporary policing issues can be better understood. His discussion of police decision-making, use of force, and militarization will assist in unpacking the more technical parts of policing. His exploration of "21st-century policing," and many of the most likely future issues in policing, provides a road map that practitioners can follow, policymakers can mandate, and community members can demand. And finally, his commentary on how all of us can advance democratic policing by stopping the shouting and starting the listening is sage advice we would all be well advised to pay attention to.

The call from some to completely eliminate policing in some communities notwithstanding, the police are here to stay. They are, in my opinion, the only thing that stands between law-abiding community members and the sociopathic predators that make up the absolute worst of our society's criminal element. Acting as society's guardians in this manner is a legitimate—in fact a noble—service to those most unable to protect themselves. However, this legitimate function in our communities loses its credibility when policing is carried out in an officious, biased, or abusive manner. Rightful, democratic policing is the result of a collaborative process and yields "co-produced" public safety (the police and the community working together). It reflects community values and treats everyone with dignity and respect. And it keeps the peace and enforces the law in a procedurally just way.

The police don't "own" policing. Communities, and the taxpayers they are comprised of, hold the ownership certificates of their police departments—whether they realize it or not. It is incumbent on all of us to facilitate, ask for, perhaps demand, the thoughtful, value-based advance of rightful, equitable policing. This requires we better understand contemporary policing. To this end, David Thomas's book gives us the information we need to be better, more responsive consumers of policing in America.

Jim Bueermann (Ret. Chief)
President, National Police Foundation
Washington, D.C.
May 30, 2018

1

History and Oppressive Police Practices against Minorities

What is the role of police in American society? Is it serving as protectors of people and defenders of citizens' civil rights? Does the police role include partnering with communities that they serve? The logical answers are a resounding "yes." Therefore, why do minority communities feel left out of those positive parts of the police equation?

Dating back to slavery and the slave patrols, law enforcement in one form or another has been viewed as an oppressor by the African American community. The stories of police abuse have been handed down from generation to generation in the African American community, and it is coupled with the fact that many African Americans have felt violated in one form or another by police today. Rooney (2010) argues: "White people living in America now are not responsible for slavery and the injustices associated with slavery. This happened before this generation was born and for anyone to dwell on the past only fuels resentment" (p. 13). Rooney's argument would have merit if African Americans were not reminded through personal experiences/contact, the media, and social media posts of police actions showing that some officers in the United States still act as if Blacks here have no rights. Depending on their location in this nation, some African Americans see police as an occupying army in their community. Conversely, I have seen social media posts where police officers argue that the "kinder, gentler police are nothing more than social workers."

Historically, American policing has not been the most desirable of professions. It has been associated with corruption, political influence, racism, ineffectiveness, abuse of civil rights, and brutality. In fact, the nature of these incidents is deeply ingrained in the psyche of many Americans, specifically the poor, the disenfranchised, and those who live in minority communities. The impact of negative police behaviors is associated with the psychology of oppression, which may or may not be the intention of those who police. This chapter examines the evolving history of American policing and its psychology and the psychology of oppression.

PURPOSE OF POLICE IN THE UNITED STATES

In 1844, New York City established the first uniformed police department in the United States. An article in the *New York Times* on January 27, 1895, outlines the evolution of the police department, dating back to the 1600s, with the first forerunner to police officers being called a *schout*. The schout never made an arrest but recommended punishment to the *burgomaster*, who was considered the mayor or chief magistrate. Beginning in 1665, the system made several changes from what is known as the "ancient Charlies," "leatherheads," and "marshals," who preceded what later became the New York City Police Department.

From an outside observer's standpoint, it would be logical to argue that a host of serious crimes were the catalyst for the growth of urban policing in the United States. New York, San Francisco, and Boston were central points drawing large numbers of immigrants from European countries in pursuit of the American Dream. Often, what new immigrants found instead of opportunity were deplorable living conditions and poverty, so many either turned to crime or became victims of crime. This problem was compounded by the large number of Blacks who began to migrate from the south then, vying for the same opportunities as the European immigrants. This apparently triggered the development of American policing.

Monkkonen (1981) offers two hypotheses in relationship to explain that emergence. One theory is that the growth of American policing was in response to a rise in crime and civil disorder. The other is that the growth of policing was in response to the need of the elite in American society for police to act as a buffer between them and what he describes as the "dangerous" class. The dangerous class is defined as the faceless in U.S. society— the paupers, tramps, and criminals—and is comprised of five groups: urban criminals, rural criminals, rural paupers, urban paupers, and tramps (p. 87). Smaller cities did not have the problems of New York or Boston, yet they created uniformed police departments. The argument is that the police uniform became the symbol of social control and order for local governments, and that is why these smaller cities opted to establish police departments (Greene, 1996; Maguire & Radosh, 1996).

But who was in control of the police, why, and to what end was not always such a laudable matter. Policing in its early origins was influenced by the rule of politics and corrupted by the local political leadership. One example is the history and influence of Tammany Hall politics, the New York City "political machine" that always had a certain number of police jobs in exchange for political favors. Even in 1936, August Vollmer, who began in 1905 as a California town marshal, was later police chief, and is considered the father of American policing, recognized that reform was almost nonexistent except for large police departments that had the capability to provide training. He was outspoken about the lack of professionalism and the corruption in policing. Vollmer (1971) argued that the poor quality of personnel was the weakest link in American policing and described political influence as a burden (pp. 4–6).

MODERN AMERICAN POLICE SCANDALS

Germann, Day, and Galatti (1976) describe 300 years of policing prior to 1978 as "operations that have ranged from the most sordid to the most splendid, and with practitioners whose capacity and character have spanned a continuum from the most incompetent and corrupt to the most brilliant and edifying" (p. 74).

The observations of Germann et al. (1976) and Vollmer (1971) in regard to professionalism help us to understand that policing does not happen in a vacuum, nor is it independent of society. In fact, it is just the opposite: What has happened in America across history culturally has had a direct impact on the profession of policing. The history of modern policing may best be examined by considering a host of commissions that have demanded change.

- *Kerner Commission, 1967*

The 1960s in the United States was a time of social change on all fronts. The generation we now know as baby boomers was on college campuses opposing the Vietnam War; other elements included the hippie generation, draft dodgers, and the counterculture. Some were members of groups like the Students for a Democratic Society, which initially promoted civil rights, voting rights, and urban reform, although they were most noted for their opposition to the Vietnam War. Students marched on college campuses, burned their draft cards, and participated in peaceful protests such as sit-ins; in some cases, groups such as the volatile Weather Underground participated in acts of terrorism. Finally, illegal drugs such as marijuana, LSD, and heroin were introduced to college campuses. The theme of the day was "Make Love, Not War!" (Barber, 2008; Leen, 1999).

The antiwar protests of the 1960s were marked by years of civil disobedience and many clashes with the police. One of the most violent clashes with police was during the 1968 Democratic Convention in Chicago. There were five days of riots, with protesters attempting to march to the convention. Rioters and innocent bystanders alike were beaten by police, an action televised around the world (Kush, 2004; Walker, 1968). The most haunting clash of that period was the shootings at Kent State University in 1970. Kent State College students were peacefully protesting the Vietnam War, more specifically the U.S. bombing of Cambodia. In response to the protests, the Ohio National Guard was sent to Kent State for crowd control. Instead of crowd control, Ohio National Guardsmen opened fire on the protesters, killing four unarmed students (Hensley, 1981; Rosinsky, 2008).

In the south, the civil rights movement was beginning. The movement officially began with the landmark decision in *Brown v. Board of Education of Topeka, Kansas,* in 1954, and a number of significant events during the years that followed forced the issue of equality: 1955, Rosa Parks refused to move to the back of the bus; 1957, Central High School in Little Rock, Arkansas, was integrated; 1960, in Greensborough, North Carolina, four Black students peacefully staged a sit-in at the local Woolworths lunch counter; 1963, in Birmingham, Alabama, police turned fire hoses and police dogs loose on peaceful protesters; 1963, at the March on Washington, Martin Luther King delivered his "I Have a Dream" speech; 1964, the Civil Rights Act was signed by President Lyndon Johnson; 1965, the Voting Rights Act was passed by Congress; 1965, the Watts race riots took place in Los Angeles, California; and in 1965, President Johnson signed Executive Order 1146, which was the beginning of affirmative action (Bullard & Bond, 1994; Dierenfield, 2008).

Each of the movements, although independent, moved in parallel ways, and they often supported one another. The media played a significant role in bringing these events to our living rooms. The Vietnam War was the lead story at 6:00 P.M., offering daily body counts of both the enemy and Americans. The civil rights movement also played out in the media. Although the protesters and leaders were usually peaceful and had taken a vow of nonviolence, their oppressors used violence as a tactic of fear to maintain control. There were bombings, assassinations, murders, and hangings—all of which were played out in the media for the world to see.

The 1960s was a time of turmoil in the United States. And the protectors of the day, as they are expected to be today, were the police. But all of America viewed police action associated with beating students with batons, the use of tear gas to disperse protesters, and the use of police dogs and fire hoses on civil rights protesters. The bottom line is that police action was less than professional, and often the police used excessive force. It is because of this that the police came to be seen as oppressors of the disenfranchised and as protectors of the "haves" in American society.

The Kerner Commission was established by President Lyndon B. Johnson in 1967 to examine the causes of the inner-city riots, the two most violent of which were in Detroit and Newark. The commission was tasked with answering the questions: What happened? Why did the riots happen? And what could be done to prevent them in the future?

The commission created a hierarchy of common complaints. There were a total of 12 types of complaints, with each being assigned to one of the three different levels of intensity. Police practices were the number one complaint and assigned to the first level of intensity.

The commission noted: "The abrasive relationship between the police and the minority communities has been a major—and explosive—source of grievance, tension and disorder. The blame must be shared by the total society" (Kerner Commission, 1968, p. 14). The real causes of the tension were the demands on police service due to increased crime rates and aggressive patrol practices and that the police did not provide an avenue or mechanism whereby community grievances could be heard regarding poor police practices.

A summary of the commission's findings included a detailed review of police operations; recommendations to eliminate the sense of insecurity in minority communities; instituting a series of mechanisms for community members to air their grievances against local police; developing policies to assist officers in decision-making; recruiting more Negro officers and promoting them accordingly; and developing a "Community Service Officer Program" to attract Negroes to the profession of policing (Kerner Commission, 1968, p. 15). The commission's recommendations are important because these issues, as well as others, seem central to the lack of professionalism that dates back to the beginning of the profession.

• *Counterintelligence Program (COINTELPRO), 1956–1971*

The FBI's COINTELPRO Program was charged with targeting foreign intelligence agencies operating in the United States during the Cold War. However, the mission changed in the 1960s, and the FBI became the political police in the United States. The FBI mounted counterintelligence programs to disrupt, misdirect, discredit, or otherwise neutralize the civil rights movement, Black liberation, Puerto Rican independence, antiwar, and student movements of the 1960s (Churchill and Vander Wall, 2002, p. x). Churchill and Vander Wall (2002) provide the actual letter sent by the FBI in 1964, suggesting that Dr. Martin Luther King Jr. commit suicide (p. 99). The FBI also forged letters to activists and their supporters in an attempt to destroy the activists' credibility and sway their followers. The FBI-authored articles were published in friendly media, and the media protected the FBI by taking credit for the propaganda and cartoon leaflets, which oftentimes pitted one group against another (p. xi).

Today, Generations X and Y may wonder why baby boomers are leery of the Patriot Act, which gives law enforcement unfettered access to personal records, allows wiretapping without warrants, and gives police the ability to declare individuals an *enemy combatant of the state* and place them in jail without due process. It is because of the aforementioned incidents that people are leery. The FBI in more modern times has been a strong organization with a reputation for being professional and above reproach, but conduct such as this has made many average Americans question the role of the FBI as well as its professionalism.

- *Law Enforcement Assistance Administration (LEAA), 1968*

In response to the Kerner Commission's findings, the Law Enforcement Assistance Administration (LEAA) was formed. The LEAA was funded due to the passage of the Omnibus Crime Control Act of 1968. The latter legislation was designed to assist local law enforcement in training and education and most importantly established rules limiting police authority, to prevent abuses by use of discrimination, among other actions. The goal of the LEAA was to professionalize policing by offering monies for college education, advanced law enforcement training for local officers, and the development of specialized skill sets. In addition to funding for police, funding was set aside to address other problems the Criminal Justice System was experiencing, such as programs to study alternatives to incarceration, drug treatment programs, and state court organization. The LEAA was disbanded in 1981 and is considered the forerunner to the National Institute of Justice.

- *Knapp Commission Report on Police Corruption (Knapp Commission), 1970*

The Knapp Commission was established by Mayor John Lindsay to investigate corruption within the New York City Police Department (NYPD). The commission was established in response to a 1970s' *New York Times* article that detailed widespread corruption within the NYPD. The article, "Graft Paid to Police Here Said to Run into the Millions," presented a survey in which officers spoke to the *Times* with complete anonymity and provided chilling accounts of corrupt practices. Burnham (1970) provided examples of officers paying to work good patrol zones on Sunday, and how businesspeople and criminals paid police officers to look the other way while businesses and criminals participated in illegal activity. Those who had paid the police included builders, numbers operators, and liquor dealers; the monies paid totaled millions (pp. 1, 18).

On completion of a two-and-a-half-year investigation, the commission determined that corruption within the agency was widespread. The commission described two types of officers involved: *meat-eaters* and *grass-eaters*. Meat-eaters were officers who took large sums of money without hesitation and pushed for those big dollars. Grass-eaters were more prevalent and were also considered a scourge of the department. Grass-eaters were officers who would took small amounts of money all the time. The commission noted that the grass-eaters made corruption "respectable" (Knapp Commission, 1972, p. 4). The commission also noted that such conduct destroys public confidence in police and morale within the agency.

Another concept discussed by the commission was the *rotten apple theory*. Simply put, if the department acknowledged that an officer was corrupt, then that officer would have to be removed from fellow officers and categorized. Failing to remove the corrupted officer would ruin other officers associated with the one already corrupted. The commission noted that NYPD ignored the existence of corruption in the department because there was no way to certainly determine how many of a rotten apple's associates had become tainted, and trying to do so would destroy or tarnish the agency's public image (Knapp Commission, 1972, pp. 6–7).

- *Independent Commission on the Los Angeles Police Department (Christopher Commission), 1991*

The Christopher Commission was established in 1991 after the beating of Rodney King by the Los Angeles Police Department and the Los Angeles riots. King, a Black man, was driving on a California highway when a highway patrolman attempted to stop him. He accelerated and led police on a short chase. Once stopped, he was viciously beaten by four Los Angeles police officers, while the highway patrol officers watched. King was Tased, hit 56 times with police batons, and kicked multiple times by police, resulting in a broken ankle, fractured face, and numerous cuts and bruises. The beating was videotaped. The officers were criminally charged and arrested but later acquitted by an all-White jury. That acquittal led to the 1992 LA riots.

The Christopher Commission was charged with investigating the police agency's failure to supervise in regard to complaints of excessive force, the culture and officer attitudes toward the minority community, the inability of the community to redress complaints against officers, and the lack of leadership.

The commission sent a survey to 960 officers regarding ethnic bias and excessive force. The commission received completed surveys from 650 officers, and the data was as follows (City of Los Angeles, 1991):

a. 24.5% of the 650 officers who responded agreed that racial bias (prejudice) on the part of officers toward minority citizens contributes to a negative interaction between police and the community; 55.4% disagreed; and 20.1% had no opinion.

b. 27.6% of the respondents agreed that an officer's prejudice toward a suspect's race may lead to excessive force; 57.3% disagreed; and 15.1% had no opinion.

c. The commission also noted that this issue dates back some twenty-five years to the 1965 Los Angeles riots. The *McCone Commission* in 1965 observed that there were many reasons for the riots; however, police brutality in the African American community was a recurring theme and one of the causes. In 1965, the *McCone Commission* recommended open communication between the African American community and the police (City of Los Angeles, 1991, p. 69).

- *Commission to Investigate Allegations of Police Corruption and Anti-Corruption Procedures of the Police Department (Mollen Commission), 1992*

The Mollen Commission was established in 1992 by Mayor David Dinkins to investigate corruption in the New York City Police Department. Mayor Dinkins authorized the commission with three mandates: to investigate the extent and nature of corruption within the NYPD, to evaluate the department's ability to detect and prevent corruption, and to recommend changes to enhance the department's effectiveness. The commission's investigation, which lasted 22 months, stated that corruption extended far beyond the corrupt cop. The commission discovered that corruption was allowed to exist because of officers' fears of being labeled a rat and of the potential consequences for being honest, and because supervisors were willfully blind, fearing scandal more than the acts of corruption (City of New York, 1994, p. 14).

The commission also noted that there had been a change in the type of corruption within the ranks of the NYPD. The new generation of corrupt officers was influenced by the drug trade and the explosion of crack cocaine. Those who participated were no longer grass-eaters but had become meat-eaters and were involved in brutality, sale and distribution of narcotics, and robbery of their competition. The commission described the officers as working in *crews* ranging from 5 to 10 members each. These crews participated in acts of violence that were used to earn respect, extort profit, relieve frustration, and administer street justice (City of New York, 1994, p. 34).

The commission's investigation of violence was quite interesting because the commission opted to address this subject, whereas other commissions such as the Knapp Commission had focused solely on corruption. The Mollen Commission found that brutality was common, although difficult to quantify, in large drug-infested minority communities, forthcoming when it came to the issue of corruption (City of New York, 1994, p. 58).

The issues presented in the Mollen Commission's report mirrored those in the 1972 Knapp Commission report, with one distinct difference: The type of corruption in the NYPD had changed to include crews that had become the major players. The crews consisted of meat-eaters fewer in numbers, as opposed to the grass-eaters who made it seem as if corruption and abuse were "normal." In response to the Mollen Commission findings, it was recommended that the city of New York establish a permanent independent commission to oversee corruption in the NYPD. On February 27, 1995, Mayor Rudolph Giuliani established the Commission to Combat Police Corruption.

- *Rampart Scandal (LAPD), 2000*

The Rampart Scandal was investigated by the Rampart Independent Review Committee. This committee was sanctioned by the Los Angeles Board of Police Commissioners to investigate the operations, policies, and procedures of the Los Angeles Police Department as a result of the Rampart Scandal. The investigation was an examination of an anti-gang unit known as the Community Resources against Street Hoodlums (CRASH). CRASH was very successful in reducing violent crime. The officers were given great latitude in order to accomplish this goal, but doing so cost the LAPD due to a host of scandals that shook not only the law enforcement community but also the citizens they served. The bottom line is that there was no trust left because of the unit's actions.

The behaviors of the officers in CRASH were exactly the same as those investigated by the Mollen Commission in New York City five years earlier. After the Christopher Commission's report, the LAPD had set out to change from what it described as the professional police model to the community policing model. The *professional police model* is defined by the LAPD as being focused on crime fighting with minimal contact with the public (City of Los Angeles, 2001, p. 7). The *community policing model* is a system focused on fostering collaboration and trust, where police, community members, and businesses form a partnership to address crime in that region. However, the transition to community policing never took place. The administration was never sold on the concept and never made it an agency priority. As a result, it was business as usual, with the community complaining that the LAPD had never used community resources to create partnerships. The most notable observation regarding management was that the administration managed the department from the top down rather than promoting collaborative partnerships and problem-solving (City of Los Angeles, 2001, p. 7).

Because the LAPD's style of policing had never changed and CRASH was given great latitude, a particular type of officer was selected for the unit, and a particular culture was bred in the unit. Three separate incidents brought CRASH officers to the forefront: a bank robbery committed by CRASH officer David Mack; the theft of narcotics from an evidence locker by CRASH officer Rafael Perez; and allegations of excessive force made against Crash officer Brian Hewitt, as well as other members of the unit (City of Los Angeles, 2001, p. 44).

The Rampart Scandal Review Committee had a host of findings, but the one that stands out most is finding number three, which focused on the agency's relationship with the community. In fact, the committee noted: "LAPD's failure to treat communities as full partners in law enforcement is related to its failure to treat its officers as partners" (City of Los Angeles, 2001, p. 99).

Thomas (2008) argues that police should treat everyone justly and that there is a belief in the United States that individual citizens should be treated equally and fairly. This expectation is understood in a host of relationships, including husband–wife, employer–employee, government–citizen, police–citizen, teacher–student, and doctor–patient (p. 177). Police believe that because of their role in society, they (police) are entitled to respect, and a citizen's respect should be automatic; it does not have to be earned. From a community's standpoint, it is assumed that police would be fair and unbiased in the treatment of the citizens that the police serve. Therein lies the great divide—many agencies, officers, and segments of society feel that police are entitled to respect. Minority communities, the poor, and disenfranchised see police as a group that treats its community members unfairly, and police are a group that should be avoided, if not feared. In minority communities, police have lost their credibility and respect.

O'Hara (2005) argues that such behavior must be classified as institutional failures, and organizations that find this behavior acceptable isolate themselves, oftentimes refusing to allow outsiders in to view, challenge, or attempt to change the officer's conduct. Ultimately, this behavior is supported by professional privilege and political power (p. 149). However, this privilege is far from professional and should be considered destructive entitlement, as well as a tool of psychological intimidation, which are the underpinnings of an oppressive relationship.

PSYCHOLOGY OF POLICING

As policing began, it is safe to surmise that the selection process was far from rigorous. In fact, there were probably only three criteria: loyalty to whomever got them the job, the law be damned; the ability to handle oneself in a brawl, to quell a disturbance; and occasionally make an arrest. Missing from the aforementioned equation are training and professionalism. The psychology of an officer at that time was simply to be firm and authoritarian.

Today, police candidates complete an exhaustive examination of their character before they can be hired. The entry-level officer will experience: a written test, an oral interview, a physical fitness test, a polygraph examination (depending on the state), a background investigation, a psychological evaluation, and finally a physical examination. All of this scrutinizing is designed to select the best possible candidate for that agency. Therefore, if this determines the best candidates, why does the profession continue to have problems?

Thomas (2011a) argues that police candidates come from diverse backgrounds, which are influenced by age, gender, culture, perceptions, and their life experiences, be those worldly or very narrow (pp. 6–7). The police personality is shaped through a series of common experiences, which begin with academy training. After academy training, the police personality is further shaped through field training, type and nature of the calls for service, working in a particular community where people dislike and distrust the police, dealing with the poor and disenfranchised, taking cues from people in a particular community and how they treat each other, the daily grind of dealing with apathy of community members who refuse to take ownership of community issues and unrealistically demand police solve all of the community's problems, an officer's personal problems, politics within the agency, and the agency's culture that can best be considered a form of peer pressure that new officers must conform to or, absent that, be ostracized (Thomas, 2017). From exposure to those many experiences, officers often develop skepticism, cynicism, and suspiciousness, which creates an outward distancing that is used as a barrier/shield. This barrier is necessary to protect an officer's mental health from psychological trauma.

Police are taught to be in control and never let anyone know that they have a personal side. It is important to note, even today, the police culture is primarily male, and associated with the police culture is the male ego/machismo; any sign that an officer is not in control is a sign of weakness (Arrigo & Shipley, 2005; Blau, 1994; Bonifacio, 1991; Slovenko, 2002). Clark and White (2003) note that police view themselves as problem-solvers invulnerable to the daily grind of the job and trauma they experience, and over time they become emotionally numb.

The police personality may best be described as biphasic. The biphasic personality allows an officer to adapt to stressful situations. Essentially, every officer has two personalities: the work personality, capable of handling and adapting to stressful situations; and the off-duty officer who has a personal life (Seaward, 2009; Siebert, 1994). Ultimately, the psychology of policing breeds an officer who is suspicious, with a cold exterior, influenced by the day-to-day interaction with the public and the quality of his or her personal life. Other factors, which are rarely discussed, also influence an officer's actions and personality, which are in the agency's culture. Holmes (2000) argues that acts of brutality are shaped by the organizational culture, peer pressure, and/or challenges to an officer's authority (p. 350).

This lends itself to a host of other questions: What does an officer have to do to be accepted? What is the agency's style of policing? Is it the professional police model noted in the investigation of LAPD's CRASH Unit? Or does the agency promote community partnerships? Does the agency discipline officers for violations of policy, or does the agency look the other way? Finally, how does an officer prove his or her worth to other officers and the agency? Agency culture and peer acceptance influence and control officer outcomes. From a community's standpoint, the community's perception is the community's reality. It is important to understand, whether just or unjust, a community's impression of police everywhere is influenced by its interaction with its community's police. The community's perception is further influenced by media coverage of police locally, nationally, and across social media. It is the convergence of all of these variables that has many minority communities viewing police as an oppressor and, often, an occupying army.

PSYCHOLOGY OF OPPRESSION

Stahl (2017) states: "The injustice characteristic of oppression is not primarily a matter of outcomes, but a matter of social relationships between people or groups which are stable and permanent in nature. Oppression as an injustice affects people as members of groups" (p. 477). Using the term "oppression" and applying it to any group in the United States, especially the poor and minority communities, is akin to making the statement: "White America is responsible for slavery and they use the police as the tool to maintain control." As I noted earlier in a quote by Rooney (2010): "White people living in America today are not responsible for slavery and the injustices associated with slavery. This happened before this generation was born and for anyone to dwell on the past only fuels resentment" (p. 13). Yet, from an African American's perspective, White America is tired of hearing that Blacks have been treated unfairly. However, the sentiment of many in White America can be summed up with another quote from Rooney (2010): "They still moan about the slave trade—it ended hundreds of years ago! Get with the times, and stop using it as an excuse not to work and to get free money" (p. 13).

As a professor, I wish that I could say that these views are a thing of the past or limited to certain elements of American society. However, many of my White students harbor similar feelings, and these feelings were born out when I exposed my classes to an article written by Bryonn Bain and published in the *Village Voice*, titled "The Bill of Rights for Black Men: Walking while Black."

Synopsis of the Bain incident: Bain explains the catalyst for this article written in 2000 is the fact that he was accused of being, but was not, involved in a disturbance at a bar. Police arrested and charged Bain, although he said he was only a bystander. Bain's illegal detention and arrest enraged him so that he wrote "Walking While Black: The Bill of Rights for Black America." "The Bill of Rights for Black America" mirrors the U.S. Constitution with one exception: Black men have no rights. Bain eloquently points to the following facts: A Black man is a nigger; Whites can apprehend and/or detain Black men with impunity; being a Black man with no other evidence allows officers to illegally stop and search the person: If contraband is found, the arrest and prosecution is valid, because race defines guilt; and Blacks are not free to leave their neighborhood: To leave a designated neighborhood implies suspicious and/or criminal activity (Bain, 2012).

Bain's arguments are a reminder of how Blacks have been devalued over the years, as was noted in the U.S. Supreme Court's decision of *Scott v. Sandford*, 60 U.S. 393 (1857), also known as the *Dred Scott Decision*. In this decision, the U.S. Supreme court stated that African slaves were not citizens but property. In examining Bain's Bill of Rights, they are eerily reminiscent of the discussions that I use to have with my grandfather, who was born in the late 1800s, where he described the Jim Crow Laws of the South. Jim Crow Laws were a rule of law that Blacks had to stay in their place and Blacks could be beaten or killed at the whim of any White person. As I reflect back on those conversations that we had in the 1960s and 1970s, they were painful to listen to and hard to understand, yet the examples were and are everywhere. Jim Crow and the incidents surrounding that era, as well as the negative interactions between police and minority communities today, serve as a constant reminder that minorities must remain hypervigilant as they move through their daily lives and attempt to assimilate into American society (U.S. Supreme Court, 1857).

Years later, I developed a survey for my students asking for their opinion concerning Mr. Bain's article "The Bill of Rights for Black America." This survey had been administered to 550 students in 11 classes from 2002 to 2013. The students who participated in the survey were identified by only race, and the survey population was as follows: total number of students: N = 550; number of White students: N = 520 or 95 percent of the population; number of African American students: N = 10 or .02 percent; and number of Latino students: N = 20 or .04 percent.

PERCEPTION OF RACE SURVEY (THOMAS, 2002)

1. Can you identify with Mr. Bain's anger?
   a. N = 515 or 94% of the White students did not feel any empathy toward Mr. Bain.
   b. N = 40 or 7% which consisted of 100% of the Latino and African American populations and 10 White respondents did understand and empathized with Mr. Bain.
2. Do you find it offensive that the author uses the term "nigger?"
   a. N =440 or 80% were not offended by the use of the word "nigger." This included five African Americans and three Latinos.
   b. N = 160 or 30% of the respondents were offended by the use of the term "nigger."
3. Do you believe that most "Blacks in America" feel the same as Mr. Bain?
   a. N = 550 or 100% believed that African Americans believed that America was biased.
4. In response to question three why do think this? Choose the most appropriate.
   a. Because of slavery and they can't let go and choose to be angry.
      • N = 192 or 35% of the White respondents agreed with this statement.
   b. Because it is easier to blame their failure on the system and not take personal responsibility.
      • N = 222 or 40% of the White respondents agreed with this statement.
   c. Because number 3 is true.
      • N = 30 or 100% of the African American and Latino respondents agree with this statement.
      • N = 82 or 15% of the White respondents agreed with this statement.
   d. Because Blacks are prejudice and hate White people.
      • N = 24 or 4% of the White respondents agreed with this statement.

What is especially disturbing is that 90 percent of these students were look-ing to enter *criminal justice,* more specifically law enforcement after grad-uation. I close the subject of race in policing, justice, and injustice, with a documentary titled *Murder on Sunday Morning (2001).* This documentary is of Brenton Butler a teen-aged, African American male, who lived in a middle-class neighborhood in Jacksonville, Florida. Brenton was falsely arrested and charged with murder by the Jacksonville Florida Sheriff's Office. After his arrest, Brenton was beaten and threatened at gun point to force him to con-fess to a murder that he did not commit. Officers wrote a false confession and forced Brenton to sign it. Brenton was tried but found not guilty. This docu-mentary is a stark reminder that justice and injustice in America can depend on skin color. And that is a hard truth we must share with our children.

Parents of young Black males have what is described as "the talk" with their children. The talk is not the traditional talk that parents have with their children concerning the birds and the bees. This talk is a reminder to Black children to be suspicious of the police and not do anything that will cause police to notice them. This talk that African American parents have with their Black male children is moved by parents' fear that their child could become a police statistic, one more unjustified shooting, beating, or false arrest. Readers might imagine, if they lived in these conditions, how it would impact their psyche, sense of safety, and self-worth.

Muhammad Ali in 1967 explained the affects, when he refused to fight for this country, in "No Viet Cong Called Me Nigga." Ali declared that he was a conscientious objector and refused induction into the U.S. Army due to his religious beliefs. Shortly after Ali's refusal to enter the army, he was inter-viewed and made the following statement:

> My conscience won't let me go shoot my brother, or some darker people, or some poor hungry people in the mud, for big powerful America. Shoot them, for what? they never called me Nigga, they never lynched me, they never put no dogs on me. They never robbed me of my nationality they never raped or killed my mother and father. What I am going to shoot them for what? I gotta go shoot them poor little black people, babies, children, women. How can I shoot them poor people? Just go on take me to jail. . . . You my opposer when I want freedom! You my opposer when I want justice! You my opposer when I want equality! You won't even standup for me for my religious beliefs and you want me to go somewhere and fight and you won't even standup for me here at home. (Ali, 1967)

The consequences for Ali declaring that he was a conscientious objec-tor were that he was stripped of his heavyweight boxing titles, found guilty of dodging the draft, and fined $10,000. The prevailing sentiment among draft-eligible Black men of that day was fear if they chose to oppose the draft, even if it was for legitimate reasons such as religion. If the government would do this to Muhammad Ali, what would government do to the average poor Black man? Through example—threat intimidation—the U.S. government established the value of Black men by imposing its will despite the U.S. Constitution and the law. In reviewing Stahl's definition of oppression, it identifies power, injustice, and relationships between groups that remain constant over time and allows one group to maintain control over another. Monkkonen (1981) supports the concept of control through his second theory regarding the growth of American policing:

> The growth of American policing was in response to the need of the elite in American society for the police to act as a buffer between them and what Monkkonen describes as the dangerous class. The dangerous class is defined as the faceless in U.S. society—the paupers, tramps, and criminals—and is comprised of five groups: urban criminals, rural criminals, rural paupers, urban paupers, and tramps. (p. 87)

VICTIMS AND TOOLS OF OPPRESSION

The victims of oppression are usually defined by groups, with no one group being mutually exclusive, and oftentimes each carries its unique burden: gender, sexual orientation, race/nationality, economic status, and education. Not being mutually exclusive can be defined as a person carrying more than one identity. An example is as follows: Black women versus White women: Although both are women, Black women have to overcome two negative characteristics—race and gender. Martin and Jurik (1996) point out that cultural images and/or stereotypes differ between White and Black women, and it is because of this that Black women are treated differently based on those cultural norms and biases (p. 71).

The tools of oppression in the United States are many, and without some sort of intervention they would remain blatant and overt. The U.S. Supreme Court has played a major role in forcing the tools of oppression underground. The modern courts have been extremely forthcoming in addressing the conduct of police officers. Police have many tools at their disposal, and from an officer's perspective he or she would never classify them as tools of oppression; rather, they are necessary tools to do the job. Police will argue that they are the only group that enforces the law as it is written, and the law is a tool to prevent, intervene, or arrest a suspect once a crime has been committed. What many officers refuse to address is, depending on the neighborhood, that there are different enforcement styles. The tools of racial profiling come in many forms: police practice, agency policy, and the legislative.

Racial profiling is the application of a stereotype to selectively enforce the law. It could be dependent on a person being in the wrong neighborhood. Laney (2006) defines racial profiling as "the practice of targeting individuals for police or security interdiction, detention, or other desperate treatment based on their race or ethnicity, in the belief that that certain minority groups are more likely to engage in unlawful behavior" (p. 2). Categories of racial profiling that minority communities experience include walking while Black, driving while Black, and riding a bicycle while Black. Each is detailed with examples.

Walking while Black

As an American citizen, while out for a walk, you are stopped by police and asked: *What are you doing in this neighborhood?* Before you can answer the question, the officer answers his own question by stating: *You don't belong here.*

I know what you are thinking: "This is America, as long as I am not doing anything illegal I can be anywhere." For African Americans this is not necessarily true, be it in a community where they don't reside or in their own community. For many police officers, the mere presence of someone different is reasonably suspicious, which meets the legal criteria provided in *Terry v. Ohio,* 392 U.S. (1968), allowing officers to stop and frisk a person based on a series of observed behaviors that are less than the probable cause needed to make an arrest.

Police will often classify this as a *citizen's contact* and argue that it is within their right to stop and talk to anyone. There isn't a problem until the person refuses to stop, runs, or refuses to identify themselves. A citizen's refusal to acquiesce to the officer's demands will result in the citizen's arrest on an obscure charge such as *resisting arrest without violence or obstruction of justice.* Review these three examples and reflect on this question: If you had to deal with this fear daily, how would it impact your psyche?

- *San Diego California* (1982)—In this case Mr. Lawson, who is Black, liked to take long walks through White communities in San Diego, California. Lawson was stopped by police and demanded identification under California State Statute 647(e), which required persons to identify themselves and account for their presence when requested by a peace officer. Lawson was stopped or detained 17 times. Simply put, the mere presence of Mr. Lawson walking through these neighborhoods was suspicious to police. This practice was brought to end in the celebrated case *Kolender v. Lawson,* 461 U.S. 352 (1983). The U.S. Supreme Court heard the case and in its decision ruled, "A person cannot be required to furnish identification if not reasonably suspected of any criminal conduct" (*Kolender v. Lawson*, 461 U.S. 352, 1983). Although *Kolender v. Lawson* found that such statutes were unconstitutional, if you are a person of color, you are automatically considered suspicious.

- *New York City*—In the early 2000s the New York City Police Department (NYPD) embarked on a campaign to reduce violent crime in its city. One of the tools NYPD instituted was the aggressive use of "stop and frisk." Stop and frisk is allowed under the landmark case *Terry v. Ohio*, 392 U.S. 1, 88 S. Ct. (1968). The *Terry* decision authorizes police to stop and pat down the exterior of a person's clothing for weapons and/or contraband. The standard for such a stop is that the officer has to be able to articulate that the subject's behavior was suspicious. This requirement is much less than the standard of probable cause, which is the standard to make an arrest. Once this aggressive enforcement policy was instituted, data provided by NYPD shows that its activity was biased. To be a Black or Latino male in New York meant that you would be stopped for reasons that were less than suspicious. The numbers of Black and Latino members stopped under the NYPD policy between 2006 and 2012 averaged 525,000. Each of those years an average 50,436 persons were arrested or issued citations most often for what would be deemed minor violations of the law. During the same time period, the average number of citizens who were not involved in criminal activity was 86 percent or 425,000; 85 percent of those stopped during those years were either Black or Latino. In 2013 the NYPD was sued in federal court in *Floyd et al. v. City of New York et al.*, and the judge determined that the NYPD's stop and frisk policy was discriminatory, and NYPD was ordered to change its tactics and work with the community to develop an alternative to these practices. In response to the court decision, stop and frisk encounters have been on a steady decline, and in 2016 the NYPD recorded just 12,000 encounters (New York City Police Department, 2006–2016).

- *Jacksonville, Florida*—A study conducted by the *Florida Times Union* discovered that the Jacksonville Sheriff's Office issued pedestrian citations to Black residents, who received 55 percent of all pedestrian citations. It is important to note that Blacks comprise only 29 percent of the city's population. The data reflects that Blacks are nearly three times as likely as Whites to be ticketed for a pedestrian violation. Residents of the city's three poorest zip codes were about six times as likely to receive a pedestrian citation than those living in the city's other, more affluent 34 zip codes (Conrack, Sanders, & Rabinowitz, 2017). The Jacksonville Sheriff's Office defended this practice by stating the (jaywalking) citations are a useful crime fighting tool, allowing officers to stop suspicious people and search them for guns and drugs, regardless of the fact that a $65 jaywalking citation was a financial hardship to many who live in the targeted communities. Failure to pay the citations resulted in the suspension of the violator's driver's license and the court issuing an arrest warrant.

Driving while Black

Driving while Black is another form of racial profiling. The term finds its origins in the "war on drugs," specifically cocaine. In Florida this profile was based on the presumption that most drug dealers and couriers are Black, brown, or Latino. In addition to the color of the subject's skin, officers were trained to look for the type of vehicle being driven, driver's age, lots of gold jewelry, lots of antennas on the vehicle, a radar detector, dark-tinted windows, and meticulously following driving laws. The profile provided the visual cues, which are considered criteria. If a subject met several of the aforementioned criteria, officers were instructed to find a traffic violation that would be probable cause for a legal traffic stop. It is said that if an officer follows a car long enough, he or she will find a reason to stop the car. What happens when an officer stops a car because a taillight or break light is allegedly not working, and after the stop it is determined that there is no problem with the equipment? I had one supervisor admit when asked how he made so many DUI arrests. He stated: "You know how a taillight or break light isn't working and you pull a car over and it is miraculously working after the stop? He then went on to say that this was his ruse to begin a drunk driving investigation or drug interdiction" (D. Curths, personal communication, December 5, 1995).

The profile of the drug courier extended beyond those that were transporting drugs on the highways, moving drugs, and/or money from north to south or east and west. This profile was applied to everyone who fit one or more characteristics much like *walking while Black*. The logic for the stops is as follows: a young Black male driving a nice car that police believe he can't afford; driving in a neighborhood where a Black person doesn't belong, which is usually a code for being a Black person in a White neighborhood or a White person in a Black neighborhood; or a Black male or female driving in a high-crime area, the high-crime area usually in the Black community, a community in which the driver or the driver's relatives reside.

- *North Florida (2007–2017)*—One of the best examples that I can offer for driving while Black comes from a driving improvement instructor who resides and works in North Florida. He teaches a class where drivers have been referred, because they have suspended driver's licenses. The students are required to attend and successfully complete this course as one of the requirements before having their license reinstated. The instructor has been teaching the class for the past 10 years and advised that there is an alarming pattern. The majority of the African Americans who attend the class come from one city and all live in the African American community of that city. He has been keeping informal data and asks each attendee why they were stopped and how they ended up in his class.

The data reflects that 80 percent of the African Americans stopped were given the following reason for the traffic stop: "You are driving in a high-crime area." The officers' reasoning is void of probable cause, which is associated with traffic violations such as ran a stop sign; not wearing a seatbelt; brake lights are not working; or made an illegal left turn. The traffic stop was illegal. In most instances, the driver's license was suspended prior to the stop due to prior violations. The officer does not issue a citation for probable cause (the reason the officer made the stop), because it does not exist. The officer issues a citation for "driving while license suspended." The data reflects over 200 African American drivers in that community were arrested for driving with a suspended license. In a separate conversation with the chief of that police agency, the chief acknowledged that there is a problem, but he does not know how to address it (Thomas, 2017).

- *Gainesville, Florida*—J. Johnson, a 30-year-old Black male, owned and drove a 1980 Cadillac Coupe Deville, with tinted windows and large chrome tire rims. Johnson lived on the west side of the city, which is predominately White. However, the majority of Johnson's extended family, as well as his girlfriend, lived on the east side of the city, which is predominately Black. He was stopped 10 times by different officers, each attempting to search his vehicle claiming that he left a drug house. Johnson refused to allow the officers to search his vehicle, and at one point the officers handcuffed Johnson and searched the vehicle looking for drugs without probable cause, only to find nothing. During the 10th traffic stop, the officer issued Johnson a citation for "window tint too dark." The officer did not have a tint meter to determine if Johnson's tint was in violation of Florida State Statutes. Johnson contested the citation in court. However, prior to his court appearance Johnson asked the Traffic Unit of the Gainesville Police Department to check his window tint to determine if his vehicle was in violation. The Gainesville Police Department (the same agency that issued the citation) determined that Johnson's tint was legal. In court, Johnson challenged the citation and the officer's probable cause. The officer admitted that he did not have a tint meter but made this statement: "Your Honor, you don't understand. The defendant has been seen leaving a drug house on several occasions and he was driving in a high-crime area. We need to know what he is doing." The judge dismissed the citation and admonished the officer for his activity, noting that it was illegal (J. Johnson, personal communication, December 15, 2017).

- *Tampa, Florida*—Riding a bicycle while Black is trigger of racial profiling and stereotyping. For many in the Black community, bicycles are the primary mode of transportation due to economics. Riding a bicycle at night without a front and rear light is illegal in every state. Many officers view this population as being associated with the drug trade and acting as lookouts for corner drug dealers. There is some merit to this, but not every Black man riding a bike at night is associated with drug activity. As a result of this stereotype, it is easier to stop every Black man on a bike without a light in the Black community in the hope that the rider is in possession of drugs, weapons, or wanted on a warrant. It is recognized that it is a violation of the law, but this is a case that, with a little homework, officers can discern who is involved in the drug trade and who isn't. It is also interesting to note that the same officers who make these stops in the Black community will not stop a White male on a bicycle at night without lights.

The Tampa Police Department (TPD) found itself in such a situation when the Justice Department was asked to investigate allegations that TPD was singling out Blacks on bicycles and ticketing them. TPD argues that it was in response to bicycle thefts. The Justice Department used data from the year 2015. During its investigation, the Justice Department determined the following: Black residents made up only about 40 percent of estimated bicycle riders during that time, 73 percent of all bicycle stops were of Black cyclists; the program had no effect on reducing crime or bike theft. The Department of Justice determined these outcomes by comparing crime data from when the bike stop program was at its peak with crime data after the *Tampa Bay Times* investigation; then bike stops dropped precipitously. The Justice Department also noted that there was racial disparity in TPD's actions but not racial discrimination. The Justice Department summarized TPD's actions in the following statement:

> The bottom-line appears to be that TPD burdened Black bicyclists by disproportionately stopping them in the name of benefiting Black communities by increasing their public safety. Yet, our analyses indicate that TPD's bicycle enforcement did not produce a community benefit in terms of bicycle safety, bicycle theft, or crime generally but did burden individual bicyclists, particularly Black bicyclists in high crime areas of Tampa. (Ridgeway, Mitchell, Gunderman, Alexander, & Letten, 2016, p. 6)

Indeed, as this book is written in 2018, there have been numerous nationwide incidents where police were called to the scene when White Americans saw the presence of a minority person, not doing anything criminal or aggressive, nonetheless, as suspicious, so they expected police to make discriminatory and illegal arrests.

• April 2018, Philadelphia, Pennsylvania—Two Black men waiting to have a meeting in Starbucks spurred an employee to call police, and the men, actually entrepreneurs, were arrested for trespass, even though it is widely recognized that Starbucks is the common hub for socializing, meeting, reading, and working. Police later apologized, and Starbucks officials declared they would close their stores for a day for "diversity training" to assure no future such incident.

- April 2018, Grandview Golf course, York County, Pennsylvania—911 was called by the White co-owners twice about five Black female members who were allegedly playing golf too slowly. Police responded but did not find any crime. A state senator has called for an investigation of the club.

- May 2018, New Haven, Connecticut—A Black female student at a Yale University dormitory fell asleep in the dorm's common room, and the police were called by a White female student because the mere presence of the Black student sleeping was suspicious to her. Police questioned and performed background checks on the woman for some 25 minutes, as the accused filmed the police with her cell phone. Ultimately, police took no action.

- May 2018, Brentwood, Missouri—Two Black high school students were shopping for prom attire at the Nordstrom Rack. The clerks accused the students of stealing and called the police, and when the police arrived it was determined that nothing had been taken.

- May 2018, Ft. Collins, Colorado—At Colorado State University (CSU), two Native American high school brothers from a low-income family, boys who'd driven hours to CSU to participate in a tour of the campus, were ordered to leave after a White female parent who was on the tour called 911, because their presence made her nervous. CSU officials later said their being asking to leave was unjustified.

- May 2018, Rialto, California—Three Black women were leaving an Air Bed and Breakfast. As they were pulling their luggage to the car, a White neighbor, leery because they did not smile at or wave to her, felt that the women were suspicious and called police. The women were detained, questioned, and background-checked some 20 minutes by police and then allowed to leave uncharged.

Minorities' mere presence—normal behavior, walking, driving, shopping, playing golf, attending college, or visiting a campus—has been met with suspicion and calls to police with allegations of feared criminal behavior. Some police react justly; many do not.

POLICY AND LAW

Long before the U.S. government ever declared a *war on drugs,* the African American community fell victim to a number of social issues beyond the African American community's control and beyond the control of the police. They include poor and declining educational systems within inner cities; industry moving from American cities to foreign countries; the introduction of heroin in African American communities; rising incarceration rates of African American adults, which lent itself to the destruction of the African American family; and the police expected to deal with a series of social problems that policing was never designed to solve.

Drugs and the Decline of the African American Family

The United States was heralded as the great industrial giant beginning with Henry Ford, the introduction of the Model T, and mass production. However, the industry that built this country and supported the United States' efforts during World War II began to crumble in the early 1970s with the oil embargo, gas shortages, soaring gas prices, poorly made automobiles, and Americans' passion for foreign automobiles with better gas mileage. As factories began closing, the United States moved away from industry and manufacturing and began investing in what we know now as a prison-industrial economy (Kirchhoff, 2010; Wildeman & Western, 2010). The factors that spurred a prison-industrial complex are as follows: Unskilled laborers lost their jobs, factories closed, and the economy crashed in those communities. Some communities, cities, and states never recovered. Detroit, Michigan, is one such city. To offset the loss of jobs, the prison-industrial complex moved into communities replacing factories with prisons and their jobs.

The result was the start of a perfect storm that has lasted for decades. The loss of jobs by unskilled laborers and the influx of heroin in the Black community negatively impacted the African American family, with one or both parents attracted to the drug trade in some way. Detroit is the perfect example. *Time* magazine (1971) reported that Detroit was in the midst of an all-out heroin war for control of the $350 million heroin market; during this time there were an estimated 20,000 addicts in the city, most of them Black. There was one homicide every four days associated with the heroin wars of Detroit (p. 20). The criminal justice system responded with increased arrests, prosecutions, and incarcerations and thus began the prison-industrial economy.

In the late 1970s heroin began to die out, and powder cocaine became the drug of choice but unavailable to the poor because of the price. Cooper (2002) notes that because the prices of powdered cocaine began to drop, cartels and chemists began to experiment with various forms of cocaine and created "crack cocaine," which emerged in Los Angeles and Miami in the early 1980s, quickly becoming the drug of choice in the African American community (pp. 27–28). Crack was small, easy to conceal, and cheap as one could by a piece or a "rock" for as little as $5. In the solid form, it was smoked, creating an instant feeling of euphoria and very addictive. For the African American community and family, there was no recovery. The scourge went from heroin to crack.

With the introduction of heroin and later crack, President Nixon declared a war on drugs. Presidents Nixon and later Regan argued and believed that to interdict or eradicate drugs was impossible. Both presidents believed that the most effective way to address the drug problem was to remove the customer and establish a zero tolerance policy, with incarceration as the ultimate penalty for substance abuse (Rosenberger, 1996). This policy directly impacted the African American family as the majority of the abusers of crack were in the African American community. The impact of incarcerating one or both parents created a void and instability in the household. The victim(s) of their parent(s) incarceration were the children, and child's response usually manifest itself in behaviors described as acting out, withdrawal, anxiousness, depression, anger, frustration, failure in school, and an increased likelihood of incarceration as a juvenile and adult (Gibson, 2008; Wildeman & Westerman, 2010).

To further explain the cause and effect in the African American community, Kirchhoff (2010) notes that in the previous decades there was a 400 percent jump in incarcerations rates in the United States, and at the end of 2008 there were 2.3 million adults incarcerated in state, local, or federal facilities, with another 5.1 million on probation or parole (p. i). Prison growth was fueled by the war on drugs, lengthy prison sentences, minimum mandatory sentencing, and recidivism. Finally, data from the Bureau of Labor Statistics (2012) supports that the United States moved from an industrial society to prison economy, noting that there were approximately 770,00 people employed in the field of corrections in 2008 and that was expected to increase by 5 percent by 2020. It should be noted that the growth of corrections as an industry is slowing now, because the crime rates have been falling consistently over the past few years. However, employment opportunities in the area of probation and parole are expected to increase by 18 percent by 2020 (Lockard & Wolf, 2012).

The war on drugs did nothing more than provide law enforcement with carte blanche to harass and stop every Black male they saw based on the profile of a drug dealer, and the war on drugs exacerbated an already-tenuous relationship between law enforcement and the Black community. If you go back and examine the tactics of police in the Victims and Tools of Oppression section of this chapter, it is clear that being Black translated into suspicious activity, an increase in police contact, and a greater likelihood of being placed in the criminal justice system based on that contact. One of the best benchmarks for police–citizen contact is with juveniles, because it is a point of first contact. Police have the ability to release the juvenile or arrest the juvenile. It is also a point at which juveniles will make a judgment about police, depending on the officer's attitude and behavior.

Pope, Lovell, and Hsia (2001) support the aforementioned argument in their examination of disparity, race, and juveniles. Pope et al. completed an exhaustive literature review and found that 25 of 34 studies examined highlighted that race determine if one would be processed or provided another avenue of resolution in the juvenile justice system. Pope et al. (2001) argue that the data sets and research support the existence of disparities and bias. Yet Pope et al. are clear to point out that these disparities may be influenced by a number of other variables that have to be considered when analyzing data of this nature: inherent system bias; local policies and police practices; and social conditions that the system has no control of such as inequality, poverty, family, underemployment or no employment, and performance in school.

In a similar study, Huizenga, Thornberry, Knight, and Lovegrove (2007) examined what they classify as disproportionate minority contact of juveniles as opposed to an exhaustive literature review they analyzed data sets from three programs: the Pittsburg Youth Study, the Rochester Youth Development Study, and the Seattle Social Development Project. Huizenga et al. argue that there is definite disproportionality when it comes to the arrest and detainment of African American male juveniles. However, they point out that there are a number of other variables that may dictate how an officer must proceed at the point of contact, which means the decision may not be related to racial bias, rather agency policy: the availability of a parent or responsible guardian for the youth if an officer wanted to counsel and release; arrest record of the juvenile and or the adult the juvenile is to be released to; a victim who is willing to press charges; the crime rate in a particular neighborhood; and the agency's strategies in response to a series of neighborhood problems or partic-ular crimes (p. 42). Each of these variables individually may well influence if a juvenile will be processed or counseled and released.

In contrast, the National Center on Crime and Delinquency (NCCD) (2007) reports that there is a disparity by race when it comes to contact, arrest, referral, and detention of African American juveniles. In fact, the NCCD supports and argues that African American juveniles are overrep-resented in every category within the juvenile justice system. The NCCD provides the following data between 2002 and 2004 in regard to African American juveniles: 16 percent of all the youth in the United States are Afri-can American; African American youth account for 28 percent of all juvenile arrests, 30 percent of all juvenile court referrals, and 37 percent of all juveniles detained; 34 percent are formally processed in juvenile court; 30 percent of the juveniles are adjudicated (found guilty); 35 percent of all the juveniles are waived to adult court; 38 percent of the youth are referred to residential treatment programs; and 58 percent of youth are admitted to adult prison (p. 3). In every category African American juveniles are twice as likely to be treated more harshly than their Caucasian counterparts based on the actual percentage of juveniles. Missing in the NCCD's research are the variables noted by Pope and Huizenga.

CASE STUDY

In 1982, I was newly assigned to the Street Crimes Unit at the Grand Rapids Police Department. It was an honor, and the unit was going to afford me the opportunity to put criminals in jail. Prior to even taking our first call for service, the police chief made us go into the Black community to introduce ourselves and complete surveys concerning police/citizen contacts, satisfaction with police, crime, and what problems the community wanted this new unit to concentrate on. Each of us had a person of interest in the community, be those a source of criminal activity or activism, in addition to the local residents. One of my connections in the community was Mr. Carl, the publisher of the local Black newspaper.

Lasting Impressions of Police in the Black Community

I asked Mr. Carl what he saw as the greatest problem in the community.

He responded: "Social issues, poverty, education, a lack of jobs, and no hope for a community that had been abandoned." I listened to Carl, but I didn't truly hear him.

He did not mention a crime problem or the police and our role. I continued with the survey and asked my second question:

What can we do as a police department to address the problems in the community?

Carl replied: "You are the police you have one job and that is to be a band aid for all of the social problems. You are powerless; you can't fix anything. Your job is to protect the rich and keep us away from them. You are our oppressor." Again, I heard Carl but did not understand. I asked my final question: What is the major crime problem, are there quality-of-life issues or violence?

He said, "You don't get it, if America addresses the social problems, the rest will take care of itself."

It wasn't until 10 years later, when I again reflected on Carl's comments, that I understood. I was reminded what it was like growing up Black in the city of Detroit in the 1960s and 1970s, a painful history. I had never been arrested or charged with a crime. However, every police encounter I ever had with the Detroit Police Department between the ages of 10 and 18 was negative, or brutal.

- At the age of 10, I saw a police officer sitting in the car and approached him to ask how fast his patrol car went. The officer drew a nickel-plated 357 Magnum and stuck it to my head and told me to get lost.

- At the age of 12, I was helping a friend with his newspaper route, pulling a wagon in the street and placing the newspapers in his customers' doorways. We were stopped, detained, and threatened with an arrest for not having identification in violation of Detroit's city ordinance requiring that everyone possess some form of identification. Where does a 12-year-old get identification?
- At the age of 13, I was walking home from middle school, and a patrol car with two police officers stopped me and placed me in the back of the car. They took me in an alley, dragged me out of the car, beat me up in the alley, and left me there.
- At the age of 18, I was driving my dad's car at 9 P.M. I had just left my high school gym, where I'd been playing basketball. I was stopped by the Detroit Police Street Crime Unit for no reason. They pulled me from the car and placed me face down in the snow with a shotgun to my head, while one officer illegally searched my dad's car. They threw all of the contents from the trunk and glovebox in the street. They told me to stay face down, until they got in their unmarked car and drove off.

For many years, the Black community has been complaining about police practices and ongoing discrimination in the courts as well as sentencing. In an exhaustive review of data and reports, it was determined that, unlike the data provided for juveniles, there is no national database that details police interaction with adults. However, what does exist are data sets of police and minority community interactions in individual cities. The shooting of Michael Brown by the Ferguson Missouri Police Department and the incidents which followed that shooting are presented here because it has become the example exemplifying the Black community's complaints of maltreatment by police.

SYNOPSIS OF MICHAEL BROWN SHOOTING

Officer Darren Wilson was on patrol, and he heard a call come over the police radio about a theft in progress. Wilson observed two men walking in the street who fit the description of those described by the victim and later corroborated by the store video showing one man seen taking some cigarillos and pushing his way past the store owner without paying for them.

Wilson told both men to get on the sidewalk and then blocked them with his patrol car. The officer attempted to exit his vehicle. Accounts differ about whether Wilson struck one of the men, Michael Brown, with the car's door, or if Brown slammed the patrol vehicle door shut, preventing Officer Wilson from exiting the vehicle. An altercation ensued, with Wilson trapped in his patrol vehicle. Brown was at the driver's side window, and evidence indicates Brown struck Officer Wilson in the face. Wilson drew his firearm and fired several shots striking Brown in the hand.

Brown ran, then stopped, turned, and started to charge at Wilson. Wilson fired several more shots, stopping when Brown succumbed to his bullet wounds.

Riots followed in Ferguson, as members of the Black community felt the killing was unjust, with the belief that Brown had actually been shot in the back as he ran away.

The shooting death of Michael Brown was ruled justifiable by the grand jury and a detailed investigation and report written by the Department of Justice (Department of Justice, 2015; *State of Missouri v. Darren Wilson,* 2014).

Based on the evidence, the shooting of Michael Brown was justifiable. So was it the shooting of Michael Brown that caused the riots in Ferguson, or was there some other cause of the riots?

After the riots in Ferguson in 2014, the Department of Justice launched an investigation of the Ferguson Missouri Police Department. The results were published on March 4, 2015, evaluating the Ferguson's Police and Municipal Court Practices and making a number of observations that mirror many of the same claims found in our discussion of police scandals.

Ferguson Missouri Police Department Practices

The Ferguson City Administration relied on the police department and courts to generate revenue so the city of Ferguson could remain fiscally sound. The Department of Justice (2015) noted that the Ferguson City Administration urged then chief Jackson to generate revenue through enforcement actions. In addition to police action, the city's administration urged the Ferguson Municipal Courts to raise their fines annually to generate income to cover any shortfalls the city may encounter through lost tax revenue (p. 1). The president of the Police Foundation, Jim Bueermann argued that Ferguson City police officers were becoming nothing more than armed tax collectors (J. Bueermann, personal communication, October 21, 2015).

The Department of Justice (2015) made the following observations concerning the Ferguson Police Department's practices:

- Officers illegally stopped members of the Black community without reasonable suspicion and made arrest without having probable cause, which violated citizens' Fourth Amendment rights. The Fourth Amendment protects against unreasonable search, seizure, and arrest. The officers relied on a common charge: failure to comply with a lawful order (p. 19). This charge is a catch-all used by officers who stop individuals, and because the subject refuses to move fast enough, or do what an officer says, he or she is usually arrested. This is usually done under the guise of *officer safety* or a term rarely spoken of outside of police circles, "Pissing of the Police (POP) or Contempt of Cop (COP)" (Thomas, 2011b, p. 233).

- Arrests made for "failing to identify oneself to a police officer in the lawful performance of their duty" (p. 20). It is important to note that if the officer contact is illegal, then every action after the contact, including the discovery of evidence and the arrest, is illegal and fruits of the poisonous tree (*Nardone v. United States*, 1939).

- The use of a police-run "wanted" system, which is a system instituted by law enforcement agencies in St. Louis County. The police-run wanted system bypassed the traditional warrant system, which requires judicial approval for the issuance of an arrest warrant based on probable cause. This system allowed officers to make the probable cause determination, enter the subjects in the system, and order agencies throughout the state to arrest the subject from any jurisdiction in the state of Missouri.

- When a subject was to be arrested, most often for failing to comply, officers routinely used excessive force to make the arrest even when the subject offered minimal amounts of resistance, even verbal resistance. Ninety percent of the excessive force violations were against the Black community (p. 28). This included the use of canines when officers encountered low levels of resistance.

- Force was routinely used against vulnerable populations, such as citizens with learning disabilities or mental health conditions.

- The Ferguson Police Department's culture was such that there was no oversight of the officers' actions, and legitimate citizen complaints were overlooked, to benefit the city's financial needs.

- The group most impacted: 90 percent of all traffic citations were issued to African Americans; and 96 percent of municipal outstanding arrest warrants were for African Americans. A total of 11,610 vehicle stops were conducted by the Ferguson Police Department between October 2012 and October 2014. Of those, 85 percent or 9,875 of the stops were African Americans, yet African Americans made up 67 percent of the population (p. 64).

- Between October 2012 and July 2014, African Americans accounted for 85 percent, or 30,525, of the 35,871 total charges in the city, which included traffic citations, summonses, and arrests. During the same time period non-African Americans accounted for 15 percent, or 5,346 (p. 66).

What many like to believe is that this type of policing demonstrates practices of the past. Historically, there is a pervasive pattern within policing that has existed since the 1800s. What some members of law enforcement refuse to recognize is that their actions create a cause and effect. The mentality of minority communities and Black communities, in particular, is that of an oppressed people who have no rights. African American community members feel that they have been abandoned by the local, state, and federal governments and believe that law enforcement is a tool to protect the haves from the have-nots. The minority communities are faced with poverty, poor or bankrupt school systems, an unemployment rate twice the national average, and drugs and violence in their communities, where the police response is often similar to that of the Ferguson Police Department. The psychological impact is threefold—feeling abandoned, depressed, and oppressed. From an agency standpoint, changing the culture is essential. Yet Shusta, Levine, Wong, Olson, and Harris (2011) argue that survival within a law enforcement organization requires that one conform, and that is the reason that prejudice and bias remain unchallenged (p. 31).

What needs to be understood is that it is a relatively small percentage of officers who are involved in such activity. However, it is the actions of the few that taint every officer in this country. Finally, before you move forward, reflect on this chapter and consider the question: "If you were the victim of targeted police actions, how would this impact your psyche? How would you view the police?"

Law enforcement without oversight is very dangerous, because what history teaches us about police is this: If there is no rule/policy/law in place to guide or stop an officer's conduct he/she will exploit the missing link until it is imposed.

(Thomas, 2017)

REFERENCES

Ali, M. (1967, April 28). *No Viet Cong called me nigger*. Retrieved January 10, 2018, from https://www.youtube.com/watch?v=vd9aIamXjQI.

Arrigo, B. A., & Shipley, S. L. (2005). *Introduction to forensic psychology*, 2nd ed. Burlington, MA: Elsevier Academic Press.

Bain, B. (2012). *From the ugly side of beautiful: Rethinking race and prison in America.* Los Angeles, CA: B. Rolly Bain, Inc.

Barber, D. (2008). *A hard rain fell: SDS and why it failed.* Jackson: University Press of Mississippi.

Blau, T. (1994). *Psychological services for law enforcement.* New York, NY: John Wiley & Sons.

Bonifacio, P. (1991). *The psychological effects of police work. A psychodynamic approach.* New York, NY: Springer Publications.

Brown v. Board of Education of Topeka, Kansas, 347 U.S. 483 (1954).

Bullard, S., & Bond, J. (1994). *Free at last: A history of the civil rights movement and those who died in the struggle.* New York, NY: Oxford University Press.

Bureau of Labor Statistics. (2012). *Occupational outlook handbook: Probation officers and correctional treatment specialists.* Washington, DC: U.S. Department of Labor.

Burnham, D. (1970, April 25). Graft paid to police here said to run into millions. *New York Times,* pp. A1, A18.

Churchill, W., & Vander Wall, J. (2002). *The COINTELPRO papers: Documents from the FBI's secret wars against dissent in the United States.* Cambridge, MA: South End Press.

City of Los Angeles. (1991). *Independent commission on the Los Angeles Police Department.* Los Angeles, CA: Author.

City of Los Angeles. (2001). *Report of the Rampart Independent Review Committee.* Los Angeles, CA: Author.

City of New York. (1994). *Commission to investigate allegations of police corruption and the anti-corruption procedures of the police department: Commission report.* New York, NY: Author.

Clark, D. W., & White, E. K. (2003). Clinicians, cops, and suicide. In D. L. Hackett & J. M. Volanti (Eds.), *Police suicide tactics for prevention,* pp. 16–36. Springfield, IL: Charles C. Thomas Publishers.

Conrack, B., Sanders, T., & Rabinowitz, K. (2017, December 22). *Walking while black: Jacksonville's enforcement of pedestrian violations raises concerns that it's another example of racial profiling.* Retrieved March 1, 2018, from https://features .propublica.org/walking-while-black/jacksonville-pedestrian-violations-racial-profiling/.

Cooper, E. F. (2002). *The emergence of crack cocaine abuse.* Hauppauge, NY: Novinka Books.

Department of Justice. (2015). *DEPARTMENT OF JUSTICE report regarding the criminal investigation into the shooting death of Michael Brown by Ferguson, Missouri police officer Darren Wilson.* Washington, DC: Author.

Dierenfield, B. J. (2008). *Civil rights movement.* New York, NY: Pearson Publishing.

Germann, A. C., Day, F. D., & Galatti, R.R.J. (1976). *Introduction to law enforcement and criminal justice*. Springfield, IL: Charles C. Thomas Publishers.

Gibson, D. D. (2008). The impact of parental incarceration on African American families. *Praxis, 8,* 23–29.

Greene, J. R. (1996). *The encyclopedia of police science*. Boca Raton, FL: CRC Press.

Hensley, T. (1981). *The Kent State incident: Impact of judicial process on public attitudes*. Westport, CT: Greenwood Press.

Heroin Shooting War. (1971, June 21). *Time* magazine, *97* (25), 20.

Holmes, M. D. (2000). Minority threat and police brutality: Determinants of civil rights complaints in US municipalities. *Criminology, 38*(2): 343–368.

Huizenga, D., Thornberry, T., Knight, K., & Lovegrove, P. (2007). *Disproportionate minority contact in the juvenile justice system: A study of differential minority arrest/referral to court in three cities*. Washington, DC: Office of Juvenile Justice and Delinquency Prevention.

Kerner Commission. (1968). *Report of the national advisory commission on civil disorders: Summary of report*. Washington, DC: Author.

Kirchhoff, S. M. (2010). *Economic impacts of prison growth*. Washington, DC: Congressional Research Service.

Knapp Commission. (1972). *The Knapp commission report on police corruption*. New York, NY: George Braziller.

Kolender v. Lawson, 461 U.S. 352 (1983).

Kush, F. (2004). *Battleground Chicago: The police and the 1968 Democratic National Convention*. Westport, CT: Praeger.

Laney, G. P. (2006). Racial profiling: Issues and federal legislative proposals and options. In S. J. Muffler (Ed.), *Racial profiling: Issues, data and analysis*. New York, NY: Nova Science Publishers.

Leen, J. (1999, September 27). The Vietnam protests: When worlds collide. *Washington Post,* p. A7.

Lockard, C. B., & Wolf, M. (2012, January). Occupational employment projections to 2020. *Monthly Labor Review, 84*(1), 84–108.

Maguire, B., & Radosh, P. F. (1996). *The past, present, and future of American criminal justice,* 2nd ed. Lanham, MD: Rowman & Littlefield.

Martin, S. E., & Jurik, N. C. (1996). *Doing justice, doing gender: Women in law and criminal justice occupations*. Thousand Oaks, CA: Sage Publications.

Monkkonen, E. H. (1981). *Police in urban America, 1860–1920*. New York, NY: Cambridge University Press.

Nardone v. United States, 308 U.S. 338 (1939).

National Center on Crime and Delinquency. (2007). *And justice for some: Differential treatment of youth of color in the justice system*. Madison, WI: Author.

New York City Police Department. (2006–2016). *New York City Police Department's annual reports 2006–2016*. New York, NY: Author.

New York Police History. (1895, January 27). Growth of the department and its present proportions. Its origin the single Schout. The "ancient Charlies" and the "leatherheads"—The London system tried—Reorganization of 1870. *New York Times*. Retrieved October 17, 2008, from http://query.nytimes.com/mem/archive-free/pdf?

O'Hara, P. (2005). *Why law enforcement organizations fail: Mapping the organizational fault lines in policing.* Durham, NC: Carolina Academic Press.

Pope, C. E., Lovell, R., & Hsia, H. I. (2001). *Disproportionate minority confinement: A review of the research literature from 1989 through 2001.* Washington, DC: Office of Juvenile Justice and Delinquency Prevention.

Ridgeway, G., Mitchell, O., Gunderman, S., Alexander, C., & Letten, J. (2016). *An examination of racial disparities in bicycle stops and citations made by the Tampa Police Department.* Washington, DC: Office of Community Oriented Policing Services.

Rooney, A. (2010). *Voices: Race hate.* London: Evans Brothers Limited.

Rosenberger, L. R. (1996). *America's drug war debacle.* Brookfield, VT: Ashgate Publishing.

Rosinsky, N. M. (2008). *The Kent State shooting: We the people.* Mankato, MN: Compass Point Books.

Seaward, B. L. (2009). *Managing stress: Principles and strategies for health and well being,* 6th ed. Sudbury, MA: Jones and Bartlett Publishers.

Shusta, R. M., Levine, D. R., Wong, H. Z., Olson, A. T., & Harris, P. R. (2011). *Multicultural law enforcement: Strategies for peacekeeping in a diverse society.* Boston, MA: Prentice Hall.

Siebert, A. (1994). *The survivor personality.* New York, NY: Berkley Publishing Group.

Slovenko, R. (2002). *Psychiatry in law: Law in psychiatry.* New York, NY: Brunner-Routledge.

Stahl, T. (2017). Collective responsibility of oppression. *Social Theory and Practice, 43* (3), 473–501.

State of Missouri v. Darren Wilson. (2014). *Transcript of the grand jury.* St. Louis, MO: Author.

Terry v. Ohio, 392 U.S. 1, 88 S. Ct. (1968).

Thomas, D. J. (2002). *Perception of race survey.* Gainesville, FL. Author.

Thomas, D. J. (2008). Culture and the hostage negotiation process. *Law Enforcement Executive Research Forum, 8*(6), 169–184.

Thomas, D. J. (2011a). *Police psychology: A new specialty and new challenges for men and women in blue.* Santa Barbara, CA: Prager Publishing.

Thomas, D. J. (2011b). *Professionalism in policing: An introduction.* Clifton Park, NY: Cengage Publishing.

Thomas, D. J. (2017). *Understanding society and its impact on policing.* Gainesville, FL: Police Counseling Services, LLC.

U.S. Supreme Court. (1857). *Scott v. Sandford, 60 U. S. 393.* Washington, DC: Author.

Vollmer, A. (1971). *The police and modern society.* Montclair, NJ: Patterson Smith.

Walker, D. (1968). *Rights in conflict: The violent confrontation of demonstrators and police in the parks and streets of Chicago during the week of the Democratic National Convention of 1968.* Washington, DC: U.S. National Commission on the Causes and Prevention of Violence.

Wildeman, C., & Western, B. (2010). Incarceration in fragile families. *Future of Our Children, 20* (2), 157–177.

2

Police Culture, Misconduct, and Consent Decrees

There are more than 17,000 state, county, and municipal law enforcement agencies in the United States employing more than 750,000 sworn law enforcement officers (Banks, Hendrix, Hickman, & Kyckelhahn, 2016). The average size of an agency is five people or less. Here we detail the extensive hiring processes that new candidates experience. It is important to note that the hiring process is not the same for every agency, and oftentimes the smaller agency's process is not as demanding due to financial hardships, unless state statute mandates the preliminary steps for new officers. Throughout this hiring process, officers are reminded of such concepts as ethics and honor and are often required to display those characteristics through the academy and hiring process. Yet to survive within a particular agency, the new candidate must modify his or her value system to be accepted.

A new candidate modifies his or her personal values to gain acceptance. New candidates may learn that patterns of pervasive police misconduct are the norm and condoned by many agencies, as well as their peers. As a result, the question that often arises is, Who polices the police? The law enforcement community's response, after the Kerner Commissions report and following the riots in the 1960s, was to establish Internal Affairs Units, which are also known as the Division of Professional Standards (DPS). DPS was put into place to investigate police misconduct and citizen complaints. Minority citizens have complained that the process of filing a complaint against an officer is often fraught with the fear that officer(s) will retaliate against the complaining citizen. Other minority citizens have described the process of formally filing a complaint as the most agonizing event of their lives, noting the process is intimidating because, as complainants, they were required to appear in person at police headquarters, the same location where the violating officer/s work; as complainants they were forced to wait in the lobby of the police headquarters, which increased the complainant's anxiety level; while waiting to meet with investigators, many have encountered the officer(s) that they were there to file the complaint against. Finally, the minority community questions the outcomes of such investigations when most often the officers are cleared.

To eliminate some of the anguish and right a ship that has been viewed as running amuck, *consent decrees* were instituted after the Rodney King incident. Consent decrees are a tool used by the Department of Justice when a law enforcement agency's operational policies, acts of misconduct, and activity have become so egregious that it shocks the conscience of America and intervention is required. A consent decree is an agreement reached between the Department of Justice and the jurisdiction in violation. In as much, the agreement is a legally binding document, which is overseen by federal court. The court assigns monitors to report the progress of the agreed-upon changes. This chapter examines the psychology of police culture, the profile of officers most likely to be involved in police misconduct, early intervention programs, internal investigations, consent decrees, and collaborative reforms.

PSYCHOLOGY OF POLICE CULTURE

The police culture has many interrelated characteristics that are dependent on each other, most notably history and tradition. Other contributing characteristics are operational procedures, unstated assumptions, tools, norms, values, and habits shaped through interaction with a particular environment or many environments (Berry & Triandis, 2004). It is important to note that we, as individuals, can become enculturated into many subcultures. Beyond being an American citizen, which by itself has its own set of values, there are other variables used to define our individual cultures—race/ethnicity, biology, psychology, family, gender, peers, economic status, education, and profession. No one of the aforementioned components by itself can fully define a person's culture. We are members of many subcultures that intersect in our daily lives, imposing a unique set of values demanding we act appropriately when in a particular setting. However, society may choose one of the aforementioned cultural variables to assume they know, or judge, our culture and, hence, our value as members of society. This is stereotyping. In policing, this would be called profiling, making an assessment based on an appearance you perceive, or the feeling or hunch you get.

Law enforcement officers have many influences that impact their acculturation. First is their environment from birth to the beginning of their professional careers. New officers bring a particular value system with them and can include a hidden criminal past, racism, or substance abuse. Once a candidate enters the police academy, he or she must begin to assimilate the role of policing and the police subculture into his or her own value system. For some, this assimilation is easy. For others, it doesn't work, with evidence of that in the number of police recruits that drop out of the police academy within the first two weeks. On average, 25 percent of those who enter the police academy drop out by the end of the second week (J. Sturdivant, personal communication, December 10, 2017; Thomas, 2011).

After graduation from the academy, new officers are assessed on their ability to do the job, and the unwritten variable of being accepted by their peers translates to the assessment of the new officer's performance—decision-making under stress and trust. Acceptance into police culture is defined by law, policy, agency culture, shift assignment, squad assignment, supervisors, and peers, with each having a different expectation or standard. In what may be described as the daily routine, for a new officer's acceptance, and survival, trust must be felt by one's shift partner, squad, and supervisors.

After graduation, new officers make a decision regarding the agency where they would like to work. The new officers assess salary, action and opportunity, but few ever say that they consciously examined the culture of an organization and that was the reason they selected a particular agency. Agency culture comes into play only after new officers have worked at their first selected site and find that they don't "fit." Often, officers leave an opportunity on the table to find an organization that agrees with their personal value system. When asked why they are leaving that agency, the response is usually simply that they "don't fit." This observation is confirmed by Yearwood (2003), who noted in his study of new officers in North Carolina that the average stay of a new officer is 28 months (p. v). Orrick (2008) notes that studies in Vermont, Alaska, and Florida reveal similar results. Martin and Jurik (2006) expand on the reasoning, saying their study shows "the reasons for turnover are dissatisfaction with promotional policies, transfer policies, opportunities, management style, agency practices, and the cost of housing in particular jurisdictions" (p. 99). Acceptance into the subculture of policing means that a new officer's behavior is modified to model the behavior of the organizational culture. Unacceptable behavior may well mean that a new officer is ostracized and considered an outcast by senior officers. The agency's culture defines the standards and values by which all are judged within that organization (Bandura, 1977).

In regard to the value system/psychology of corrupt law enforcement officers, an officer's immoral behavior and/or misconduct is allowed to continue because the agency's value system is corrupted at some level and the agency turns a blind eye to officer misconduct. Champion (2001) equates immoral behavior with police misconduct and offers the following: "Police misconduct is any inappropriate behavior that is either illegal, immoral or both" (p. 3). As discussed in Chapter 1, a number of issues have affected public perception of police over the years. The image of policing has been tainted by acts of poor judgment, theft, bribery, brutality, drug dealing, extortion, gang affiliation, and even acts of murder. The end result of these acts is that public trust is no longer automatic. And the poor behavior of a few officers has created a seemingly insurmountable trust void in poor and minority communities (Bradley, 2008; Palmiotto, 2001; Reisig, 2002).

Most police bad behavior targets minority communities, as noted in Chapter 1. The mere fact that persons are Black means that they are fair game. No value is placed on those persons' value to society because they are suspected of being criminals. Who will believe them if they complain of this injustice? They violated the law by jaywalking, or riding a bike at night with no light; each "justifies" the disparity in treatment that members of these communities receive. This happens because the Black community has been complaining for hundreds of years, and mainstream America has largely tuned out Black America. The most outspoken—seemingly the norm—in mainstream White America argue that Black and minority communities are using their minority status to gain sympathy and preferential treatment. Black America perceives that "tune out" as essentially Whites saying, "Enough, we are no longer listening because you have offered no proof. Your complaints are not valid."

McWhorter (2000) adds that Blacks have been accused of peddling victimhood, which is not a new charge. Calling attention to a wrong is healthy, but to say that everything negative happens because a person is Black and without evidence fosters resentment (p. 2).

I will go a step further and argue that Black communities must become educated and stop displaying what can best be described as "Black hysteria" and making arguments without having all the facts. When an argument of race is not based on fact, not supported by evidence, then the complaint and complainant lend themselves to a lack of credibility. No credibility means that mainstream America can and will tune you out. A common belief held by many in mainstream America is that police would not be contacting people or making an arrest if the person had done nothing wrong. But this rationale is disproven with the Innocence Project's findings of over 300 wrongly convicted people being released from prison.

Not all law enforcement officers participate in unjust practices. Again, performance and acceptance are determined by agency culture and, more important, the culture of police peers at the street level. When an agency is assessed, it should be assessed on what the agency values most. Is it productivity/numbers of arrests to show the public that its officers are performing? Or is the agency a service agency where numbers are less important and rather officers are judged by the quality of police service offered, responsiveness to the community needs, clearance of cases, and community partnerships?

PSYCHOLOGY OF POLICE MISCONDUCT AND BRUTALITY

The profiles of officers who are involved in brutality have been identified by Scrivner (1994), and those persist today. These profiles were developed after conducting a survey of 65 police psychologists, who provided psychological services to and for law enforcement agencies throughout the United States (pp. 11–14). Profiles of officers involved in brutality included these factors:

1. *Chronic risk*—This group is distinguished from other groups because of personality disorders. The personality traits displayed are antisocial behavior, narcissism, and paranoid or abusive tendencies. Such ingrained personality traits and abuse may be intensified due to the high-stress nature of police work. Sixteen percent of the officers evaluated displayed personality disorders.

2. *Job-related trauma*—This group of officers have experienced job-related trauma. This should not be confused with a personality disorder. These officers are prone to excessive force because of the emotional baggage they carry due to involvement while on duty in prior incidents. In many of these cases, the trauma has not been resolved, and the traumatic emotional effects manifest in brutality. Most often this group of officers refuse to see a clinician out of fear they will be classified as mentally unfit, removed from duty, or seen as weak by their peers. Seventeen percent of those evaluated were in this category.

3. *Early career–stage problems*—This is a group of young and inexperienced officers. They are frequently seen as "badge happy," macho, and immature. Supervisors and peers see these officers as ones who will outgrow these problems. In many instances, older officers expect "He will learn after he gets his ass kicked a few times." Instead, the new officer becomes a detriment to the agency. It is believed that training and supervision will remedy the situation. What the study fails to recognize is the impact the organizational culture has on this type of officer. Eighteen percent of those evaluated were in this category.

A special note should be made here. Policing is going through a major cultural change. Since 2000, there have been a number of retirements throughout the United States, and agencies are losing veteran officers. Many in the profession see it is as a mass exodus. The exodus has created a void, leaving behind training officers with little or no experience, who are training new and immature officers, and a cadre of supervisors who lack experience, further creating a void in both leadership and training. Thus, new officers are often left to their own devices, a sort of initiation by fire.

4. *Patrol style*—This group of officers were described as heavy-handed and exuding a dominant command presence. They use force to show that they are in control, and this has become a norm. These officers refuse to allow their authority to be challenged without recourse. Many of these officers evolve from early career–stage officers to this style. Twenty-one percent of those evaluated developed patrol styles that incorporate the use of force without cause as a norm.

5. *Personal problems*—Not all officers with personal problems fit this category. This profile is based on an officer's inability to adjust to a personal loss such as divorce, separation, or a perceived reduction in status. In fact, this group previously functioned fine, until their personal life suffered a negative impact. Twenty-eight percent of those evaluated were in this category.

These profiles are far from finite and are limited in their scope. However, the early career–stage officers and the patrol-style officers are what have been identified in each of the commission reports and studies cited earlier. Although limited in number, these two categories comprise 38 percent of the respondents' data. Even if the real percentage was 10 percent, the numbers are significant and clear with the advent of social media, body cameras, in-car video, and surveillance cameras at every corner. Yes the actions of the few taint every officer in the United States. And without corrective action, the agency appears to condone this behavior, fostering a culture of abuse, albeit unintentional or not.

THE INTERNAL AFFAIRS PROCESS

The internal affairs process is questioned by those outside an organization. "Police investigating the police? How can we trust them? And who investigates the internal affairs police?" To police, those in internal affairs are seen as headhunters. The most common perception of internal affairs investigators is that the investigators have an agenda, they are looking to get promoted, or investigators get personal satisfaction in the termination of their fellow officers.

The following, for example, are excerpts from the Alachua (FLA) County Sheriff's Office Directive 122, which establishes the roles and responsibilities of the Office of Professional Standards (Internal Affairs):

a. **Chief Inspector** is in charge of the Office of Professional Standards and has the responsibility, among other duties, for conducting internal investigations, and reports directly to the Sheriff. One function of this Office is to provide fact-finding assistance to the Sheriff and his/her staff by providing a systematic, objective and impartial method of investigating citizen and employee complaints of all employee misconduct (civilian and sworn personnel).

b. **Inspectors** assigned to the Office of Professional Standards and are responsible for:

1. Conducting Administrative Inquiries arising from employee misconduct or lack of performance and have full authority to discharge this responsibility.

2. On occasion, conducting criminal investigations prior to commencement of the administrative inquiry.

3. Investigating Category One Use of Deadly Force incidents.

4. Investigating any matter as directed by the Sheriff.

c. An employee who is the subject of an administrative inquiry will cooperate with and assist Inspectors, recognizing that internal investigations are conducted under the immediate authority of the Sheriff.

In any internal investigation, complaints can come from five sources: citizens, civilian employees, sworn employees, supervisors, and suspects. Often when citizens call to complain about an officer's conduct or to determine if what they observed was proper police procedure, their inquiry is answered and a complaint is never filed.

Those complaints that are filed can be addressed in one of two formats. If the conduct is criminal, then an agency must perform two separate investigations, one criminal and the other administrative.

a. **Administrative Investigations** are performed by Internal Affairs and, depending on findings, with recommendations for discipline or no discipline. Internal investigations are unique in that an officer is **compelled** to cooperate with the investigator, since it is an administrative investigation and no criminal charges can be filed. Unlike criminal cases, Miranda Warnings do not apply. This is supported in the U.S. Supreme Court decision **GARRITY v. NEW JERSEY, 385 U.S. 493 (1967), 385 U.S. 493**. Garrity provides that an officer must cooperate. However, the information that is provided to Internal Affairs during the administrative investigation cannot be used against the officer in a criminal investigation.

b. **Criminal Investigations**—If there is a possibility that criminal charges can be filed against an officer as a result of the same incident, then the agency **must initiate a separate criminal investigation and the information cannot be shared between investigators**. For an agency to avoid allegations of impropriety, an outside agency should conduct the criminal investigation. However, in larger agencies this is rarely done.

c. **Outcomes for Administrative Complaints:**

1. Unfounded—The act or acts complained of did not occur or did not involve agency personnel.

2. Not-sustained—Insufficient evidence to clearly prove or disprove the allegation/complaint. It does not mean that the incident did not occur. It means there was not enough evidence to support the complaint.

3. Sustained—The preponderance of evidence clearly proves the allegation/complaint.

4. Exonerated—The act or acts did occur, but were justified, lawful and proper.

5. Exonerated due to policy failure—A finding or conclusion which indicates policy, procedure, rule, or regulation covering the situation was non-existent or inadequate.

Early Intervention Programs

Some law enforcement agencies have recognized that officer misconduct and acts of brutality may be more than the agency's culture, rather a response to a series of stressors that may be job related, involve the officer's personal life, and/or may be a combination. Scrivner (1994) identified two of these typologies as job-related tendencies and personal problems. Thomas (2017) states:

> Officers are exposed to a number of traumatic incidents. What we don't know is how each of these incidents impacts the officer's mental health over time and/or how much is too much. Each officer has a different series of coping mechanisms and as outsiders looking in we don't know when the officer's coping mechanisms have failed or when the officer is overwhelmed. What we do know about human behavior is that if stressors are not addressed they will manifest and be expressed in some way, for some it may be: acts of brutality, domestic violence, substance abuse/alcoholism, depression, anxiety, marital infidelity, suicide or a combination of any or all of the aforementioned. (para. 10)

In response to these stressors, some agencies have implemented a section in their internal affairs policy known as an Early Intervention Program (EIP) or Early Warning System. The Tampa Police Department has implemented such a program, and it is detailed in *Standard Operating Procedure 651.1* (2016), which states, "The early intervention program is designed to assist employees who are engaging in a pattern or practice of problematic behavior or experiencing underlying issues that are affecting their job performance" (p. 1).

The goal of an EIP in agencies that use such a system is to examine every officer's performance in totality through a weekly audit conducted by internal affairs by reviewing the following performance indicators: citizen's complaints, use-of-force incidents, service-related inquiries initiated by internal affairs, division discipline, failing to appear in court, and/or three or more complaints involving off-duty assignments. The audit is run weekly, and officers must have three or more of any of the aforementioned performance indicators within a 90-day period. The information is forwarded from internal affairs to the officer's immediate supervisor.

The officer's supervisor is tasked with completing a thorough investigation and is required to make a determination of whether the performance indicators are stress related, a training issue, or no issue at all. There are two options if stress is not a determining factor: department discipline, mandated remediation training, and/or both to correct the officer's behavior. However, if it is determined that stress is the cause, depending on the agency, a recommendation can be made that the officer attend some form of counseling. Depending on the agency, its policy or union contract may prevent mandatory psychological counseling. In other agencies, officers can be mandated to attend counseling.

In reviewing the internal affairs process and EIPs, it would appear that the institution of American law enforcement has all the necessary tools to address officer abuse and misconduct. Every community should be able to rest in peace knowing that the police are effectively policing themselves. Before we move to the discussion of consent decrees and their necessity, review this scenario and reflect on the outcome.

SUSPICIOUS VEHICLE

Police Action Legal or Illegal

It is 2 A.M. on a Monday morning in a rural Florida County. Deputy Mark Smith is on patrol driving eastbound, and Deputy Smith observes a black Chevrolet pickup truck pass him traveling westbound occupied by a lone White male driver. Smith initiates a U-turn and is now westbound directly behind the black pickup truck. Both vehicles stop at a traffic light, and the pickup turns northbound. Smith activates his overhead lights, and the driver of the pickup truck refuses to stop. The pickup is not speeding; in fact, the driver is driving perfectly, with no indications of being impaired;

he just refused to stop. The pickup truck continued until it pulled into the driveway of a house. From the time Smith activated his overhead lights until the pickup stopped was exactly one minute. Smith exited his patrol car with his firearm drawn and ordered the driver to get on the ground. The driver asked why he was being stopped, and once Smith observed that the driver was unarmed, Smith drew his Taser, walked up to the driver, and shot the driver in the chest with the Taser. The driver offered no resistance during this encounter. Once the Taser was activated, the driver fell to the ground on all fours. Then Smith kicked the driver in the center of his back, forcing the driver to the ground. Smith continued to activate his Taser intermittently until the driver was handcuffed. Again, the driver never offered any resistance. The only thing the driver did was not stop until he drove into his driveway.

The driver's wife advised that the driver had a brain injury and was taking Tegretol to control seizures. When the driver asked again why Smith stopped him, the deputy responded that he had a taillight out. In reviewing the deputy's in-car video, it was later seen that the taillights and brake lights were functioning fine.

When backup arrived, they searched the interior of the pickup and the covered rear. When the driver asked what he was under arrest for, Smith listed fleeing and attempting to elude, a misdemeanor; and resisting arrest without violence, a misdemeanor; and the driver was issued a citation for defective equipment, taillight out.

The driver filed a formal complaint. In the interview of Smith, the internal affairs investigator who questioned him supplied and wrote responses in the proper legal verbiage when Smith's answers were not complete. Ultimately, Smith was exonerated and promoted to the rank of sergeant (*John Dupler v. Mark Hunter Sheriff of Columbia County et al.*, 2016).

Everything from start to finish in this incident was illegal: the traffic stop, the use of force, the arrest, and search of the vehicle, yet Smith was rewarded. The driver has now filed a federal lawsuit against the agency and Sergeant Smith. Is this an example of an agency's culture that is supported by the administration? Did the internal affairs process fail? Why would you promote someone who violated a citizen's constitutional rights? Again, who is policing the police?

CONSENT DECREES

Consent decrees are relatively new tools when it comes to modern policing. They officially began in 1994, after the beating of Rodney King in 1991 by Los Angeles police officers, the acquittal of those officers involved in the beating, and the Los Angeles riots that followed the officer's acquittal. Congress authorized the Department of Justice, under Federal Statute 42, Chapter 136—Violent Crime Control and Law Enforcement, Subchapter IX—State and Local Law Enforcement. Part B—Police Pattern or Practice, Sec. 14141—Cause of Action, to address patterns and practices of police misconduct. This statute gave the Justice Department the authority to sue state, county, or municipal governments in federal court and seek injunctive relief for pervasive patterns of police misconduct. The statute specifically addresses "police patterns and practices," including a culture that is tolerant or permissive of police misconduct. The first case was against the city of Pittsburgh, Pennsylvania, where it was determined that the Pittsburgh Police Department engaged in a pattern or practice of "excessive force, false arrests, and improper searches and seizures, grounded in a lack of adequate discipline for misconduct and a failure to supervise officers" (U.S. Department of Justice, 2017, p. 3).

Examples of Consent Decrees

Although consent decrees are ultimately an agreement among the Justice Department, a law enforcement agency, and the governmental entity, local law enforcement hates any form of federal oversight. Law enforcement administrators argue that this is a local problem and the local agency knows what's best for its citizens. The consent decree allows an agency to publicly save face by not admitting guilt. Yet the findings and the remedies clearly indicate that the agencies are guilty. Several consent decrees were selected, and their summaries are presented for your review. Examine the findings and make the determination; have crimes been committed, or is guidance the only thing needed?

- *Los Angeles Police Department 2000*—After the Los Angeles Police Department (LAPD) Rampart Scandal in 2000, the Department of Justice initiated a consent decree with LAPD and the city of Los Angeles. Although the consent decree did not specifically address that police agency's culture, it is clear that the consent decree was aimed at changing a culture that was indifferent to the community it served. Stone, Foglesong, and Cole (2009) provided a summary of the LAPD Consent Decree:

  a. Create a new data system that tracks the performance of every sworn officer and alerts supervisors to signs that individual officers are headed for trouble.

  b. Create new definitions, new rules, and new management systems governing the use of force by police officers.

c. Create new systems for tracking police stops of motor vehicles and pedestrians, breaking down the patterns by race and ethnicity, by the reasons for the stops, and by the results of the stops in terms of crime detected.

d. Create new management procedures in the LAPD's anti-gang unit and its other special divisions, tightening the management of "confidential informants" and otherwise increasing checks against possible corruption (p. 5).

- *New Orleans Police Department (NOPD) 2010*—The Justice Department's investigation found a pattern or practice described as serious, systemic, wide-ranging, and deeply rooted. This describes the NOPD's agency culture. In a March 2011 letter from the Assistant U.S. Attorney General's Office to the mayor of New Orleans, Mitchell Landrieu, the Justice Department discovered the following in its investigation and found the following patterns and practices of unconstitutional conduct and/or violations of federal law:

a. Use of excessive force; unconstitutional stops, searches, and arrests, and biased policing.

b. Racial, ethnic, and LGBT discrimination; national origin discrimination-systemic failure to provide effective policing services to persons with limited English proficiency; and gender-biased policing-systemic failure to investigate sexual assaults and domestic violence.

c. Failed systems for officer recruitment, promotion, evaluation, and inadequate supervision.

d. Inadequate training.

e. Ineffective systems of complaint intake, investigation, and adjudication.

f. A failed off-duty paid detail system.

g. Failure to engage in community-oriented policing and a lack of sufficient community oversight.

h. Inadequate officer assistance and support services (T. E. Perez, personal communication, March 16, 2011, pp. 2–3).

   The Department of Justice made a point of recognizing the devastating impact of Hurricane Katrina on the city of New Orleans, yet made it clear that the patterns and practices of police misconduct existed long before Katrina.

- *The Cleveland Police Department (CPD) 2015*—The Justice Department's investigation found a pattern or practice described as serious, systemic, wide-ranging, and deeply rooted. In addition, CPD failed to meet the obligations of a 2004 agreement with the Justice Department. The 2004 agreement had not been enforced by the court. In the investigation of CPD, the Justice Department found the following:

a. Unnecessary and excessive use of deadly force, including shootings and head strikes with impact weapons; the unnecessary, excessive, or retaliatory use of less-lethal force, including electronic control weapons, chemical spray, and fists; excessive force against persons who are mentally ill or in crisis, including in cases where the officers were called only for assistance; and the employment of poor and dangerous tactics that place officers in situations where avoidable force becomes inevitable and place officers and civilians at unnecessary risk.

b. Engage in a pattern or practice of unlawfully stopping, searching, and arresting persons in Cleveland.

c. Failure to adequately review and investigate officers' uses of force; fully and objectively investigate all allegations of misconduct; identify and respond to patterns of at-risk behavior; provide its officers with the support, training, supervision, and equipment needed to allow them to do their jobs safely and effectively; adopt and enforce appropriate policies; effectively deploy resources; and implement effective community policing strategies at all levels of CDP (*United States v. City of Cleveland*, 2015, pp. 4–5).

• *Baltimore Police Department (BPD) 2017*—The investigation and filing of the consent decree were a result of the death of Freddy Gray in 2015 while in BPD custody being transported to jail. Subsequently, community riots occurred. The Justice Department's investigation found that the legacy of "zero tolerance" street enforcement, along with deficient policies, training, and accountability systems, resulted in conduct that routinely violated the Constitution and federal antidiscrimination law and detailed the following:

a. BPD conducted stops, searches, and arrests without meeting the requirements of the Fourth Amendment.

b. Focusing enforcement strategies on African Americans, leading to severe and unjustified racial disparities in violation of Title VI of the Civil Rights Act and the Safe Streets Act.

c. Used unreasonable force in violation of the Fourth Amendment.

d. Interacting with individuals with mental health disabilities in a manner that violates the Americans with Disabilities Act.

e. BPD violates the First Amendment by retaliating against individuals engaged in constitutionally protected activities. Officers frequently detain and arrest members of the public for engaging in speech the officers perceive to be critical or disrespectful.

   BPD officers use force against members of the public who are engaging in protected speech.

f. Arrests—two categories of common unconstitutional arrests by BPD officers: (1) Officers make warrantless arrests without probable cause; and (2) officers make arrests for misdemeanor offenses, such as loitering and trespassing, without providing the constitutionally required notice that the arrested person was engaged in unlawful activity.

g. BPD fails to collect data on a range of law enforcement actions, and even when it collects data, it fails to store it in systems that are capable of effective tracking and analysis. BPD does not use an effective early intervention system to detect officers who may benefit from additional training or guidance to ensure that they do not commit constitutional and statutory violations (U.S. Department of Justice, 2016, pp. 8–10).

h. The findings in the BPD investigation have not been formalized because Attorney General Jeff Sessions has made some major changes to the role of the Justice Department overseeing local law enforcement.

Consent Decree Policy Change

Consent decrees have been viewed as a tool utilized by the Obama administration and then attorney generals Eric Holder and Loretta Lynch, to force change in law enforcement agencies where needed. Law enforcement officials despised the Obama administration's efforts and felt that the federal government had no business interfering in local affairs. This was no more evident than in 2014, when Attorney General Eric Holder was the keynote speaker at the International Association of Chiefs of Police Conference (IACP) in Orlando, Florida. The chiefs all but booed Holder and showed total disrespect for Holder's office and the Justice Department's interference in local matters. This was evidenced again, when President Obama was the keynote speaker at the 2015 IACP Conference. The chiefs did not respect President Obama; the room was less than half full. Obama's message was in support of law enforcement but clear that police misconduct must not be tolerated.

That changed with the election of President Trump and the appointment of Attorney General Jeff Sessions. In a March 31, 2017, memo, Attorney General Jeff Sessions outlined a new direction for the Justice Department in regard to overseeing local law enforcement, a return of local law enforcement fully into the hands of local police agencies. The key points of the Sessions memo are as follows:

- Law enforcement officers perform uniquely dangerous tasks, and the Department should help promote officer safety, officer morale, and public respect for their work.
- Local law enforcement must protect and respect the civil rights of all members of the public.
- Local control, and local accountability are necessary for effective local policing. It is not the responsibility of the federal government to manage non-federal law enforcement agencies.

- The misdeeds of individual bad actors should not impugn or undermine the legitimate and honorable work that law enforcement officers and agencies perform in keeping American communities safe.

- The collection and analysis of timely, reliable statistics on crime and criminals are essential for effective law enforcement strategies.

- Recruitment and training of law enforcement officers should focus on making law enforcement a rewarding career, and attracting and retaining well qualified personnel.

- Collaboration between federal and local law enforcement is important, and jurisdictions whose law enforcement agencies accept funding from the Department are expected to adhere to the Department's grant conditions as well as to all federal laws.

- The Deputy Attorney General and the Associate Attorney General are directed to immediately review all Department activities including collaborative investigations and prosecutions, grant making, technical assistance and training, compliance reviews, existing or contemplated consent decrees, and task force participation in order to ensure that they fully and effectively promote the principles outlined above. Nothing in this Memorandum, however, should be construed to delay or impede any pending criminal or national security investigation or program. (J. B. Sessions, personal communication, March 31, 2017)

Collaborative Reform Initiative for Technical Assistance

Collaborative reform is another tool designed to provide state, local, territorial, and tribal law enforcement agencies with critical technical assistance tailored to the needs of the agencies' problems. Agency participation is voluntary. The project is grant funded through the Justice Department's Community Oriented Policing Services (COPS) Office.

Participating agencies and/or the Justice Department identify areas of assistance to best suit their needs, which include subjects ranging from community policing to the use of force and de-escalation training. The goal of the technical assistance program is to provide agencies with the training and technical assistance to address a problem or a series of problems.

The difference between collaborative reform and consent decrees is that collaborative reform is not overseen by a court, such as in the case with the Las Vegas Police Department:

- *Las Vegas Metropolitan Police Department (LVMPD) 2011*—This process involved a critical review of officer-involved shootings by LVMPD officers. The process was begun in response to a five-part newspaper series published in the *Las Vegas Review Journal* in December 2011, titled "Deadly Force: When Las Vegas Police Shoot, and Kill" (Stewart, Fachner, King, & Rickman 2012, p. 4). The entire focus of the LVMPD reform addressed the use of force, specifically deadly force. Between the years 2002 and 2011, LVMPD averaged 17.9 officer-involved shootings (OIS) per year, with two higher than average—24 OIS in 2006 and 25 OIS in 2010. Some of the findings and recommendations were the following:

a. LVMPD does not conduct department-wide fair and impartial policing training that includes a focus on deadly use of force. In addition to the community perception of biased interactions in incidents of deadly force, review of agency data found that 7 out of 10 (70%) OISs involving unarmed suspects were Black. Six of nine (66%) OISs that began as officer-initiated stops involved Black subjects.

b. Officer-initiated stops are more likely to result in the shooting of an unarmed suspect more than any other type of contact. This is what is termed as "Lawful but Awful" meaning that the officer's reasons for contact do not meet the standard of suspicious or probable cause. The contact falls under the classification of police citizen contacts. The subject flees for an unknown reason; the officer chases. The officer and the subject get into a struggle; the officer fears that he or she may be seriously injured or killed and shoots the subject.

c. Supervisors were not required to respond to calls of armed person(s).

d. The objectively reasonable officer doctrine established by *Graham v. Connor* was not clearly specified in the LVMP Use of Force Policy. Reasonable officer doctrine asks the question: Would an officer with similar years of experience and background have responded the same given the same or similar situation?

e. The LVMPD did not have an intermediate-force level identified in its Use of Force Policy, meaning the use of electronic weapons, impact weapons/batons, or pepper spray.

f. De-escalation was discussed in the Use of Force Policy but not emphasized. Most policies mandate that an officer "must de-escalate when control is established" (Stewart et al., 2012, pp. 124–128).

Collaborative Reform Policy Change

The Collaborative Reform Initiative Program and the grants process was administered by the Justice Department's COPS Office until December 2017. However, with the Trump administration came change, and the collaborative reform process is now supervised by a number of organizations that answer to membership, as opposed to organizations that embody independence in their fact-finding.

It is important to note that when an organization is responsible to its membership, there are times when the organization is responsible for defending the actions of a member(s), such as a chief who has made a poor decision or an officer who is involved in questionable activity. If the member organizations are responsible for the collaborative process, then they may well be more responsive to their constituents than what is best for policing. It may be argued that the outcomes of such a process do nothing more than reinforce negative behavior that the Justice Department has cited as "serious, systemic, wide-ranging, and deeply rooted" (Stone et al., 2009, p. 5). Policing often is shrouded in a culture that refuses to change and is based on tradition. Wadman (2009) supports this argument:

> Change is evolving and needed in the very organization whose responsibility is to sustain the current traditions and cultural values of society. However, it is important to keep in mind, as new theories and practices emerge, the police departments of America are still organized to support the goals of our long held commitment to a social value system of the past rather than one that is in a state constant flux and ever evolving. (p. 25)

COMMUNITY POLICING—A FAILED ATTEMPT AT CHANGE

Organizational culture is much like that of society. The profession of policing is a subculture, and if closely examined we see it is a mirror of our society. In its beginnings, it was a subculture that was strictly a White male club. Over time, it has been forced to change and look more like the community in which it serves. Schein (2004) explains:

> Perhaps the intriguing aspect of culture as a concept is that it points us to phenomena that are below the surface, that are powerful in their impact but invisible and to a considerable degree unconscious. In that sense, culture is to a group what personality or character is to an individual. We can see the behavior that results, but often we cannot see the forces underneath that cause certain kinds of behavior. Yet, just as our personality and character guide and constrain our behavior, so does culture guide and constrain the behavior of members of a group through the shared norms that are held in the groups. (p. 8)

Community policing is a style of policing where citizens trust the police. It requires a partnership between the community and the officers. The most commonly used phrase associated with community policing is: "Working in partnership with the community."

The initial concept of community policing began in the late 1970s and early 1980s as an experiment to bring back old-fashioned foot patrols or what is known as the "Beat Cop." The need for such a program was born out of two concerns from the community: a rise in the violent crime rate and a series of volatile incidents that occurred nationally throughout African American communities. Most notable of the incidents was the shooting of unarmed Black males who had committed nonviolent felonies and were fleeing the scene. It wasn't until 1985 and the celebrated case of *Tennessee v. Garner* that the fleeing felon rule was abolished. In essence, the return of foot patrols/beat cops had as much to do with public relations as it did with protection and security. Trojanowicz and Bucqueroux (1998) offer the following:

> The C.S. Mott Foundation of Flint, Michigan invested millions of dollars in implementing foot patrols citywide. Trojanowicz a professor at Michigan State University trained the Flint officers to become community-based problem solvers, collaborating with formal and informal leaders of the community. At the same time, Professor George Kelling of Northeastern University was monitoring a similar initiative sponsored by The Police Foundation in Newark, New Jersey. (p. 3)

Foot patrols/beat cops evolved into the philosophy that we now know as *community-oriented policing*. Community policing includes the development of external partnerships with community members and groups. In addition, community policing addresses organizational changes that should take place in a police agency (e.g., decentralized decision-making, fixed geographic accountability, agency-wide training, personnel evaluations) designed to support collaborative problem-solving, community partnerships, and a general proactive orientation to crime and social disorder issues. Central to the implementation of community policing is a commitment by the administration *demanding* the implementation of the program. The administration has to have *buy in* from every individual in the department, including patrol officers and supervisors. Anything short of this commitment means a failed attempt to change in cultural ideology.

In addition to the foot patrol/beat, Professor Herman Goldstein of the University of Wisconsin developed the concept of problem-oriented policing (POP) in conjunction with the Scanning-Analysis-Response-Assessment (SARA) model, which are concepts that go hand in hand with the concept of community policing. "Problem-oriented policing is not community policing; problem-oriented policing is a method for analyzing and solving crime problems. When done well, community policing provides a strong overarching philosophy in which to engage in POP, but community policing that fails to incorporate the principles of POP within it, is unlikely to have a substantial impact on reducing crime" (Center for Problem-Oriented Policing, 2018, para. 1).

The components of SARA are essential in addressing a problem within a neighborhood; some of the more common problems are abandoned homes, prostitution, drugs, auto theft, burglary, and robbery. The acronym SARA is defined as follows:

1. *Scanning*—The stakeholders need to research the problem, gathering as much information as possible. They can use crime analysis, police reports, victim interviews, and news accounts. The idea here is to collect as much data as possible.

2. *Analysis*—Analyze the data that they have gathered. Determine the how and why such a problem exists. In doing the analysis, often the researcher will find a cause and effect.

3. *Response*—Here is where you determine how to solve the problem. It is considered brainstorming. The caveat is that whatever is decided must be legal, ethical, and doable. You will often find that the pubic has many misconceptions regarding police authority.

4. *Assessment*—This is the final phase of any project: to look back and determine how successful your plan of action was. When discussing success, let's say eliminating drugs from a neighborhood and the associated crimes, what most likely has happened is that the crime has been displaced to another location (Center for Problem-Oriented Policing, 2018, para. 1). The question administrators have to ask is: Do I have the resources to continue to displace crime until it is eradicated or moved? Typically, what we find is law enforcement is understaffed and often lacks the necessary resources to continue sustained efforts.

COMMUNITY POLICING IN ACTION

One of the most challenging and rewarding positions in policing is that of being assigned to a neighborhood and developing a true partnership between police and community members. Community policing is so much more than making arrests. It can include assisting the neighbors to receive city services that have been allowed to erode due to neglect; working with the city to open a recreation center abandoned and closed for years; creating a summer basketball program for the kids aged 6 to 14 and supervising those games; forming partnerships with businesses in the city so that they will fund antidrug, sports, or tutoring programs; attending neighborhood watch meetings so that residents have input into police efforts; and assisting and organizing neighborhood cleanups. When you read this list, you may wonder how police involved have time to police. But community policing can make police work a lot easier. In one case, for example, officers made 300 arrests for sale and possession of crack cocaine in a six-month period. Information that officers had received to make many of those arrests came from the neighborhood where they were assigned for community policing programs.

Community policing has many meanings, and it depends on the agency or the administrator as to how they want to define it. However, when it comes to implementation of the principles and practices of community policing, agencies sometimes bastardize the true definition, and the alternatives are policing at its worst, which means aggressive policing, violating citizen's rights, and is fraught with police misconduct. It is because the term has so many meanings that the community is confused and wary. Kappeler and Gaines (2011) assert the following concerning the current state of community policing and its failure:

Police departments across the country are using saturation patrols, undercover operations, field interrogations, and other highly visible enforcement tactics under the guise of community policing and call it community policing. Police managers maintain that these tactics are efforts to "take back the streets" or regain control over areas that *have* been lost to crime. (p. 39)

CONCLUSION

Policing is an institution that has been suspect for the mistreatment of minority citizens dating back to slavery and brought to fruition after the 1967 riots, with a series of innovations that President Johnson mandated. Here we are today, and still the culture of law enforcement overall has not changed and fails to change to meet the ever-changing values of the communities it serves. After the Rodney King beating, the Justice Department was given tools to force cultural changes within law enforcement, through consent decrees and collaborative reform agreements, both excellent tools because the agencies were made accountable.

However, due to Attorney General Jeff Sessions's view of local government and local police best "policed" by themselves, the Justice Department will no longer use one of the tools, despite the fact that evidence exists that consent decrees are needed. Law enforcement has proven that it is unwilling to change. And there is an old saying in psychology: "The best predictor of future behavior is past behavior."

In a similar but less-dramatic fashion, Sessions directed that the use of collaborative agreements be managed by membership organizations that are often defending the very same officers or organizations who are violating citizens' rights. And such actions are described by the Justice Department often as serious, systemic, wide-ranging, and deeply rooted.

So we return to the question asked at the start of this chapter: "Who is policing the police?"

The answer is "no one."

REFERENCES

Alachua County Sheriff's Office. (2015). *Alachua County Sheriff's Office Directives.* Gainesville, FL: Author.

Bandura, A. (1977). *Social learning theory.* Englewood, CA: Prentice-Hall.

Banks, D., Hendrix, J., Hickman, M., & Kyckelhahn, T. (2016). *National sources of law enforcement employment data.* Washington, DC: U.S. Department of Justice.

Berry, J. W., & Triandis, H. C. (2004). Cross U.S. Department of Justice. Cultural psychology. In C. Spielberger (Ed.), *Encyclopedia of applied psychology.* Atlanta, GA: Elsevier.

Bradley, R. (2008). *Public expectations and police perception.* London, UK: Research, Development and Statistics Directorate.

Center for Problem-Oriented Policing. (2018). *Step 5: Be true to POP.* Retrieved January 21, 2018, from http://www.popcenter.org/learning/60steps/index.cfm?stepNum=5.

Champion, D. J. (2001). *Police misconduct in America: A reference handbook.* Santa Barbara, CA: ABC-CLIO.

John Dupler v. Mark Hunter Sheriff of Columbia County et al. (2016). Case No.: 3:16-CV-191-J-34MCR.

Kappeler, V. E., & Gaines, L. K. (2011). *Community policing: A contemporary perspective.* New York, NY: Elsevier.

Martin, S. E., & Jurik, N. C. (2006). *Doing justice, doing gender: Women in legal and criminal justice occupations.* Thousand Oaks, CA: Sage Publications.

McWhorter, J. H. (2000). *Losing the race: Self-sabotage in black America.* New York, NY: The Free Press.

Orrick, D. (2008). *Recruitment, retention, and turnover of police personnel; reliable, practical, and effective solutions.* Springfield, IL: Charles C. Thomas Publisher.

Palmiotto, M. J. (2001). Police misconduct and minority citizens: Exploring key issues. In M. J. Palmiotto (Ed.), *Police misconduct: A reader for the 21st century*, pp. 58–71. New York, NY: Pearson Publishing.

Reisig, M. D. (2002). *Satisfaction with police: What really matters*. Washington, DC: National Institute of Justice.

Schein, E. (2004). *Organizational culture and leadership*. San Francisco, CA: Jossey-Bass.

Scrivner, E. (1994). *The role of police psychology in controlling excessive force*. Washington, DC: National Institute of Justice.

Stewart, J. K., Fachner, G., King, D., & Rickman, S. (2012). *Collaborative reform process: A review of officer-involved shootings in the Las Vegas Metropolitan Police Department*. Washington, DC: U.S. Department of Justice.

Stone, C., Foglesong, T., & Cole, C. M. (2009). *Policing Los Angeles under a consent decree: The dynamics of change at the LAPD*. Cambridge, MA: Harvard Kennedy School.

Tampa Police Department. (2016). *Written directives: Standard Operating Procedure 651.1*. Tampa, FL: Author.

Tennessee v. Garner, 471 U.S. 1 (1985).

Thomas, D. J. (2011). *Professionalism in policing: An introduction*. Clifton Park, NY: Cengage Publishing.

Thomas, D. J. (2017). *Mental health triage: A tool for law enforcement officers*. Retrieved from https://www.calibrepress.com/2017/12/mental-health-triage-tools-leos-pt-1/.

Trojanowicz, R., & Bucqueroux, B. (1998). *Community policing: How to get started*. Cincinnati, OH: Anderson Publishing Company.

United States v. City of Cleveland. (2015). Case: 1:15-cv-01046.

U.S. Department of Justice. (2016). *Investigation of the Baltimore City Police Department*. Washington, DC: Author.

U.S. Department of Justice. (2017). *The civil rights division's pattern and practice police reform work: 1994–present*. Washington, DC: Author.

Wadman, R. C. (2009). *Police theory in America: Old traditions and new opportunity*. Springfield, IL: Charles C. Thomas Publishers.

Yearwood, D. L. (2003). *Recruitment and retention study series: Sworn sheriff's personnel*. Raleigh, NC: North Carolina Governor's Crime Commission.

3

The Psychology of Bias and Racism in Policing

There is a long-held belief in the minority community that police are biased in their decision-making. This belief system is historical and dates back to the southern sheriff and the sheriff's participation in slave patrols. These ideas have been passed on from generation to generation and today have become more polarizing with the shooting of unarmed Black men who have in many instances done nothing wrong. Parents of African American male youth describe having "the talk," a conversation with their African American male children to keep them from becoming a police statistic or an accident due to racial profiling.

Since bias and racism are at the core of some allegations of police misconduct, we examine the psychology associated with implicit bias; examine the limitations of psychological testing to identify bias in police candidates; and examine implicit bias testing, agency policies, subculture policing, and variables that influence police decision-making. Several case studies and/or vignettes are presented to assist readers in understanding how and why an officer's decision-making can be influenced.

PSYCHOLOGY OF IMPLICIT BIAS

Researchers have argued that racism/bias is implicit in nature. Implicit bias is also known as implicit social cognition, which is associated with stereotypes that impact our decision-making (Staats, Capatosto, Wright, & Jackson,

2016). These stereotypes are subconscious in nature and cross many lines and beliefs in regard to gender, sexuality, orientation, race, disability, and/or socioeconomic status. Implicit bias is similar to the biases that we are aware of and hide with one primary distinction: Implicit bias is buried in our subconscious, whereas the biases we are aware of (explicit biases) are controlled cognitively. To present explicit bias publicly may be political suicide or career ending. Implicit bias is present in or subconscious, is subtle, and is not something that we can reflect on. Implicit bias is developed through repeated exposure over time, through teachings, through environmental influences, and through media portrayals.

A classic example is the Clark Doll Experiment (1939). The Clark Doll Experiment asked Black children to choose between a black doll and a white doll. The dolls were exactly the same except for skin color. The experiment was conducted in Springfield, Massachusetts, where the public-school system and nursery were racially mixed. The study participants were 119 Black students—66 Black girls and 53 Black boys, between the ages of six and nine—with two dolls, one white and one black. The researchers asked the following questions in the order listed: (1) Show me the doll that you like best or that you'd like to play with; (2) show me the doll that is the "nice" doll; (3) show me the doll that looks "bad"; (4) give me the doll that looks like a nice color; (5) give me the doll that looks like a colored child; (6) give me the doll that looks like a Negro child; and (7) give me the doll that looks like you (Sokol, 2014).

The results are as follows: 72 percent chose the white doll as the doll that they would prefer to play with; 68 percent chose the white doll as the "nice" doll; 71 percent identified the black doll as the "bad" doll; 63 percent chose the white doll as having a "nice color"; 61 percent chose the black doll as the doll that looked like them. The third question was the most damning because most of the Black children picked the black doll as the "bad" one (Sokol, 2014). The Clark Experiment was used as an example because many question whether our subconscious impacts our decision-making without a person ever realizing why he or she made that decision. The ideal factor in having children choose is that they do not have the cognitive wherewithal to attempt to mask their decisions or the cognitive process to answer with "political correctness." Many had no idea why they made choices that they did.

One of the key components of implicit bias begins with stereotypes. In the case of police, stereotyping is designed to assist an officer in the assessment of potential threats. Assessing a threat is based on several factors: an officer's knowledge of the subject, nature and type of calls taken in that particular patrol zone, behavioral cues, and a profile or stereotype of what the officer believes who is most likely armed or who will attack the officer. Armed with that information, researchers argue that an officer's cognitive processes are primed with a racial stereotype known as racial priming. Draine and Greenwald (1998) argue that the longer an individual has to make a decision, the less likely there are errors, which are influenced by implicit bias and/or racial priming. When decisions are made under time constraints, the errors associated with implicit bias/racial priming increase; this process is called speed criterion (pp. 301–303). In their findings, Draine and Greenwald were able to show that under time constraints subjects made repeated errors associated with racial priming (p. 301). During the speed criterion process, responses can be categorized in one of two categories:

- *Proper decision* was made under duress and limited time. This may be the result of repeated exposure to a situation(s) and the ability to draw from those experiences.
- *Improper decision* was made under duress and limited time. This decision may be because the decision maker is under or in a situation that the subject views as causing serious injury and/or death. The subject had little experience to draw from, and his or her decision was influenced by implicit racial bias. The stereotype is that of a young Black male between the age of 15 and 35, in a neighborhood known for violence and drug dealing. When approached, the officer asks for identification; the Black male reaches for his wallet, and the officer responds by shooting the subject. Police officers have been responsible for the shooting of a number of unarmed Black men, most recently in the shooting of Philando Castile, although the circumstances were slightly different. Castile was legally armed when stopped by police. During the traffic stop, Castile advised the officers that he was armed and that he had a valid concealed weapons permit. From the beginning of the traffic stop, the officers had their firearms drawn and also had the tactical advantage. When the officer requested Castile's identification, Castile reached for his wallet and the officer shot and killed him. This could have been avoided by requesting Castile to step out of the car and then handcuff him. After handcuffing Castile, officers could secure his firearm and obtain Castile's identification.

The law recognizes sudden movements that are called "furtive movements," which can be construed as dangerous to the officer. Officers do not have to wait to see a weapon because it is recognized that once the suspect's weapon appears, officers are at a disadvantage. However, this rarely happens when an officer has instructed the subject to do something, such as produce identification, and the officer with weapon drawn has the tactical advantage.

Therefore, why did the officer make this decision? Did race play a factor in the shooting of Castile?

Payne (2001) noted in his research that when racial cues are associated with weapons, then race will be a predictor in decision-making. Payne developed two experiments to determine if race would influence perception in regard to weapons, as well as misidentify subjects who may or may not be armed. In the first experiment, with no time constraints to shift from incident to reaction, subjects identified guns faster when primed with Black faces than when compared with White faces. Participants misidentified tools as guns more often when primed with a Black face than with a White face (p. 181). The analysis of Draine and Greenwald (1998) and Payne (2001) offers some insight into the concept of threat assessment and police decision-making.

SCENARIO

Traffic Stop/Open Container

Two state troopers, Trooper Smith and Trooper Williams, are working assigned to I-75 and running radar at 2 A.M. They observe a Black male driver pass them drinking a beverage from a can. The troopers suspected the driver was drinking beer, given the time of night. The bars had just closed. The troopers stop the car to investigate what the driver was drinking, and it was determined it was a can of Coke. The driver was identified as John Ford. Trooper Smith was at the driver's window conducting the stop, and Trooper Williams was on the passenger side of Ford's vehicle acting as backup. Trooper Smith requested Ford's driver's license, registration, and proof of insurance. Ford advised Trooper Smith that his wallet with the information was in a zippered pouch. Ford was having difficulty opening the pouch, so Trooper Smith asked Ford to give the pouch to Trooper Williams so he could retrieve the paperwork from that pouch. Trooper Williams unzipped the pouch and saw a gun inside. Trooper Williams panicked, yelling "gun!" Trooper Smith, who was standing at the driver's side door, looking at Ford's hands, saw no gun but had drawn his weapon in response to hearing Trooper Williams yell "gun!" Trooper Smith fired three shots, striking Ford in the head and chest. Ford was pronounced dead at the scene.

Troopers Smith and Williams were veteran troopers, each with 10 years' experience.

Trooper Smith is Black and Trooper Williams is White.

1. Were the reactions of both troopers based on the urgency of the situation?
2. Can the troopers' decisions be tied to racial priming/stereotyping?
3. Was this is a justifiable shooting?

THREAT ASSESSMENT BY POLICE—DOES IT FOSTER IMPLICIT BIAS?

"Threat assessment" has long been a term associated with terrorism, executive protection details, stalking, domestic violence, and serial killers. However, it goes far beyond the scope of those entities. In every officer–subject encounter there is some degree of assessing the potential threat to an officer or others. From a tactical standpoint, officers are usually at a disadvantage, because officers are usually in a reactionary posture, with limited knowledge of the situation or subject that they are encountering. The subject that an officer encounters usually has intimate knowledge of his or her past deeds, will know if an arrest warrant exists, will know if he or she has just committed a crime, or if he or she is currently involved in a crime that officers have stumbled upon. Holbrook (2004) argues that threat assessment is fluid, ever changing, and unique to a particular situation or set of circumstances (p. 555). During threat assessment, within seconds, there are several variables that an officer must process to assist him or her in his or her decision-making: the subject's behavioral cues, the officer's skill level, and the officer's ability to react to a perceived threat.

During any encounter, an officer must read the subject's behavioral cues. The process begins with a visual scan of the subject's outer clothing, looking for any unusual bulges that might identify a weapon, for example, an outline of a gun under a shirt. The next most important component is the subject's hands: Are they visible? Finally, attention is given to the subject's verbal and nonverbal cues, which are possible indicators of violence. The verbal cues could be loud, angry tone of voice, profanity, and/or threatening words. The nonverbal cues include a red flushed face, hyperventilation, rigid body, clenched fists, and/or shaking (Florida Department of Law Enforcement, 2008; Garwood, 2005; Murray, 2004). These are possible indicators, but nothing is absolute.

As discussed in earlier chapters, law enforcement officers enter the profession with a number of biases. Some are explicit, meaning they are aware of and have no problem expressing the bias. However, other biases—especially those that new candidates possess—are implicit, and the candidate may have never recognized the effects of implicit bias and its influence on his or her decision-making, because implicit bias lies in the subconscious. And implicit bias influences on decisions are triggered when decisions are made under stress.

In new candidates' training there are examples of White trainees calling Black trainees "niggers" in shoot/don't shoot scenarios and White trainees using excessive force such as the application of chokeholds on Black trainees.

Interestingly, the trainees have never been trained in the application of a chokehold. Likewise, Black trainees have called White trainees "crackers or White motherfuckers" in similar circumstances. When both groups have been interviewed separately, each expressed the need to control the subject and believed that swearing was a way to let the subject know that the trainee was serious. Neither group knew why they used racial slurs in response to the training scenario. In fact, both groups advised that the statements were spontaneous and they were unaware they made the statement until the conclusion of the scenario. The use of racial slurs was uncontrollable; the trainees were aware that their performance was being evaluated.

As the trainees are exposed to more scenarios, their confidence builds, and they are able to make fairly good decisions under stress. From a practical standpoint, it is impossible to train for every situation and the many variables that may arise in a law enforcement officer's career. The best a trainer can hope for is that the trainees will go beyond what they have been taught at the academy, continue to train, read, and further develop their knowledge base and skill set. It is important to note that the street poses a series of new challenges, threats, and stressors that training can't always stage:

- A drug task force is involved in a foot chase with a Black male suspect after an illegal drug sale. A Black officer catches and tackles the fleeing suspect, and in the process of handcuffing the Black male suspect, a White officer slides in to assist the Black officer and states to the suspect: "You can't run now nigger, I got you." The White officer made the statement, disregarding the Black officer's presence, without thought of political correctness.

- A White officer makes a traffic stop of a White male driver. The White male driver has a suspended driver's license. The White officer advises the driver that he could arrest him but won't unless the officer finds illegal contraband in the car. The White officer issues a citation and releases the White male driver, allowing him to drive the car illegally away from the scene. Two days later, the same White officer is working in the Black community and stops a 65-year-old Black male, who is disabled and needs a cane to walk. The Black male driver's license is suspended. The White officer advises the Black male that he is under arrest, handcuffs and searches the Black male driver, and then places him in the back of his patrol car. The White officer searches the car and finds nothing. The officer issues the driver two citations and has dispatch call the driver's relative for someone to come to the scene, to take possession of the vehicle. The 65-year-old Black male driver was taken to the county jail and booked for driving with a suspended license. With all things being equal, why was the Black male treated differently?

- A White officer working in the White community makes a traffic stop and determines that a White male driver is wanted on a felony warrant for armed robbery. The officer orders the White male driver out of the car, places him under arrest, handcuffs, searches, and transports the White male to jail. The same officer days later is working in the Black community and makes a traffic stop on a Black male driver. The officer determines that the Black male is wanted on a misdemeanor warrant for possession of less than 20 grams of marijuana. The White male officer orders the Black male out of the car at gun point, advises the driver he is under arrest, and threatens the Black male driver with the following statement: "Nigger if you so much as move I will kill you." The officer handcuffs the Black male, searches him, and transports him to jail. Compare the differences in the crime warrants and the disparity in the use of force. When asked why the difference, the officer stated: "Black people need to understand that I mean what I say and the only way they do is when I swear at them." When asked about the use of the racial slur, the officer was unaware that he used it but admitted that he was not surprised. When asked if he was afraid of Black people, he replied: "I believe Black people are more of a threat, so it is important that I show them who is in control."

- The agencies' training unit was made aware that several patrol squads had been using racial slurs when interacting with the Black community. To address the issue, the training unit commander asked a Black officer assigned to the training unit to speak with each of the squads in question, in closed-door meetings prior to regular training officially starting. The Black officer was well respected as a police officer and was responsible for training the entire agency in diversity issues. In each of the meetings, the Black officer openly discussed the use of racial slurs, in particular the use of the word "nigger," during arrests. The Black officer advised that he understood profanity may be necessary to use but just avoid using racial slurs. In each meeting, there was at least one officer who stated: "You are trying to tell us what to do. We do what we need to do." Again, the Black officer stated he understood the use of profanity at times but advised the officers to stop using racial slurs. Several officers responded, in essence all saying: "We will do what we feel is necessary." When the Black officer asked why the officers felt compelled to use racial slurs, they could not offer an explanation. The meetings ended with the Black officer advising the officers that this meeting was an attempt to address a problem before someone ended up in Internal Affairs for the use of racial slurs. Each of the four meetings ended the same, with officers standing by their use of racial slurs.

THE ORIGINS OF IMPLICIT BIAS

Implicit bias originates with learning. If we review the findings of the Clark Doll Experiment, it is clear that the children are not coached and are void of politically correct pretenses. Therefore, how are their choices imprinted or learned? Often it is through simple associations: All kids are taught to associate the color black with bad or evil and to associate the color white with good or positive. Every American child learns these associations, and for a child to apply these to race is not surprising. Black and white become a simple way to make associations that become building blocks for a child's cognitive development.

But media assists with those associations. Consider the symbols in Westerns, the bad guys wear black hats and the good guys wear white hats; in Star Wars, Darth Vader is black-covered and evil, while Princess Leia wears white and is seen as noble, honorable, and angelic. The news media and the Internet provide largely negative images of African Americans involved in violent crime. And the images that a Black child sees of White America are completely opposite. Black kids believe White America is privileged, rich, in the best schools, in an environment void of poverty, and with two-parent families void of violence.

What is the source of these images? If you were a child with limited input and examples, what would you choose? Which doll would you choose? And how would you make the determination between good and evil? How does the repeated exposure to these images impact a child's conscious and subconscious?

As we get older, we learn to suppress or mitigate our biases and define what is politically correct. However, there are a number of other issues that build on the implicit bias imprint: More than media, they include positive and/or negative interaction with others from a different race, gender, or sexual orientation; environment with peer and family belief systems; employment; and court decisions, which may affect one's quality of life in the areas of employment, housing, and education. This list is not inclusive of every influence that might have an impact on implicit bias, and the baggage moves with us from adolescence to college years and professional career. However, the original imprint of good and evil resides in our subconscious.

Correll et al. (2007b) apply the logic that police who are trained to handle shoot/don't shoot scenarios should be much better at discerning the differences between subjects who are armed and unarmed, and the professional police officer would make fewer errors in judgment (p. 1008). Correll et al. found that police officers made substantially fewer errors when making shoot/don't decisions, and nontrained community members made significantly more errors, when engaged in the same shoot/don't shoot scenarios. Racial bias was discovered and displayed through the time it took officers and civilians when engaged in some scenarios. Less time was required to make a decision to shoot or not when both groups engaged armed Black targets and unarmed White targets. In contrast, a delay occurred when both groups engaged unarmed Black targets and armed White targets.

Admittedly, the research is unable to recreate all environmental variables that occur and influence an officer's decision-making. In essence, the laboratory setting is sterile and controlled. In a second study conducted by Correll, Park, Judd, and Wittenbrink (2007a), the goal was to manipulate the accessibility of stereotypes by linking Blacks to concepts of danger and crime. Seventy non-Black undergraduate students were randomly assigned to read about either Black or White criminals. After reading the articles, the students participated in a series of shoot/don't shoot scenarios. The data showed that reading the articles racially primed the participants before engaging in the scenarios, which link Blacks to danger and crime, and can significantly impact shooter bias. However, no evidence of shooter bias was indicated when the participants engaged the White criminal targets in the shoot/don't shoot scenarios (pp. 1107–1108).

The second Correll experiment is very similar to racial priming that influences an officer's decision-making process. In police officers, racial priming is subtle and buried in the officers' subconscious. Some variables that can impact an officer's decision-making are interaction with citizens in the officer's patrol zone; the amount and frequency of violence witnessed by the officer; the number of times that an officer and fellow officers have been assaulted; and an officer's confidence in his or her skill set when dealing with acts of violence. We tend to view officers and their actions in isolation, like an officer's behavior is based on conscious decision, not implicit bias.

Often, post-incident evaluations fail to acknowledge that officers are human beings who have personal problems and baggage that can/may influence their behavior. Some of the less publicized stressors are relatively common, and every adult experiences these at some point in his or her life: financial problems, problem with children, personal/family illnesses, divorce, domestic violence, substance abuse/alcoholism, health concerns, depression, anxiety, and issues with anger management (White & Honig, 1995).

When discussing implicit bias, it can be argued that this is just theory and there is no evidence to prove it actually exists. To take it a step further, James, Klinger, and Vila (2014) developed a series of shoot/don't shoot scenarios that were filmed in high definition to enhance realism, scenarios that were designed to test civilians in deadly force decision-making. A primary purpose of the experiment was to map the neurophysiological responses of the participants. Each participant was fitted with an electroencephalogram (EEG) device to monitor the brain's alpha wave activity. Alpha waves are normally suppressed in situations that appear threatening. The EEG coupled with shoot/don't shoot scenarios gave the researchers a "read" on what was happening in the participants' subconscious.

James et al. noted that the participants—civilians, with 85 percent of the group Whites—responded to Black suspects with more suppressed alpha waves—signaling higher levels of perceived threat—than when presented with White or Hispanic suspects. These findings suggest participants held subconscious biases associating Blacks with threats and violence. When the participants were presented with White and Hispanic suspects, their alpha wave suppression system was slower to arouse and less intense (pp. 334–336). It is important to note that this experiment did not include law enforcement personnel, so the results are not necessarily generalizable to police officers.

Another Explanation of Poor Police Decision-Making

Thomas and Barringer (2013) argue that race plays a major role in a police officer's perception of his or her personal safety and in an officer's use-of-force decision-making. Thomas and Barringer asked the following question: Is the use of excessive force by police officers determined by officer bias and/or the combination of racial socialization, as well as police socialization? They developed a survey and met with 150 officers in the southeastern United States. To ensure confidentiality, the researchers received permission from each of the agency's training divisions, explained the survey, announced that participation was voluntary, answered any questions that the officers had regarding the purpose of the survey, and confirmed that their answers would be confidential. The researchers stood by while the surveys were completed and then collected the surveys upon completion. Of the 150 surveys distributed, 115 surveys were returned, and 90 were completed and utilized in the data analysis. Despite the researchers' assurance that confidentiality would be maintained throughout, 35 officers refused to participate. The reason most often cited was fear that the administration would obtain the information and use it against the officers. The remaining 25 surveys could not be used because the participants did not complete the full survey; thus, there was insufficient data.

The participants were identified by race only. Gender was not tracked in this survey. The following is the demographic composition of the survey population. There were 90 participants: 79 (88%) were White, and 11 (12%) were Black. The survey examined officer preparation, skill development, emotions, race and threat assessment, police–community interaction, witness to or involvement in excessive force, and reporting excessive force. The resulting data that was most interesting follows:

- Ninety percent of the participants experienced apprehension, anxiety, and fear when it came time to making an arrest. This response was in anticipation of the subject physically resisting after the subject was advised that he or she was under arrest.

- Forty percent of the officers had either witnessed or participated in excessive force.

- Sixty percent of the White officers had never witnessed or committed any acts of excessive force.

- Seventy-three percent, or 58, of the White officers felt that race did make a difference, most notably in their interactions with young African American and Latino males. This group further noted that is because these groups disrespect the officers the most. They insult the officers with racial epitaphs and refuse to comply with the officers' requests. The officers also noted that these are the communities where the violent crime rate is the highest.

- One hundred percent, or 11, of the African American officers surveyed stated race made no difference, and they viewed everyone they contacted as posing the same potential threat. The finding was the same for 27 percent, or 21, of the White officers.

- One hundred percent, or 11, of the African American officers noted that although their responses were not based on race, they had not been accepted by either the White or African American communities. There was an expectation that there would be some hostility in the White community. However, many noted that they had been viewed as traitors in the African American community. This may explain why African American officers view everyone as a potential threat.

- One hundred percent, or 90, of the officers have never reported an excessive force incident. They all stated that being "a rat" is not an option because it could ruin their careers. (Thomas & Barringer, 2013, pp. 112–114)

Thomas and Barringer (2012) noted similar findings in another study of police attitudes and perceptions when it comes to race and the use of force. The theme is universal that officers, minority or otherwise, who witness or participate in acts of excessive force will not report them. In addition, those most likely to fall victim to these acts are the poor and/or are members of minority communities. The motivations for excessive acts are usually precipitated by acts of disrespect or motivated by fear and anxiety during an arrest situation. Holmes (2000) argues that there is very little difference when it comes to acts of brutality within minority communities, noting that race is not a factor. Instead, acts of brutality are shaped by the organization, peer pressure, and/or challenges to all officers' authority (p. 350).

Holmes and Smith (2008) hold that diversifying a police agency does not necessarily mean that the end result will have a positive impact on the community (p. 135). The long-standing belief is that because an officer is from a minority community, the minority officer will relate to the residents better than a White officer. There is very little evidence to support this hypothesis. The fact is that minority officers usually come from working- and/or middle-class neighborhoods and have views similar to those of their White counterparts (Williams & Murphy, 1990).

PSYCHOLOGICAL TESTING AND BIAS

Psychological instruments to assess the mental health of police candidates have been utilized for years. A mental health clinician usually administers a written examination, which addresses many facets of a new candidate's personality. The instrument can also assess if the candidate exhibits, or has, a psychopathology. In addition to the written examination, the new candidate should participate in a face-to-face interview with a mental health clinician. I say "should" because not all mental health clinicians offer this service or agencies required it. The interview is designed to address any results of the written examination which might appear as anomalies. It gives the candidate an opportunity to discuss the anomalies and provide explanations. In addition to addressing any identified problems, the mental health clinician should review the results of the candidate's polygraph examination and background investigation before the interview. Examining the additional documents offers a much clearer picture of the candidate's personality. If there are anomalies in either the background information or polygraph, often they are confirmed through psychological testing. What psychological tests and interviews can't determine is if the candidate is a racist or is subconsciously primed with implicit bias.

In regard to implicit bias, the most popular test to date is the Harvard *Implicit Association Test (IAT)*. The IAT offers an opportunity for test takers to determine if they have an implicit bias in the following areas: disability, Native Americans, sexuality (gay/Lesbian), weapons, gender career, skin tone, religion, Asian, Arab Muslim, age, race, weight, presidents, and gender science. I was asked to provide in-service training to officers in the area diversity. In each of the sessions, the participants took the *Harvard Weapons IAT*, which requires the participant to recognize White and Black faces and pair them with images of weapons or harmless objects. Prior to administering the test, I assumed that all participants Black, White, male, and female would have similar scores. In fact, they did, meaning that they showed very little if any bias.

The general IAT is based on how quickly one can identify the threat and respond by pushing a button. The IAT and similar tests are subjective at best and cannot be used to identify if a subject has implicit bias. Bias is not a psychological impairment or pathology, as defined by the American Psychological Association. It is because of this that specialized testing used to identify implicit bias has not been utilized in the assessment of police candidates.

AGENCY POLICIES AND AFFIRMATIVE ACTION

Law enforcement agencies have policies that forbid discrimination in any form, which means that open bias, discrimination, and/or harassment exhibited by officers are strictly forbidden. The policies do not address implicit bias. Where I see officers' biases most evident and outwardly expressed is when an agency applies affirmative action during the hiring of new candidates, transfers from patrol to specialized units, and during the agency's promotional process from officer to sergeant, lieutenant, or captain.

Race and Gender: The Internal Subcultures of Policing

Law enforcement is a subculture that mimics society. Officers are grouped based on specialties or job task, such as detectives, patrol, supervision, and administration. The road less discussed in policing is the subcultures of race and/or gender and their impact on the profession, the individuals, and the agency. There is no doubt that every profession has a dark side, and such issues are not unique to policing. In fact, the issues of race and gender continue to play out in America daily as this country increasingly becomes more divisive.

Affirmative Action

The term "affirmative action" has a negative meaning in many circles. Today, affirmative action is being attacked in every state as it relates to education, employment, and equitable treatment. Affirmative action is usually examined by the mainstream of an organization and viewed as negative and with suspicion. Rarely is affirmative action examined through the eyes of those who are hired under the program. Therefore, is there a psychological impact and burden on those who are hired under this system? Some of the comments most often made by rank-and-file officers in regard to affirmative action are the following:

1. All we are doing is lowering our standards to hire Blacks and women.
2. They are not qualified; that is why we never hired them in the past.
3. Women don't belong in policing; they need to be home having babies and taking care of the house.

4. What is going to happen when a woman gets in a fight? They are weak and will need a male officer to come to take care of what they cannot handle.

5. Most Blacks are drug dealers, and that means when we hire them they will learn all of our tactics and use them against us.

6. You need to watch those Black officers, because they will be giving breaks to their friends.

AFFIRMATIVE ACTION

Response of the Rank and File

A law enforcement agency recognized that it had a problem in that all of its officers were White males. Fearing that the Department of Justice would step in and order the agency to hire minorities, the agency developed a campaign to aggressively hire and train qualified minority candidates. During academy training, the first Black recruit was advised by his fellow classmates: "If you ever got into trouble and called for help, you are on your own. We will not be there to back you up." On successful completion of the Field Training Program, the Black officer attended mandatory in-service training, where the agency set aside an hour to discuss the decision to make the agency diverse and representative of the community that it served. The senior officers began to openly disagree with the new policies on affirmative action. The most damning comment made by one of the White male officers, in front of the Black male officer and everyone in the room, was: "Why do we have to hire niggers? They aren't qualified and they don't belong here." Other officers supported the comments by stating that they agreed. The Black officer got up and left the room in protest. He learned later that one of his field training officers stood up for the Black officer but was shouted down. During the entire time the Black officer was assigned to his shift, his supervisor made rude comments and called the Black officer a "nigger" when speaking to White officers. The use of racial slurs and mistreatment were brought to the attention of agency administrators; nothing was done, and the Black officer resigned and moved to another agency.

Affirmative action legislation was designed to give minorities and women an opportunity to enter the workforce in careers where access had been denied or extremely limited. The origins of affirmative action began in 1966 when President Lyndon B. Johnson issued Executive Order 11246. It was later passed into law, in 1972, and is now known as the Equal Employment

Opportunity Act, which extended coverage to state and local governments. The caveat to this act is if an entity public or private utilizes government funding, then it must adhere to the legislation. The legislation in its simplest form meant that all things being equal—same test scores and qualifications—the minority would receive preference in hiring.

There is no doubt that there have been governmental abuses when it comes to affirmative action, and hiring under the guise of affirmative action continues to fuel debate. Agencies have been accused of hiring less-qualified applicants. The term "qualified" is often vague and ambiguous, left for interpretation by those who place a value on successes that may be irrelevant.

What does the word "qualified" mean to you? What qualifications predict police success? Is it academics and success in the academy? Is it an unsullied lifestyle prior to entering the academy? Is it scoring in the upper 10 percent of new officer candidates on the agency entrance exam? Is it a college education? Is it common sense and good decision-making?

Take a moment and play the role of an administrator. Choose from the aforementioned list of questions: Which question or questions will you use to determine who is the most qualified candidate for your agency? Officers should possess cognitive skills and higher-order thinking, and these skill sets should be coupled with reasoning, judgment, and inferential thinking. But how do you determine if a candidate has them?

The abuses of affirmative action are most often associated with an agency attempting to meet quotas established by a decree by the Department of Justice or as a result of a federal lawsuit. The most common complaint against affirmative action is that agencies are required to meet specific quotas and by doing so lower their standards.

AGENCY ABUSE

Affirmative Action

What Would You Do?

You are a Black officer and have a reputation for being the best field training officer in the agency. The lieutenant in charge of the Field Training Program trusts your judgment so much that he has asked you on several occasions to evaluate trainees to determine if they are worth salvaging or if they should be terminated. If they can be salvaged, the lieutenant has you develop a training plan to address their shortcomings. If they do not possess the necessary skills to become a successful officer, then the lieutenant uses your observations and reports as the means for termination.

You have been at the agency for seven years and finally get transferred to training to become the lead trainer responsible for the high-liability aspects of training, which encompass firearms, defensive tactics, and driving. During your tenure, you are aware that the agency has hired less-than-qualified minorities. In fact, there have been accusations that these individuals were given the test questions after failing the entrance examination two or three times. There have also been allegations that the females who did not pass the entrance exam had sexual relationships with the personnel lieutenant and were hired.

While assigned to training, one of your fellow officers (Officer Smith, a Black officer) is in serious trouble. In fact, when he was hired, Officer Smith did not have to complete the Field Training Program. He was moved directly to Neighborhood Services because they needed him for community outreach. In discussing the matter with the personnel unit, it was determined that Officer Smith took the examination three times and failed miserably on the writing sample as well as the oral interview. However, on the third attempt he passed each aspect of the exam with a score of 100 percent. The personnel lieutenant stated that he helped him prepare but did not give him the answers.

You have been in training approximately six months, and there have been several budget cuts. Officer Smith's position in Neighborhood Services has been returned to patrol. Before Officer Smith can go back to patrol, he must successfully complete the Field Training Program, the program that he was exempted from once hired. The department is divided, and several accusations have been made that the Field Training Program is racist; because of this Officer Smith will never pass the process. You have been approached by the chief and the union to leave the training program for the first phase of Officer Smith's training and return for his final phase of training. The department is attempting to address the issues of racism and use you to protect them in case a lawsuit is filed.

Reflection Questions

1. How do you feel about the preferential treatment that this candidate received?

2. Do you believe that he should have completed the Field Training Program before moving to a specialty unit?

3. How does this impact your reputation, and how others view you as a Black officer?

4. What do you believe the White officers are saying about this matter and if it is fair or not?

5. Do actions such as these give affirmative action a bad name?

6. How do you feel about the chief's request?
7. Is the agency admitting that it is racist by making such a request?
8. How did all of the other Black officers make it, if the system is so racist?
9. Why has the union approached you in this matter?
10. What would be the best way to resolve this matter?
11. If you choose not to participate and ignore the chief and union, will it have a negative impact on your career?

The senior Black officer in this scenario refused to leave training to participate in this matter. In fact, he asked these questions of the chief and command staff: Are you saying that the system is racist? If so, where is the foundation to support the allegation? Does that mean that all of the Black officers who came before me, the Black officers who have come through the system since I have been here, are victims of a racist system? After meeting with the chief and command staff, it was agreed that the Black officer would be assigned to the Field Training Program with no special consideration, and the Black training officer would remain in training. The situation was closely monitored, and at the end of the first phase (four weeks), the Black officer resigned before he was terminated. It was clear that he was over his head, having been at the agency for more than three years; he was, nonetheless, incapable of writing a basic police report. A final note: The union approached the senior Black officer in this matter because they trusted his opinion, and it was their belief that the senior Black officer would do what was right, regardless of politics or race.

Administrators who participate in these and similar acts fail to realize that such actions do nothing but hurt the credibility of those minorities already on staff and who have had to fight to gain the respect of their White counterparts. Although policing is considered a subculture by itself, it is also one that has several subcultures, divided by race or gender. Keep in mind that at the very least a new minority hire is being judged by a minimum of two subcultures: White males and their own subculture be it Black males, women, Latino, Asian, and so on. Their respective subculture views them more harshly, because the failure of a new member candidate could damage the reputation of that particular subculture. The questions most often posed by the minority subcultures are the following: Will the new minority candidate fit in? Is the new minority candidate smart? If it is a female, is the new minority candidate a whore?

Each of these subcultures has worked to gain the respect of its peers and, in many cases, has had to work harder to be accepted. In the Black community it is known as "the Black tax," which means that Blacks have to work twice as hard as Whites to be accepted and to receive the same recognition as their White counterparts. However, if you were to examine this concept, you will find that all successful minorities have a similar belief system, and it would be fair to call it a "minority tax."

From a psychological standpoint, think of the burden and pressure that each new minority candidate feels when hired. A fear of failure, the need to assimilate, the need to prove themselves to be accepted, and a need to be more knowledgeable. Everyone is judging, and the minority wants acceptance. What is the psychological cost? Does this mean that the police culture is more powerful than one's own value system? Does this mean that police culture supersedes determinants of race and implicit bias?

BLACKS AND WOMEN IN POLICING

The aforementioned discussions and scenarios offer a list of excuses used by the establishment to keep the profession pure, White male. Those statements are the same stereotypes and attitudes that forced the federal government to enact Affirmative Action Legislation and demand that hiring practices change. Yet the attitudes and biases remain in policing today, be they explicit or implicit. Bolton and Feagin (2004) provide the following excerpt from their text *Black in Blue,* which illustrates the perception that White police officers have of Blacks:

> My white riding partner and I learned something. He said to me one time, we were riding along one day and just out of the clear, blue sky just started talking about a whole lot of things and he says, "You know what I've learned since you and I have been riding together?" And I said, "What's that?" And he said, "You know, I found out that you have a family and that you feel about them just about the way I do about mine." He says, "I've also found out you have about the same moral values that I have, but I was raised to think that you were different." He said, "I've felt like black people were stupid and dumb and, you know, didn't know anything about anything." And he says, "You know, you and I talk about all kinds of things and a lot of times you know a lot more about it than I do." (p. 11)

The history of Blacks in law enforcement has not been well documented. However, the history begins in the late 1800s. Abel (2006) classifies the years of progress in policing for Blacks in the following manner: 1891–1920, the beginning; 1921–1940, step by step; 1941–1960, antagonist of social change; 1961–1980, gender and social boundaries; and 1981–2003, who is next.

Prior to 1968, policing was an exclusive club defined by race and gender. Simply put, you had to be a White male in order to be accepted, and this is why affirmative action was necessary. As Abel (2006) explained:

> Policing New York City is a white man's job, a white policeman remarked for Battle to hear. "He won't be here long. It's one thing to force yourself in where you're not wanted, but it's another thing to be able to stay there." (p. 17)

The nature of policing as an exclusive club could not have been made clearer in the past practices of the Atlanta Police Department. Black officers were denied participation in the agency's supplemental retirement plans, a benefit afforded to White officers. Greene (2006) adds that, because of this practice, Black retirees who worked in the 1950s and 1960s receive some $700 per month less than their White colleagues.

Blacks in policing are rarely discussed openly in the African American community, as many in the African American community see Black officers as traitors. It is not uncommon to hear Black officers called "Uncle Toms" or "the Whiteman's nigger," because they have chosen to enforce the law. What the community is expressing and believes is that Black officers will be heavy-handed and unfair. That is not without some merit. Some Black officers feel that in order to be accepted by their White counterparts they have to intimidate and brutally attack members of the African American community. This feeling of mistrust and contempt toward Black police officers is outlined in a conversation detailed in a documentary filmed at Fredonia State University entitled *Behind the Badge*:

> Being a black police officer is difficult. My dad hated the fact that I became an officer. He stated: "You went to college to become a police officer what a waste. In fact, all I can say is that you have become a useless piece of shit. You could do anything and you choose to be a cop. They have been beating our asses since the beginning of time. Why would you do something so stupid? Nothing good will ever come of this. I will pray that you come to your senses."

Women in Policing

The history of women in policing is more concise but similar to that of Blacks in policing, and much of what pertains to Black officers pertains to female officers. Schulz (2004) provides six eras from which women's roles evolved from specialized gender roles and were replaced by demands for equality: (1)

Forerunners: The Matrons, 1820–1899; (2) The Early Police Women 1900–1928; (3) Depression Losses, 1929–1941; (4) World War II and the 1940s; (5) Paving the Way for Patrol, 1950–1967; (6) Women become Crimefighters, 1968–Present. Fletcher (1995) supports that there are similarities in the experiences of Blacks and women in policing with the following quote:

> Seattle is a very politically liberal city. If the city of Seattle and the politicians hadn't mandated affirmative action, there would be very few blacks, and very few Asians, and there would be even less women on the force today. When I came on, there were very few women. It was very outwardly hostile by some people. They were very verbally abusive and tried to discourage you every chance they got. Where now, I find that the discrimination is a lot more subtle, a lot more insidious, actually. It's political correctness now. It's p.c. It's p.c. to say "Yes we want women, yes we want minorities, yes we want this cultural diversity—we want to appreciate everybody's diversity." And everybody mouths the words, but I don't feel that they're quite living the words yet. It's kind of like, even abusive parents tell their kids that they love them. (p. 205)

There is a stigma attached to the accomplishments of a minority because of the exclusivity of the police "club" (White males). If a Black male or female is promoted, the first thing that many of the club members say is that he or she was promoted because of his or her race or gender without looking at what that individual had accomplished as an officer. This goes back to the issue of the minority tax. How much does one have to pay in order to be accepted? Fletcher (1995) saw this same reaction decades ago:

> Every time I've gone up in rank, I've gotten a jealous reaction from some men. Every time. And I finally thought that would go away. And it has happened every time. When I made lieutenant, before we got the list back as to who was where in rank order, one of the guys came up to me and said, "Wherever you are on the list, I just hope that I'm one in front of you." And I said, "Why?" And he said, "Cause you know they're not gonna pass up an opportunity to promote a woman. And they have to get to me to get to you." (p. 210)

The final step in the approval process is that a new hire needs to understand how he or she is going to be accepted. The question that the club has: How will a Black officer handle himself or herself, if I am fighting a Black suspect? Will the Black officer help? How will a female officer handle a fight? Will a female become emotional when she is investigating a death? The club waits for feedback from one of its members. If the minority officer performs well under pressure, then the minority officer can be trusted to perform in those situations. However, it needs to be understood that the minority will not gain full access to the club because there is still the stigma of being a minority. Imagine it—you were hired because you were a minority, you were promoted because you were a minority, and you are never really trusted or accepted by the mainstream because you are a minority. The bias is there, both implicit and explicit. The impact of such a stigma/stereotype is the same in society as it is in policing. Policing has a hierarchy of acceptance although unwritten and subculture rank in the following order: White males, minority males, females, and gay males. Fletcher describes the hierarchy in the following manner: White males on top; Black males and minority males; White females; Black females are the least accepted; and gay males.

CONCLUSION

Police have been accused of being biased for years. The minority community argues that police departments hire officers who are racist, and racism is the reason for the brutality, mistreatment, and killing of unarmed minority men. Police stand on the principle that they have been acting appropriately by responding to the needs of minority and poor communities where much of the violence occurs. This situation can best be described as the great divide; the minority community argues that things have never changed, and law enforcement argues that its actions are necessary.

Implicit bias is also known as implicit social cognition, which is associated with stereotypes that impact our decision-making (Staats et al., 2016). These stereotypes are subconscious in nature, cross many lines, and believe in regard to race and gender. When subjects have the ability to take their time and cognitively process information, their stereotypes and biases are hidden. Implicit bias gets exposed when decisions are made under pressure, such as the shoot/don't shoot scenarios and the examples of officers blurting racist statements out when making an arrest. In legal terms, these statements are what is defined as "an excited utterance," an unplanned statement made by a person in response to a startling or shocking event or condition (Saltzburg, 2007, p. 267). Officers understand the consequences of explicit bias and only express explicit bias when they are with friends and trust that the offending officer's confidences will not be betrayed. The only time explicit bias rears its ugly head is during the hiring process and promotional process. Those participating in either of the processes don't believe their statements are either sexist or racist. Yet these discussions often take place behind closed doors or are whispers in the hallway.

In addition to learned biases, explicit or implicit, a law enforcement officer's decision-making is influenced by a number of factors: interaction with citizens in the officer's patrol zone; the amount and frequency of violence witnessed by the officer; the number of times that an officer and/or fellow officers have been assaulted; and an officer's confidence in his or her skill set when dealing with acts of violence.

The final piece of this equation is the acculturation of the officer. What does the agency require the officer to do, to be accepted as one of the group? Acceptance and trust are limited, with race and/or gender being factors or barriers that limit a minority officers' complete acceptance into the fraternity of policing. Culture is a major factor in an officer's decision-making. When dealing with the public, an officer's race has little bearing on behavior; it is the officer's desire to be accepted by mainstream officers.

It is impossible to say that implicit bias is the reason an officer makes a bad decision or that the officer is racist. The brain should be looked at as a computer, with data being received from multiple sources. Some information is processed and discarded; other information is stored and used immediately, and some information is stored in our subconscious unknowingly. The only way to impact the problem is through training. However, those on the receiving end of the training must see the value in the lessons being taught and have a willingness to change. Changing attitudes begins by changing the organizational culture.

REFERENCES

Abel, R. L. (2006). *The black shields*. Bloomington, IN: AuthorHouse.

Bolton, K., & Feagin, J. R. (2004). *Black in blue: African American police officers and racism*. New York, NY: Routledge.

Correll, J., Park, B., Judd, C., & Wittenbrink, B. (2007a). The influence of stereotypes on decisions to shoot. *European Journal of Social Psychology, 37*, 1102–1117.

Correll, J., Park, B., Judd, C. M., Wittenbrink, B., Sadler, M. S., & Keesee, T. (2007b). Across the thin blue line: Officers and racial bias in the decision to shoot. *Journal of Personality and Social Psychology, 92* (6), 1006–1023.

Draine, S. C., & Greenwald, A. G. (1998). Replicable unconscious semantic priming. *Journal of Experimental Psychology: General, 127*, 286–303.

Fletcher, C. (1995). *Breaking and entering*. New York, NY: HarperCollins Publishers.

Florida Department of Law Enforcement. (2008). *Florida basic recruit training program. Vol. 2: High liability* (2008:4). Tallahassee, FL: Author

Garwood, R. J. (2005). *Thanks for listening*. Bloomington, IN: AuthorHouse.

Greene, K. (2006, January 16). Retired black cops pressure Georgia for pension equity. *Wall Street Journal*, p. C 5.

Holbrook, R. M. (2004). *Political sabotage: The LAPD experience, attitudes towards understanding police use of force*. Victoria, BC: Trafford Publishing.

Holmes, M. D. (2000). Minority threat and police brutality: Determinants of civil rights complaints in U.S. municipalities. *Criminology, 38* (2), 343–366.

Holmes, M. D., & Smith, B. W. (2008). *Race and police brutality: Roots of an urban dilemma*. Albany: State University of New York Press.

James, L., Klinger, D., & Vila, B. (2014). Racial and ethnic bias in decisions to shoot seen through a stronger lens: Experimental results from high-fidelity laboratory simulations. *Journal of Experimental Criminology, 10,* 323–340.

Murray, K. R. (2004). *Training at the speed of life, volume one: The definitive textbook for military and law enforcement reality based training*. Gotha, FL: Armiger Publications.

Ormsby, R. (Producer/Director). (2002). *Behind the badge* (Documentary). Fredonia, NY: Fredonia State University.

Payne, B. K. (2001). Prejudice and perception: The role of automatic and controlled processes in misperceiving a weapon. *Journal of Personality and Social Psychology, 81,* 181–192.

Saltzburg, S. (2007). *Trial tactics*. Washington, DC: American Bar Association.

Schulz, D. M. (2004). Invisible no more: A social history of women in U.S. policing. In B. R. Price & N. J. Sokoloff (Eds.), *The criminal justice system and women: Offenders, prisoners, victims, and workers,* 3rd ed., pp. 483–494. New York, NY: McGraw-Hill.

Sokol, J. (2014). *All eyes upon us: Race and politics from Boston to Brooklyn*. New York, NY: Basic Books.

Staats, C., Capatosto, K., Wright, R. A., & Jackson, V. W. (2016). *State of the science: Implicit bias review*. Columbus, OH: Ohio State University.

Thomas, D. J. & Barringer, T. A. (June 2012). Law enforcement officers: Perspectives on race, credibility, and community. *Law Enforcement Executive Forum, 12*(2), 53–63.

Thomas, D. J., & Barringer, T. A. (2013). Police perceptions of race, personal safety, and use-of-force decision making. *Law Enforcement Executive Forum, 13*(2), 108–119.

White, E. K., & Honig, A. L. (1995). Law enforcement families. In M. I. Kure and E. M. Scrivner (Eds.), *Police psychology into the 21st century,* pp. 189–206. Hillsdale, NJ: Lawrence Erlbaum Associates.

Williams, H., & Murphy, P. (1990). *The evolving police strategy: A minority view*. Washington, DC: U.S. Department of Justice.

4

Police Decision-Making—Law, Policy, and Psychology

The public questions the factors that influence a law enforcement officer's decision-making process when it involves making an arrest with the use of force. Depending on the community, it has been argued that police are selective and justify the treatment of citizens and suspects based on the nature of the crimes that occur in that community. However, police decision-making is based on two factors: state statutes and the agency's policies and procedures. The policies and procedures are usually much more restrictive than state statutes. And there is a third variable that we have discussed at length in previous chapters, the organization's culture, which can best be defined by the agency's style of policing.

This chapter examines the role of the law and its limitations in regard to an officer's ability to make an arrest; department policies and their limitations in guiding an officer in the decision-making process; officer perceptions in decision-making; the use of a decision matrix to explain an officer's decision to use physical force excluding deadly force; and the warrior mentality. In addition, readers have an opportunity to examine successes and failures and apply the law to a number of scenarios presented.

THE LAW AND POLICE DECISION-MAKING

An officer's ability to use force is defined in state statutes. The use of force is most often associated with making an arrest for a criminal violation. Most state statutes read similar to Florida State Statute 776.05, Use of Force in Making an Arrest, which specifies three circumstances in which an officer is justified in using force:

1. In defense of self or another while making an arrest
2. When retaking felons who have escaped
3. When committed to arresting felons fleeing from justice

Reflect on the aforementioned set of circumstances in which an officer can use force. Can you conceive of a situation when force is not associated with an arrest? It is important to note that the first level of a police officer's use of force is associated with the mere presence of a uniformed officer on the scene; it is classified as officer presence. Elements of officer presence are identification of the police uniform and the deterrent effect that the uniform has on preventing crime (Box, 1983; Olsen, 2001; Shpayer-Makov, 2002).

Defining Force

The use of force is dictated by a series of circumstances. In most cases, police react to a situation or attempt to prevent further damage or harm. The most important component associated with the use of force is the concept of reasonableness, which may have infinite interpretations. In essence, the term "reasonable" is one void of clear meaning, and that was addressed by the U.S. Supreme Court in *Graham v. Connor,* 490, U.S. 386 (1989). The *Connor* decision established a doctrine that I refer to as the "Reasonable Officer Doctrine" (Lippmann, 2006; Urbonya, 1998; Williams, 2005). The doctrine requires an examination of the facts, as the officer perceived them at the time, not after the fact. The *Graham* decision prescribed the following criteria for determining reasonableness: the severity of the crime, whether the suspect poses an immediate threat to officers or others, and whether the suspect is resisting arrest or attempting to evade arrest by flight.

To prepare officers for the application, control, and response to unarmed subject threats is police defensive tactics. Police defensive tactics encompass a number of empty hand skills, the use of intermediate weapons, and ultimately the use of deadly force (Alpert & Dunham, 2004; Rahtz, 2003; Thomas, 1989; Walker, 2005). The root of most defensive tactics techniques is martial arts, which encompasses a number of striking techniques, kicks, control holds, pressure points, and handcuffing. A key to every proper use of force encounter is that officers must not take the attack, or subject's resistance, personally. The officers must avoid anger and learn to control their fear during use-of-force encounters. Anger and fear are a recipe for disaster; they trigger an officer to lose control.

When the public views a police–subject encounter, often it appears that an officer is beating a subject. What the public doesn't understand is that there are no magical techniques and there is not a place on the body that an officer can touch which will render a subject defenseless and stop any acts of aggression. That said, an officer must establish control of a combative or armed subject within the rules of reasonableness. In almost any instance, a kick to the groin or a strike to the throat would stop an aggressor. However, based on the encounter, an officer is limited in the application of these techniques, because the techniques could cause serious injury and/or death (Dantzker, 2005; Kennedy, 1995; Lawrence, 2000; Waddington, 1991).

As you examine the officer's response levels, understand that no tactic is 100 percent effective, and this includes a firearm, often requiring an escalation of force by an officer to establish control of a resisting subject. The type and level of force an officer uses are dictated by a subject's actions. Today, force is best defined and described for all to understand through a use-of-force decision matrix or a force continuum. However, many agencies have removed use-of-force decision matrix from their policy manuals, despite the fact that they are great tools. The logic behind the removal of the decision matrix is that trainers argue that officers become confused and hesitate when it comes to responding to a subject's aggression. Allegedly, the officers are attempting to process the subject's resistance level and correlate that to their use of force during the time of the encounter. In fact, the decision matrix is designed to explain the encounter after the incident has occurred. This is a training issue, not a decision matrix issue. Most, if not all, continuums have been developed by trainers, agencies, or state training commissions as a visual tool to explain the concept of force and are unique to their respective needs (Dantzker, 2005; Neyroud, 2008; Walker, 2005). However, all define force and resistance using similar terms and definitions. Thomas (1989) identifies and defines a subject's level of resistance and an officer's response to the subject's resistance as shown in Figure 4.1.

Definitions associated with the levels of force and resistance are given next. As you read them, understand that an officer cannot establish control of a subject if the officer uses a level of force that corresponds to the subject's level of resistance. For example, an officer has sufficient evidence to make an arrest for disorderly conduct when a subject is drunk, in public, is verbally abusive, and refuses to leave an establishment. The officer advises the suspect that he is under arrest and the subject continues to argue and refuses to comply and acknowledges that the officer has placed the suspect under arrest. To establish

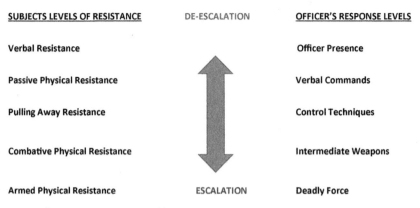

SUBJECTS LEVELS OF RESISTANCE	DE-ESCALATION	OFFICER'S RESPONSE LEVELS
Verbal Resistance		Officer Presence
Passive Physical Resistance		Verbal Commands
Pulling Away Resistance		Control Techniques
Combative Physical Resistance		Intermediate Weapons
Armed Physical Resistance	ESCALATION	Deadly Force

Figure 4.1   Force continuum/decision matrix

control and handcuff the suspect, the officer must place his hands on the suspect, have the suspect turn around, and handcuff the suspect. Based on the decision matrix, the officer used empty hand control in response to a suspect's verbal resistance. If the officer were to stand there and continue to argue with the suspect, and the suspect refused to comply, then all you have is a shouting match.

In order to effect an arrest, the officer must have a legal reason to be at the location in question; the suspect must have violated the law, providing the officer with probable cause to make the arrest. In the aforementioned scenario, most officers usually look to have a person leave an establishment or get off the street as opposed to arresting them. The officer must have the ability to move one step above the subject's level of resistance in order to establish control; this is known as 1 + 1 in use-of-force encounters.

DEFINING THE FORCE CONTINUUM/DECISION MATRIX

Subject's Levels of Resistance

I. *Verbal resistance*—It occurs once police arrive at a scene. The subject becomes verbally abusive or begins to challenge the officer's authority.

II. *Passive physical resistance*—It is a subject's failure to respond to police requests and offers no overt physical acts of aggression toward the officer, nor does the subject attempt to flee.

   Example: A crowd is involved in an unlawful assembly. The officer orders the crowd to disperse, and the crowd responds by sitting in the middle of the street blocking traffic. The subject offers no physical resistance other than sitting.

III. *Pulling-away resistance*—An officer has made physical contact with a subject with the intent to arrest the subject. The subject responds by pulling away. The subject offers no overt physical aggression toward the officer. The subject is attempting to defeat an officer's arrest attempt by pulling away from the officer's grasp or control.

IV. *Combative physical resistance*—The subject's level of violence has escalated, and he or she is now attacking the officer with hands, fists, or feet. The objective is to injure the officer and escape.

V. *Armed physical resistance*—The subject's level of violence is such that the subject intends to cause great bodily harm and/or death to the officer. The subject may be using any of a variety of weapons: a knife, firearm, automobile, and so on.

Officer's Levels of Response

I. *Officer presence*—It is the officer's arrival at a scene or call for service. This could also be interpreted as deterrence while on patrol. The key here is that the officer has not attempted dialogue, and this level of force is associated with the officer's uniformed presence.

II. *Verbal direction*—The officer directs a subject to do something. Examples: "Move over here so we can talk." "Leave or go to jail." "Place your hands behind your back you're under arrest." "Get on the ground." "Stop resisting."

III. *Control techniques*—These are techniques that require physical contact with a subject.

They are often utilized to establish control of a subject who is offering some form of physical resistance. The techniques can be categorized in the following manner:

a. Pain compliance—These are techniques that are used to get a subject to stop resisting. They are often used when a subject engages in forms of passive or pulling-away resistance. These techniques are not designed to cause injury but compliance. Examples: nerve pressure points or joint locks.

b. Takedowns—These are techniques that require an officer to physically take a subject to the ground. The probability of injury increases based on the technique employed, how aggressively the technique is applied, how active the subject resists, and the surface that the subject and officer are going to land on.

c. Striking—Striking techniques are the most violent of the empty hand techniques when deployed. Strikes include kicks, punches, and the use of elbows and knees. The areas that an officer can strike are nonlethal. However, if the officer needs to stop an attack, which could cause great bodily harm or death to the officer, the officer can escalate and attack targets that are considered lethal/deadly in nature. Examples of lethal/deadly targets are groin, eyes, temple, spine, and throat.

IV. *Intermediate weapons*—These are weapons that an officer deploys to stop combative physical resistance. Within the past 10 years there has been a growing trend to move intermediate weapons above empty hand control techniques. The belief is that once verbal resistance begins, it will soon be followed by some form of physical resistance. By deploying intermediate weapons early in the confrontation, control is established sooner, reducing the potential for injury to the officer and subject. The categories of intermediate weapons are:

a. Impact weapons—These are weapons that an officer uses to strike a subject. Until the 1960s these were known as "night sticks." Today the correct term is baton, and the officer has many choices. However, the type of baton and system used with them are often dictated by an agency's policy. Potential for injury is minimal if the officer strikes muscle mass. However, if the targets become bones and joints, then the potential for serious injury is greatly enhanced. Baton strikes do not work each time a baton is deployed, sometimes requiring multiple strikes. Examples of impact weapons are side-handle baton, straight baton, and collapsible baton.

b. Oleoresin capsicum (OC spray)/pepper spray—OC spray is an aerosol spray that is sprayed on the subject's face. The focal points of the spray are the nose, the eyes, and the top of the head. The objective of the spray is to temporarily incapacitate a subject by affecting his or her ability to breathe and see. Depending on the manufacturer, incapacitation is temporary and lasts at best half an hour. As with the deployment of batons, OC spray is not effective in every case. In fact, once OC spray is deployed, an officer should wait until the subject is affected before attempting to establish control. Potential for injury or long-term aftereffects are minimal. However, there has been some controversy surrounding the use of OC spray, associating its deployment with resisting subject's deaths. Chan et al. (2001) determined that "OC exposure and inhalation do not result in significant risk for respiratory compromise or asphyxiation, even when combined with positional restraint" (p. 3). It should be noted that this study was completed in controlled laboratory conditions, with the participants wearing goggles and void of the stressful conditions a subject experiences during an arrest. The question remains, why has death been associated with the use of OC spray?

c. Electronic devices—These are designed to disrupt a subject's neuromuscular system by rendering them helpless, sending an electrical current through the subject's body. Electro-muscular disruption devices are designed to limit the potential for serious injury to the officer and the subject. However, as with OC spray there is controversy surrounding the use of electronic devices. Most, if not all, of the controversy is associated with subjects who have died during the deployment of an electrical device. A 2008 National Institute of Justice study indicates that such weapons are not risk free and that there is no conclusive medical evidence that indicates a high risk of serious injury or death due to the deployment of an electronic device (p. 3). Studies conducted by Taser International have all been done in a lab and during police training conditions which are sterile. Again, the sterile laboratory environment does not take into account the fear and anxiety subjects experience when resisting arrest.

V. *Deadly force*—This is employing a weapon with the intent to cause great bodily harm or death. Deadly force is the last resort and is deployed only if the officer has no other options. In most cases, deadly force is associated with the use of a firearm. However, other options can include the use of empty hand techniques, baton strikes, and, in rare cases, the use of a motor vehicle.

WHY DOES AN OFFICER USE FORCE?

The primary objective of the use of force is to establish control. From a legal standpoint, there is no other purpose for an officer's actions (Alpert & Dunham, 2004; Ivkovich, 2000; Tyler & Huo, 2002). If we reexamine Florida State Statute 776.05, it identifies three conditions in which an officer can use force: stop a threat, stop a felon who has escaped, or arresting a felon who is fleeing. The statute is specific to felons, but it is important to note that all arrests, be they felonies or misdemeanors, may require that some force be used. Force may be as simple as verbal direction, the application of handcuffs where there is no resistance, or as severe as the use of deadly force.

The concept of control carries with it two important components: escalation and de-escalation. An officer can escalate the use of force to establish control of a subject. However, the officer must de-escalate once control is established (Dobkin, 1996; Geller & Toch, 2005; Goodwin, 2002; Walker, 2005).

FACTORS INFLUENCING USE OF FORCE

Officer/Subject Factors

Desmendt (1982) describes what has become known as officer/subject factors, arguing that the use of less-than-lethal force may involve a number of variables that are evaluated based on the nature of the confrontation, the officer's observations, assessment of the subject, and the officer's beliefs at the time of the incident. Desmendt's argument is supported by the U.S. Supreme Court decision, *Graham v. Connor,* which is discussed earlier in this chapter. The *Graham* decision went one step further and applied reasonableness to all of use-of-force encounters. The most important factor in any use-of-force incident is the officer's interpretation of the encounter. The officer's assessment and interpretation begin before the encounter. The officer's assessment continues through the encounter, and the level of force is adjusted to address the subject's level of resistance. Finally, the assessment occurs post encounter, most often during the report writing (Arrigo & Shipley, 2004; Blum, 2000; Florida Department of Law Enforcement, 2008; Michigan State Police Training Academy, 2004; Rahtz, 2003). Walker (2005) notes that there is more to an officer's use of force than officer/subject factors and argues that the use of force is closely correlated to the nature and types of calls for service, race of the suspect, and the suspect's actions (p. 189).

Threat assessment and interpretation are essential in an officer's ability to react to a situation. If an officer is unable to assess a situation properly or is not mentally prepared, it inhibits the officer's ability to react to the threat. Therefore, assessment and interpretation are integral components in the use-of-force equation and are associated with one's ability to process information cognitively (Lachman & Butterfield, 1979). Proper decision-making with limited errors is dependent on an officer's ability to recognize a threat, process the information, and respond with the appropriate level of force. Cannon (1915) was the first researcher to detail the components of stress responses/fight or flight. Cannon described fight-flight/stress response in four stages:

- *Stage 1*—Some sort of stimulus is sent to the brain by one or more of the five senses: seeing, visual cues such as body movement or hands in the pockets; smell, the smell of gunpowder or blood; touch, during a pat down the feel of a weapon or contraband; hearing, the sound of a gunshot or a loud verbal dispute; and taste, the taste of something sweet or sour.
- *Stage 2*—The brain processes the stimulus and categorizes the information as a threat or nonthreat.
  a. *Threat*—The body's autonomic nervous system activates preparing to defend (fight) against the threat or flee (flight). The fight response is associated with anger and aggression. The flight response is associated with fleeing, hiding, and/or freezing.
  b. *Nonthreat*—If the stimulus is categorized as a nonthreat, the response stops.
- *Stage 3*—The body stays in the threat mode with all systems aroused until the threat no longer exists.
- *Stage 4*—The threat is neutralized and the body's systems return to normal, return to homeostasis. Oftentimes because of the high states of arousal, it takes time for hormones such as adrenaline and cortisol to be reabsorbed in the body, with officers experiencing nervousness and hypervigilance.

SCENARIO I

Threat Assessment

You receive a call of a Black male selling drugs on a street corner. The caller provides dispatch with a perfect physical description, including the subject's clothing. You arrive on scene, park in the shadows, and observe the suspect on the corner. Several pedestrians approach the suspect, and as the pedestrians approach the suspect, they exchange greetings and shake hands. You do not witness a transaction of drugs or money. However, you decide to investigate and approach the suspect. As you talk to the suspect, you ask him to take his hands out of his pockets. He does but keeps placing his hands in his pockets despite your repeated requests. Fearing that the subject is armed, you ask if you can pat him down. The suspect agrees, but before you can secure the suspect, suddenly he reaches into his pockets. You attempt to trap his hands in his pockets, but before you can stop the suspect, he draws a handgun from his right jacket pocket and what you discover later as crack cocaine from his left jacket pocket. You disarm the suspect and place him under arrest.

1. Did you have a legal authority to be on the corner and approach the suspect?
2. Was the suspect selling drugs, and if so, can you describe what a drug deal looks like?
3. On approaching the suspect, was there anything suspicious about his behavior?
4. Did you have the legal authority to pat the suspect down for weapons and contraband?
5. Would you have done anything differently? If so what?
6. Did you properly assess the threat?

USE OF FORCE—PHYSIOLOGICAL AND PSYCHOLOGICAL RESPONSES

Prior to this discussion, we addressed the guidelines and defined force. It would be great if our discussion could be limited to those factors, but it can't. The most important factors are the officer and the subject at the time they cross each other's path. In our society, there is an expectation that an officer will act professionally in the execution of his or her duties. In saying this, there are a number of false perceptions: Officers do not possess biases; officers possess the necessary skill sets to apprehend a suspect and control a threat; officers do not experience fear when involved in an encounter; officers do not take threats and insults personally; and officers are always objective. If this were the case, why are officers charged with brutality?

The Human Element

The officer–subject encounter becomes much more complex because the human element offers an infinite number of possibilities. Thomas (1989) argues that when an officer encounters a suspect, the officer will face one of three possible personality types: cooperative, potentially uncooperative, or combative. Remsberg (1986) describes these personality types as yes, no, and maybe. Thompson (1993) classifies these personalities as the nice, the difficult, and the wimp. Knowing that you will encounter one of the three personalities, would you treat every person the same or would you adjust your behavior to match that of the subject? As you reflect on this question, remember the subject has the advantage at the beginning of most encounters.

SCENARIO II

Cooperative, Positionally Uncooperative, or Combative

You are on patrol and find a subject prowling behind a business at 2 A.M. When you approach the subject, you notice that he has hands in his pockets. You ask the subject to remove his hands and he refuses. You advise the subject that you need to pat him down for the subject's safety and your safety. The subject agrees to the pat down. You handcuff the subject, advising him that it is temporary until your investigation is complete. As you begin to pat the subject down and reach for his crotch area, he pulls away. When you reach for the crotch area a second time, the subject attempts to block your efforts a second time. Finally, you take the subject to the ground, complete the pat down, and recover a .357 Magnum from the subject's crotch.

1. Did you have reasonable suspicion to believe that criminal activity was afoot when you first observed the subject?
2. Were you suspicious of the subject because he refused to remove his hands from his pockets when you requested that he do so?
3. How would you classify the subject's personality: cooperative, potentially uncooperative, or combative?
4. Who had the tactical advantage in this scenario, you or the suspect?

Fight or Flight

When faced with these situations, officers and subjects alike have to deal with the human physiological and psychological response known as fight or flight (Cannon, 1915; Cotton, 1990; Pfaff et al. 2007). Since the police are on the front line and called on to protect the public, police have no duty to retreat and, in many cases, must perform their duty (Waddington, 1991). The subject has options, including challenging the officer both verbally and physically. If the subject is a true predator, then the subject may be better prepared than the officer in any encounter.

Grossman (1996) adds two additional, not previously discussed, components to the fight or flight syndrome. Grossman's model describes the human encounter as fight or flight, posture, or submit (pp. 5–7). As the encounter begins, rather than flee, the subject postures and argues with the officer. During this phase, the subject shows no respect for the officer or the officer's authority. This is a decision point for many officers. If there is no arrestable offense, what are the officer's options? In many cases, an officer will respond by giving the suspect two options: leave or go to jail. The officer knows that there is no violation of the law, but the subject's actions are leading the officer down a decision-making path rarely discussed outside of the police culture known as "pissing off the police" or "contempt of cop" (Rudovsky, 1997; Zeisel & Kaye, 1997).

If the subject continues to argue and challenge the officer's authority, the subject is often arrested and charged with a minor misdemeanor similar to breach of the peace or disorderly conduct. Two things have occurred during the posturing phase: a challenge to an officer's authority and the officer challenging the subject's credibility on the street. The bottom line is a loss of respect or an attempt to "save face." Thompson (1993) addresses the issue of face-saving by attempting to get officers to understand that they will always have the last action, the ability to make an arrest. By allowing the subject to blow off steam and leave, an officer allows the subject to save face and reduces the potential for violence (pp. 76–77).

If during the posturing phase an arrest is imminent, then the options are flight, fight, or submit. If the subject leaves before the officer announces that the subject is under arrest, then the situation is resolved. During the arrest, the subject has two options: fight or submit. Submission is the preferred method. However, a summary of 20 years of data taken from the FBI Uniform Crime Report: Officers Killed and Assaulted between 1996 and 2016 offers insight into the number of officer assaults and injuries annually. On average, there were 59,000 assaults committed against police officers each of those years. In addition, during this same time period, officers sustained 16,000 injuries, and this includes every category of assault with a suspect's personal weapons (hands, fists, and feet) (Federal Bureau of Investigation, 2017).

Physiology of Fight or Flight

Cannon (1915) is the father of the stress response also known as fight or flight. In his research, Cannon (1915) observed that when the body experiences acute stress, it moves to a state of readiness prepared to respond to the perceived threat by either fleeing or fighting. In preparation to respond, the body mobilizes several bodily systems: an increased heart rate; increased blood pressure; increased breathing; blood rerouted to the large muscle groups (arms and legs); increased blood sugar in preparation for the muscle to work; increased fatty acid mobilization to feed the muscles while at work; decreased clotting time in case of injury and blood loss; increased muscular strength, decrease in abdominal and intestinal blood flow which can result in the stomach or bowels emptying in preparation for battle; and an increase in the perspiration rate to keep the body cool under stress. The physiological responses are controlled by the autonomic nervous system, meaning that we have no control over them; the physiological response is automatic.

Anger and Its Impact on Decision-Making

Lerner and Keltner (2001) note in their research that emotion-related appraisal tendencies may link stable traits (e.g., fearfulness or hostility) to the ways an individual interprets, acts on, and creates specific social interactions. Anger exacerbates risk seeking, causing people to perceive less risk. It is important to note that excessive risk aversion could have a catastrophic ending, if the officer underestimates the subject's abilities in the encounter.

I have found the excessive aversion belief system in some police candidates whom I have administered the 16PF Protective Services Plus Instrument during preemployment psychological evaluations. The 16PF is an inventory designed to assess personality traits of a person. The final report offers an assessment of 16 traits, with each trait scored on a scale from 1 to 10, with 1 being the lowest and 10 the highest possible score. An average score is in the range of 4 to 7. The 16 personality traits examined are warmth, reasoning, emotional stability, dominance, liveliness, rule consciousness, social boldness, sensitivity, vigilance, abstractedness, privateness, apprehension, openness to change, self-reliance, perfectionism, and tension (Institute for Personality and Ability Testing, 2001).

The 16PF Plus examines additional personality traits utilizing pathology-oriented scales, and these traits are scored utilizing the same 1 to 10 scale. The pathology-oriented scales examine psychological inadequacy, health concerns, suicidal thinking, anxious depression, low-energy state, self-reproach, apathetic withdrawal, paranoid ideation, obsessional thinking, alienation/perceptual distortion, thrill seeking, and threat immunity (Institute for Personality and Ability Testing, 2001).

Examining the pathology scale, there are two indices that when paired together clearly indicate risk aversion—thrill seeking and threat immunity. Thrill seeking is the first category; a score of eight or above indicates that a candidate will take unnecessary risks and place others in harm's way. Oftentimes the candidate does not recognize that he or she possesses this belief system. Threat immunity is the second category; a score of eight or above indicates that the candidate does not believe that he or she can die.

To confirm that these indices are, in fact, correct, they are addressed in a series of scenario-based decision-making questions, which usually confirm the results. When examined more closely, the candidates are not angry but express a sense of entitlement. In fact, the candidates fail to exhibit fear or anger and usually have very low scores in the areas of apprehension, self-reproach, and tension. If identified, these candidates are rejected because of their distorted belief system and the fact that they are a danger to fellow officers as well as the public.

Fear and Its Impact on Decision-Making

Fear should be considered a roadblock in one's decision-making process, an inhibitory emotion (Topalli & Wright, 2014). Fear acts much like anger to fuel different but still extreme responses. Fear triggers the activation of memories associated with danger and inhibition, as opposed to provocation and frustration that are associated with anger. Fear serves as a fundamental survival instinct, warning and acting as an interrupter of a goal or task (Fridja, 1986). Just as anger exacerbates risk-taking behavior, fear does just the opposite; it impedes risk-taking behavior and, in some instances, can cause panic, freezing, and errors in decision-making.

Chapter 3 provides a detailed discussion regarding the role of race/implicit bias/stereotyping and its impact on decision-making. Draine and Greenwald (1998) offer a model similar to fight or flight. In their argument, Draine and Greenwald note that the longer an individual has to make a decision, the less likely he or she is to make errors in decision-making that are influenced by implicit bias and/or racial priming. When decisions are made under time constraints, which is called speed criteria, the errors associated with implicit bias/racial priming will increase (pp. 301–303). In their findings, Draine and Greenwald were able to show that when limiting the amount of time by which a subject has to make a decision, the subject made repeated errors, which were associated with racial bias/stereotyping (p. 301). During the speed criterion process, responses can be categorized in one of the three categories:

- *Proper decision* was made under duress and limited time. This may be the result of repeated exposure to a situation(s) and the ability to draw from those experiences.

- *Improper decision* was made under duress and limited time. This decision may be because the decision maker is extremely stressed or in a situation that the subject views as causing serious injury and/or death. The subject has little experience to draw from, and the subject's decision was influenced by implicit racial bias.

STEREOTYPE

Profile Black Male

1. Black male between the ages of 15 and 35.
2. Clothes loose, baggy, wearing pants below the hips, underwear visible, expensive gym shoes, wearing a baseball cap backward and/or a hoody.
3. The loose-fitting clothes are designed to hide a firearm, drugs, or both.
4. Gold front teeth with hair an Afro, deadlocks, or bald.
5. Listens to gangsta rap music; plays it loudly while driving with deep bass that shakes other vehicles as they pass or sit behind them.
6. Driving a car that is an older make and model with big tires and expensive rims. The car may need a paint job and body work or has a custom paint job, or he may be driving an expensive car such as a BMW, Lexus, or Mercedes.
7. If driving a vehicle, he is likely to have a suspended driver's license, no insurance, or the vehicle's license plate is expired or illegal in some way.
8. Another mode of transportation may be a bicycle because the subject has a suspended driver's license.
9. More than likely, the young Black male is wanted on a warrant of some type.
10. The young Black male is, or will probably be, a criminal.

The Case of Philando Castile

The shooting of Philando Castile was a stereotype-triggered case. Prior to being shot and killed during a traffic stop, Castile had been stopped by police in the Minneapolis area 52 times and issued 86 citations, over half of which were dismissed by courts (Associated Press, Minneapolis, 2016). Castile was stopped for a broken taillight. Castile was legally armed when stopped by police. During the traffic stop, Castile advised the officers that he was armed and that he had a valid concealed weapons permit. From the beginning of the traffic stop, the officers had their firearms drawn and had the tactical advantage. When an officer requested Castile's identification, as Castile reached for his wallet, the officer shot and killed Castile. This could have been avoided by requesting Castile step out of the car, then handcuffing him, securing his firearm, and then obtaining his identification.

The law recognizes sudden movements that are called "furtive movements" and can be construed as dangerous to the officer. Officers do not have to wait to see a weapon because it is recognized that once the suspect's weapon appears, officers are at a disadvantage. However, this rarely happens when an officer has instructed the subject to do something, such as produce identification, and the officer has the tactical advantage. Why did this officer make this decision? Was race a factor in the shooting of Castile?

- *Mental stall/freezing* occurs when, under duress and limited time, the subject is unable to make a decision, right or wrong. Ultimately, the subject has not taken the time to process information similar to the incident in question. For police officers, this could result in death because they are frozen and unable to respond accordingly. Another possibility is that the officer will make an error in decision-making because the officer believes that he or she must do something. Is racial priming/stereotyping a possibility in this category?

SCENARIO III

I Don't Know What to Do

A police officer makes a traffic stop on a late model F 150 pickup truck. The driver of the pickup truck exits his vehicle and approaches the officer, meeting the officer between both vehicles. The driver/suspect chest bumps and pushes the officer. The officer deploys his Taser, shooting the suspect with the Taser, but it has no effect on the suspect. The suspect then punches the officer twice, and the officer does nothing. The suspect walks toward his pickup truck, starting to enter the truck and leave the scene. However, the suspect changes his mind and returns to grab the officer by the throat and chokes the officer, pinning the officer between the truck's open door and the truck's frame. A second officer arrives on scene, deploys her Taser and, again, that does not work. The original officer is still being choked. When the Taser does not work, the second officer begins striking the suspect with her Taser. A third officer arrives on scene and takes the suspect to the ground and handcuffs him.

1. What happened to the first officer? Was it mental stall, or was the officer afraid?
2. What was the appropriate level of force when the suspect began choking the officer?
3. When the second officer arrived on the scene and her Taser failed, what would have been the proper response after Taser failure?
4. Did the second officer experience mental stall?
5. Why did this happen, and what would you do to prevent this in the future?

VIOLENCE MODELS IN RESPONSE TO STIMULI

D. Thomas (2014) argues that there are many models and classification systems that have been used to explain violence. In policing, reactive violence is violence that is designed to protect or stop. It is violence that is spontaneous and in response to an immediate threat (Thomas, D. 2014, p. 60). Note that reactive violence is not always in response to an act of violence; it may be in response to disrespect and committed spontaneously in a fit of anger and/or rage. Again, this is known as contempt of cop or pissing off the police. Reactive violence is prone to a number of errors due to a number of inputs. For police this may include fear, anger, stereotyping, zone assignment/calls for service, officers injured or assaulted, neighborhood's response to police, personal belief system, and agency culture.

Proactive violence is a form of violence that is planned and predatory in nature. This is the type of violence that a SWAT (special weapons and tactics) team perpetrates when it is taking a violent subject into custody. Further, this type of violence is the violence perpetrated by officers when they are confident of their skills or they have the time to make a weighed decision, such as knowing a suspect is wanted and potentially armed. The knowledge is based on fact, not primed due to race or stereotype.

Decision Fatigue and Its Impact on Decision-Making

The concept of "decision fatigue" has rarely been applied to police decision-making. Integral to decision fatigue is a construct known as ego depletion. Ego depletion has two components, will power and self-control, and through a series of lab experiments Masicampo and Baumeister (2008) determined that will power and self-control have finite limits of energy. The research findings noted that when you make a number of decisions during the course of a day, that act (decision-making process) will, in fact, exhaust a decision maker's will power reserves, ultimately compromising self-control (Govorun & Payne, 2006; Masicampo & Baumeister, 2008; Thomas, T. L., 2014).

Danzigera, Levavb, and Avnaim-Pessoa (2011) conducted a study regarding judicial decision-making and who was likely to receive favorable decisions. Their data shows that the likelihood of a ruling in favor of a prisoner spikes at the beginning of each session—the probability of a favorable ruling steadily declines from 0.65 to nearly 0 and jumps back up to 0.65 after a break for a meal (p. 6890). Also, research indicates that as the quality of the decisions erode, the decision maker chooses habit over logic and/or reason. Decision fatigue is not limited to judges. Experimental research has shown that decision fatigue impacts individuals from every walk of life and profession.

As noted earlier, self-control is a component of ego depletion. It is hard to fathom that self-control and will power require the use of energy. It has always been that poor self-control was more the lack of mental toughness. Self-control is when one consciously makes an effort to change a form of behavior, a belief system, or feeling. Self-control minimizes negative behaviors and maximizes positive interaction and political correctness. To exhibit these behavior patterns takes energy, because an individual is constantly working to keep the negative belief system under wraps. Chapter 3 provides examples of officers blurting out racial epitaphs spontaneously when under duress, indifferent to their audience. The factors that impact self-control, and ultimately decision fatigue, are many and require the use of stored energy because filtering them out requires thinking and conscious effort. Such factors include stressors such as noise, crowds, and habits and conditions, including excessive smoking, drinking, and eating; dieting; delayed gratification; and mood regulation (Muraven & Baumeister, 2000, pp. 249–251).

The studies of decision fatigue have never been conducted using police officer participants. However, Govorun and Payne (2006) did assess ego depletion as it relates racial prejudice through a series of shoot/don't shoot scenarios. The population tested was 72 introductory psychology students, which included 62.5 percent males and 37.5 percent females. Race/ethnicity of the participants is as follows: 84.7 percent European American, 8.3 percent African American, 4.2 percent Hispanic, 1.4 percent Asian, and 1.4 percent identified as "other." Initial analyses showed that sex and race had no main effects or interactions, but these variables were not included in the primary analysis. Govorun and Payne determined that depletion manipulation (laboratory depletion of self-control) had an adverse impact on the participants' ability to cognitively control their responses but did not impact automatic responses. Simply put, due to self-control depletion, the participants reverted to habits as opposed to using logic and conscious thought. Govorun and Payne also concluded depletion manipulation (laboratory depletion of self-control) did not affect automatic stereotyping bias but does impact the cognitive processes required to suppress politically incorrect belief systems. Finally, Govorun and Payne stated: "Automatic associations are more likely to guide behavior when one's resources are depleted. As a result, stereotypical errors result more frequently among participants who have a strong automatic bias and are depleted" (p. 128).

SCENARIO IV

Stalker

After midnight, a call comes in about a stalker who beat and raped his ex-girlfriend. The ex-girlfriend advises officers that the suspect is the father of her child and that she ended the relationship two months prior to this incident. Since the breakup, the suspect has been harassing the victim by making threatening phone calls, text messages, showing up at the victim's place of employment, slashing her tires, and breaking into her house on two separate occasions. The victim believed that this would stop and she did not report any of the previous incidents to the police. On this night, the suspect broke into the house, beat, and raped the victim at gunpoint. Midnight shift officers could not locate the suspect. The dayshift was given information and possible locations where the suspect might be located. A dayshift patrol unit located the vehicle, with the suspect sitting in his vehicle. The officer parked in front of the suspect vehicle, blocking the suspect's ability to drive off. The officer's vehicle was parked at a 45° angle facing the suspect vehicle driver's side. The officer was aware that the suspect could be armed and, while facing the suspect, the officer signaled for the suspect to raise his hands. The suspect snatched his hands from the dashboard quickly exiting his vehicle. At the same time, the officer exited his vehicle drawing his firearm. The suspect was armed with a handgun and pointed it at the officer. The officer shot and killed the suspect.

The suspect was a well-dressed White male. In the officer's interview the officer stated what made the difference in his response was the information that the suspect could be armed. The officer also stated that if he didn't have the information, and judging the suspect based on race and clothing alone, he (the officer) would have approached the suspect without ever drawing his firearm, and it probably would have cost the officer his life. The officer stated that the suspect's race, clothing, vehicle, and personal hygiene were disarming and not that of a traditional suspect. What did the officer mean by "traditional suspect"?

The Warrior Mentality

There has been an argument in America that the mentality of police officers has changed from that of being service oriented and personal to becoming impersonal and detached as if the officers are fighting a war. The media has argued that policing has become militarized with armored vehicles, black tactical uniforms, and ballistic helmets. The public and media view this as a move to separate police from the public. What no one understands is that mental conditioning, police culture, and basic human instinct all play a role in the officer's psyche.

Reflect on this. You have just made the decision to become a police officer. Your background is middle class, and you have bachelor's degree; you have never been in a physical fight and never been exposed to violence; and you have witnessed acts of violence vicariously through media sources. You enter the police academy, and your trainers begin to teach you about a winning mind-set, going home at night, and being prepared for sudden attacks that officers experience. To prepare you for the potential threats, you are taught defensive tactics and firearms, both 80 hours of individual instruction, and they are perishable skill sets, the latter meaning that over time your ability to recall and apply the skills diminishes if you do not practice. In the academy, you learn about crime scenes, victims, suspects, constitutional law, the Bill of Rights, and your role in protecting citizen's rights.

Upon graduation from the academy, you are assigned to field training and your indoctrination is initiation by fire. You are witness to victims of murder, rape, child abuse, and fatal car accidents; assist family members of victims;

and interview and arrest suspects who have committed atrocities that you have only seen on television.

SCENARIO V

A Defining Moment in Your Career

You are in your first week of field training. You are investigating a domestic violence call. You interview both parties and determine that there is no act of violence. The girlfriend wanted the boyfriend to pack his stuff and move out. This is what many would say is a fairly routine situation. The suspect is willing to move his belongings, complies with all of your requests, and puts you at rest. In essence, his attitude and behavior are psychologically disarming. Your training officer completes a warrants check on the boyfriend/suspect. The information that you receive is that the suspect is wanted on a warrant for attempted murder. He had the advantage; he knew that he was wanted. Your training officer approaches the suspect and advises him that there is a warrant for his arrest. The suspect asks what the warrant is for.

When the training officer responds, assault with intent to commit murder, the suspect explodes, attacking you, briefly knocking you unconscious. You and your training officer are then in a fight for your life. During the fight, both of your portable radios are lost. Family members stand by, watching. The suspect attempts to pull your firearm from the holster. You respond by knocking the suspect down and beating his head on the floor, freeing his grip from your firearm. Your training officer gets a handcuff on the suspect and pulls on the suspect's arm until the suspect gives up screaming in pain. You are transported to the hospital and cleared to go back to work. On reflection you recognize that you almost died.

1. Did you do anything wrong?
2. Were you prepared for what happened?
3. Was something missing in your approach to this suspect?
4. Do you develop a warrior mentality now? If so, what does that mean?

There is a great debate today concerning the police officer's mind-set, is the officer a warrior or guardian? When you think of the term "warrior," what are the words that come to mind? Researchers use a number of adjectives to describe a warrior, or a warrior's mind-set; many are described as a belief system, which all should strive for. "Bushido" is a Japanese term that characterizes the Samurai's Code of Honor, loosely translated means "way of the warrior," and is described in Japanese literature dating back to the year 1180 (Cunningham, Reich, & Fichner-Rathus, 2014). Cunningham et al. (2014) list Bushido's eight virtues as justice, courage, mercy, politeness, honesty, honor, loyalty, and self-control (p. 747). As you reflect on these virtues, do you believe that these are characteristics an American police officer should exhibit? Are they all inclusive, or would you add anything? Do you believe that the virtues provide balance and equity to the police warrior mind-set?

The guardian mind-set focuses on returning to a day before 9/11, when police protected the rights of citizens. More important, the guardian mind-set requires that police are fair and impartial in their decision-making. Sheriff Sue Rahr (2011) operationalized a procedural process for training street officers through the acronym LEED: L = listen; E = explain with E = equity; D = dignity. With the LEED model "officers are trained to take the time to listen to people; explain what is going to happen and how the process works; explain why that decision was made so the equity of the decision is transparent; and leave the participants with their dignity intact" (Rahr & Rice, 2015, p. 3).

Some of the researchers have asked the question: Why have police adopted such a harsh attitude? And if the police are at war, who are they at war with? I find these arguments interesting because, for as long as I can remember, we have had a war on drugs and law enforcement has been at the front line of that war. Since 9/11, law enforcement has been actively involved in the War on Terror at home and has been training to respond to nuclear, biological, and/or chemical attacks. Finally, law enforcement has been at the front line of every mass shooting in this country. Therefore, when researchers ask who law enforcement is at war with, just look around at the threats and the officers' responsibilities. Also, in the beginning, the so-called domestic wars that law enforcement has fought on the streets of the United States were originally fought by specialized units or SWAT teams. However, because of the immediacy, the need for rapid response, or by dumb luck, these wars are no longer unique to SWAT. These wars have the ability to impact every officer, daily, as they interact with the public. Finally, the term "war" is not one selected by law enforcement. "War" is a policy decision that emanates from the White House, used to describe to the ends to which we as a country will go to stop what is believed to be a threat or harm to our society.

CONCLUSION

Over the past several years, I have been critical of the warrior mentality in policing. I associated the warrior mentality with poor decision-making, police brutality, and the shooting of unarmed Black men. With the number of officer deaths related to ambush in 2015, 2016, 2017, and early 2018, I have had to reflect on the term "warrior mentality." There is little difference in the terms "warrior mentality" and "officer survival." In analyzing the virtues of Bushido, Bushido is a true warrior's mind-set that encompasses LEED. The most difficult time trainers have had, and will have, is to teach officers that being in control does not mean that officers must be abusive and use racial epitaphs. Officers must understand that stress and duress will place their decision-making on autopilot, suppress their cognitive safeguards, and often-times expose the officers' true belief system, which can manifest itself in a number of decision-making errors where racial bias can and will rear its ugly head. To offset these potentially negative outcomes, it is important for officers to train, even after graduation from the academy and beyond in-service train-ing. Ongoing training is an investment, designed to assist officers in harness-ing their fears and in mastering their defensive tactics skills, firearms skills, and communication skills because each is perishable. Continual training is the key to preparation, confidence, and mastering the fear, which creates errors in officer decision-making when under duress. Finally, officers need to find a way to evaluate their actions daily.

Thomas (2017) developed an evaluation tool for Calibre Press designed to assist officers in assessing their mental health on a daily basis. It uses the acronym "REST" and is a great tool to personally assess/evaluate an officer's daily mental health and performance on calls.

R: *Reflection*—Find quiet time after you get home and review your day. Reflect on your calls for service and if one or several were stressful. Self-reflection is deep; oftentimes we find things that we don't like. The one thing I will say, be honest with yourself, and this should be done while you are alone and without drinking.

E: *Evaluate*—During your reflection, if you determine that there was a call(s) for service that caused you undue stress, evaluate your performance. Attempt to find the source of the stressor. Here are some examples: Are you lacking a skill set? Were you afraid? Is something in your personal life spilling over into your professional life causing poor performance? Are you exhausted/fatigued? Have you suffered a loss of some sort? And/or have you or a fellow officer been a victim of a physical assault or attack?

S: *Symptoms*—This is what are you feeling as a result of your evaluation. "Feelings" is a nasty word, and male law enforcement officers have difficulty using this word. It's okay to have feelings; however, where we get into trouble is denying them. Two things that we must understand are to keep our feelings bottled up is self-destructive and the longer we keep them bottled up, the more they will impact our performance. No matter how much we attempt to contain our feelings, they will find a way to be exposed usually through outbursts of uncon-trolled and unwarranted verbal abuse and/or unwarranted and unnecessary excessive force. *True symptoms are* anxiety, depression, inability to sleep, obsessive repetitive thoughts, intrusion of thoughts, worrying, withdrawal from those close to you, and excessive absences from work. *Words associated with feelings are* "fear," "powerless," "anger," "distrust," "disillusioned," "overwhelmed," "isolated/lonely," "numb," and "sad." Don't be afraid to use these words or others that describe your feelings.

T: Triage—Triage should be done as needed. The goal is not to become overwhelmed and resolve those feelings as soon as you can. It is important to have a network to share your feelings. One of the greatest sources for triage is your significant other or spouse. It is the one person that you can trust and bare your soul to. Your spouse will never understand if you don't give him or her a chance. The alternative is shutting your significant other out and chance losing him or her. Historically, law enforcement officers count on other officers to hear them out. This is bad practice because it is usually done while drinking. Discussions with fellow officers while drinking minimizes poor decisions and reaffirms bad behavior, and the daily trauma is never resolved. In fact, in these situations, what happens is the officer's true feelings and behavior are never addressed, which could lead to consequences that can be catastrophic.

REFERENCES

Alpert, G. P., & Dunham, R. G. (2004). *Understanding police use of force: Officers, suspects and reciprocity.* New York, NY: Cambridge University Press.

Arrigo, B. A., & Shipley, S. L. (2004). *Introduction to forensic psychology: Issues and controversies in crime and justice,* 2nd ed. Burlington, MA: Elsevier Academic Press.

Associated Press, Minneapolis. (2016, July 9). *Philando Castile has been stopped 52 times by police.* Associated Press. Retrieved February 11, 2008, from http://minnesota.cbslocal.com/2016/07/09/philando-stops/.

Blum, L. N. (2000). *Force under pressure: How cops live and why they die.* New York, NY: Lantern Books.

Box, S. (1983). *Power, crime, and mystification.* New York, NY: Tavistock Publications.

Cannon, W. B. (1915). *Bodily changes in pain, hunger, fear, and rage: An account of recent searches into the emotional excitement.* New York, NY: D. Appleton and Company.

Chan, T., Vilke, G. M., Clausen, J., Clark, R., Schmidt, P., Snowden, T., & Neuman, T. (2001). *Pepper spray's effects on a suspect's ability to breathe.* Washington, DC: National Institute of Justice.

Cotton, D. H. G. (1990). *Stress management: An integrated approach to theory.* New York, NY: Brunner/Mazel.

Cunningham, L. S., Reich, J. J., & Fichner-Rathus, L. (2014). *Culture & values: A survey of the humanities*. Boston, MA: Wadsworth Publishing.

Dantzker, M. L. (2005). *Understanding today's police*. Monsey, NY: Criminal Justice Press.

Danzigera, S., Levavb, J., & Avnaim-Pessoa, L. (2011). Extraneous factors in judicial decisions. *Proceedings of the National Academy of Sciences, 108* (17): 6889–6892.

Desmendt, J. (1982). *The physical intervention paradigm for enforcement and corrections*. Nokesville, VA: Protective Safety Systems.

Dobkin, B. A. (1996). Video verite: Language and image in the interpretation of power. In M. E. Stuckey (Ed.), *The theory and practice of political communication research*, pp. 84–94. Albany, NY: SUNY Press.

Draine, S. C, & Greenwald, A. G. (1998). Replicable unconscious semantic priming. *Journal of Experimental Psychology:* General, 127, 286–303.

Federal Bureau of Investigation. (2017). *2017 Law enforcement officers killed and assaulted*. Washington, DC: Department of Justice.

Florida Department of Law Enforcement. (2008). *Florida basic recruit training program: High liability*, volume 2 (2008:4). Tallahassee, FL: Author.

Fridja, N. H. (1986). *The emotions*. New York, NY: Cambridge University Press.

Geller, W. A., & Toch, H. (2005). *Police violence: Understanding and controlling police abuse of force*. New Haven, CT: Yale University Press.

Godwin, C. (2002). Professional vision. In D. Weinberg (Ed.), *Qualitative research methods*, pp. 281–312. Hoboken, NJ: Wiley-Blackwell.

Govorun, O., & Payne, B. K. (2006). Ego-depletion and prejudice: Separating automatic and controlled components. *Social Cognition, 24*(2): 111–136.

Graham v. Connor, 490, U.S. 386 (1989).

Grossman, D. (1996). On killing: *The psychological cost of learning to kill in war and society*. Boston, MA: Little, Brown and Company.

Institute for Personality and Ability Testing. (2001). *Qualification training for the 16PF questionnaire*. Champaign, IL: Author.

Ivkovich, S. K. (2000). Challenges of policing democracies: The Croatian experience. In O. Marenin & D. K. Das (Eds.), *Challenges of policing democracies: A world perspective*, pp. 45–86. The Netherlands: Gordon and Breach Publishers.

Kennedy, E. A. (1995). Teaching martial arts to law enforcement personnel. In C. A. Wiley (Ed.), *Martial arts teachers on teaching*, pp. 131–141. Berkeley, CA: Frog Books.

Lachman, J. L. & Butterfield, E. C. (1979). *Cognitive psychology and information processing: An introduction*. Hillsdale, NJ: Lawrence Erlbaum.

Lawrence, R. G. (2000). *The politics of force: Media and the construction of police brutality*. Berkeley, CA: University of California Press.

Lerner, J. S., & Keltner, D. (2001). Fear, anger, and risk. *Journal of Personality and Social Psychology, 81*(1): 146–159.

Lippmann, M. R. (2006). *Contemporary criminal law: Concepts, cases, and controversies.* Thousand Oaks, CA: Sage Publications.

Masicampo, E. J., & Baumeister, R. F. (2008). Toward a physiology of dual-process reasoning and judgment: Lemonade, willpower, and expensive rule-based analysis. *Psychological Science, 19* (3): 255–260.

Michigan State Police Training Academy. (2004). *Criminal law and procedure: A manual for Michigan police officers.* Lansing, MI: Author.

Muraven, M., & Baumeister, R. F. (2000). Self-regulation and depletion of limited resources: Does self-control resemble a muscle? *Psychological Bulletin, 126* (2): 247–259.

National Institute of Justice. (2008). *Study of deaths following electro muscular disruption: Interim report.* Washington, DC: U.S. Department of Justice.

Neyroud, P. (2008). Policing and ethics. In T. Newburn (Ed.), *Handbook of policing,* 2nd ed., pp. 666–692. Portland, OR: Willan Publishing.

Olsen, M. (2001). *State Trooper: America's state troopers and highway patrolmen.* Paducah, KY: Turner Publishing Company.

Pfaff, D.W., Martin, E. M., & Ribeiro, A.C. (2007). *Relations between mechanisms of CNS arousal and mechanisms of stress,* Stress, 10:4, 316–325.

Rahr, S., & Rice, S. K. (2015). *From warriors to guardians: Recommitting American police culture to Democratic ideals.* Washington, DC: National Institute of Justice.

Rahtz, H. (2003). *Understanding police use of force.* Monsey, NY: Criminal Justice Press.

Remsberg, C. (1986). *The tactical edge: Surviving high-risk patrol.* Northbrook, IL: Calibre Press.

Rudovsky, D. (1997). Police abuse: Can the violence be contained? In M. D. McShane & F. P. Williams (Eds.), *Law enforcement operations and management,* pp. 249–286. New York, NY: Garland Publishing.

Shpayer-Makov, H. (2002). *The making of a policeman: A social history of a labour force in metropolitan London, 1829–1914.* London, UK: Ashgate Publishing.

Thomas, D. (1989). *Defensive tactics manual,* 2nd ed. Grandville, MI: Author.

Thomas, D. (2014). *Understanding violent criminals: Insights from the front lines of law enforcement.* Santa Barbara, CA: Praeger Publishing.

Thomas, D. (2017). *Mental health triage: A tool for law enforcement officers.* Retrieved February 17, 2018, from https://www.calibrepress.com/2018/01/mental-health-triage-pt-2/.

Thomas, T. L. (2014). *Cutting edge to success: Personal development and time management skills that will change your life.* Chapel Hill, NC: Lulu Publishing Services.

Thompson, G. J. (1993). *Verbal judo: The art of gentle persuasion.* New York, NY: Quill Publications.

Topalli, V., & Wright, R. (2014). Affect and the dynamic foreground of predatory street crime: Desperation, anger and fear. In J. L. Van Gelder, H. Elffers, D. Reynald, & D. Nagin (Eds.), *Affect and cognition in criminal decision making,* pp. 42–57. New York, NY: Routledge Publishing.

Tyler, T. R., & Huo, Y. J. (2002). *Trust in the law: Encouraging public cooperation with the police and courts.* New York, NY: Russell Sage Foundation.

Urbonya, K. R. (1998). Dangerous misperceptions: Protecting police officers, society, and the Fourth Amendment right to personal safety. In M. M. Ross & American Bar Association (Eds.), *Sword and shield revisited: A practical approach to 1983,* pp. 259–349. Chicago, IL: American Bar Association.

Waddington, P.A.J. (1991). *The strong arm of the law: Armed and public order policing.* New York, NY: Oxford University Press.

Walker, S. (2005). *The new world of police accountability.* Thousand Oaks, CA: Sage Publications.

Williams, G. T. (2005). *Force reporting for every cop.* Sudbury, MA: Jones & Bartlett Publishing.

Zeisel, H. Z., & Kaye, D. H. (1997). *Prove it with figures Empirical methods in law and litigation.* New York, NY: Springer Publications.

5

Deadly Force Decision-Making— Law, Policy, and Training

The use of deadly force is a police officer's nightmare. There are two prevailing public attitudes concerning the use of deadly force. Unfortunately, this debate is divided by racial lines and often void of logic or reason. The White community argues that police have a right to defend themselves and support the use of deadly force, with the belief that police use firearms only when absolutely necessary. The Black and minority communities argue that they are victims and police unjustly shoot people of color even when the person of color follows the officer's instructions.

Annually, police in the United States shoot and kill an estimated 1,000 people in the line of duty. However, there is no official data collection system such as others operated by the FBI or the Department of Justice. This is interesting because the FBI records every assault and homicide made against a law enforcement officer in the United States but not killings by police. Data regarding the use of deadly force by police is collected only by the *Washington Post* and *Guardian* newspapers, respectfully. And the data collected by both newspapers does not account for the number of citizens who are shot by police and survive.

This chapter begins by providing the historical foundation and the context by which police can use deadly force by first examining the fleeing felon law and compare it to the current standard of law established in the *Tennessee v. Garner* and its many interpretations. The reader will briefly revisit threat assessment fight or flight, and the three categories of officer-involved shootings (OISs). The reader will examine the most common words used in almost every police shooting, "I was in fear for my life," and attempt to answer the questions: What do those words really mean and when should they be applied? This chapter offers a number of case studies as examples concerning OISs, providing the reader with the guidelines to categorize the shootings. The reader will be exposed to police privilege versus Black hysteria, the concept of damaging the brand; and Black Lives Matter versus Blue Lives Matter. Finally, readers will review a discussion concerning the importance of interpreting deadly force encounters with police, and they will have an opportunity to examine three sides of the subject, looking through the lenses of the respective communities: White, minority, and law enforcement officers.

THE LAW AND DEADLY FORCE

Prior to 1985, the law of the land in the United States was that officers could shoot any person who committed a felony, armed or unarmed, violent or nonviolent, and who was fleeing from the scene of the felony they committed. This rule was a rule of law known as the fleeing felon rule. The fleeing felon rule, defined in its simplest terms, means when a subject commits any felony he or she can be shot to stop escape (Fyfe, 1996; Kleinig, 2008; Lippman, 2007; Walker, Spohn, & DeLone, 2007). As an example, the state of Michigan has a statute titled Larceny (theft) in a Building, MCL750.360 (felony); there is no dollar value associated with this act of larceny. The statute reads:

> Any person who shall commit the crime of larceny by stealing in any dwelling house, house trailer, office, store, gasoline service station, shop, warehouse, mill, factory, hotel, school, barn, granary, ship, boat, vessel, church, house of worship, locker room or any building used by the public shall be guilty of a felony. (Michigan State Legislature, 1931)

SCENARIO I

Larceny in a Building

You are a new officer, on patrol prior to 1985, and the fleeing felon rule is in effect. You are dispatched to the local 7-11 for a call about a juvenile stealing a candy bar from the store. You are just around the corner, and dispatch gives you a physical description of a Black male subject, about

10 years old, 5 feet, 100 pounds, wearing a red plaid shirt and blue jean shorts. Dispatch also advises that the subject has no weapons and did not threaten the clerk. As you arrive, you observe the subject running from the store with what appears to be a candy bar in one hand and a bag of potato chips in the other. The store clerk steps outside and states: "That's him, officer stop him!" You order the subject to stop and he continues to run. You shoot the subject in the back killing him.

Reflective Questions

1. Although the law and department policy allow you to shoot a fleeing felon, is the law and policy in conflict with your personal value system?

2. Would you shoot the juvenile? Or would you fear that if you didn't you would be labeled a coward and ostracized by your fellow officers? Not fit into the culture.

3. Do you believe that the value of a human life is worth more than a candy bar and a bag of potato chips?

The change in the use of deadly force was the result of a 1985 landmark Supreme Court decision known as *Tennessee v. Garner*, 471 U.S. 1 (1985). The circumstances of the *Garner* case were similar to those in Scenario I. In that decision, the Supreme Court ruled that an officer *cannot use* deadly force to apprehend a nonviolent felon. It also stipulated that officers can use deadly force only in defense of themselves or others (pp. 7–22).

Why the change in policy and law? At the time our forefathers adopted English Common Law, there were very few felonies. Today, our society has evolved, so has our sense of morals, and this change from English Common Law met that we value life over property. In essence, the fleeing felon rule shocked the conscience of American citizens; the Supreme Court heard the cries and recognized that life was more precious than property.

It is not enough to address *Garner*. When discussing deadly force, the next logical step is to examine circumstances in which deadly force is used and attempt to answer the age-old question: Are police trained to shoot to kill? Take a moment and reflect on some of the circumstances in which you could see yourself using deadly force. Do any of your reflective thoughts match the following set of circumstances: man with a gun; woman attacking an officer with a pair of scissors; officer being attacked with a screwdriver; suspect is biting an officer's thumb off and the officer is passing in and out of consciousness; a suspect is in the act of stabbing a woman as the officer enters the residence; a suspect armed with a baseball bat and charges the officer; and a suspect has taken a hostage and is threatening to shoot the hostage. The circumstances and list of possibilities are infinite. It is important to note that the use of deadly force is a highly personal decision and unique to each officer regardless of law or agency policy. There are two constants concerning police and the use of force: law enforcement officers have no duty to retreat, and their duty is to act. The second most notable constant is in American society; police are the only individuals legally authorized to kill another; within those guidelines, the crime of murder is excused, and such killings are ruled justifiable homicide.

THREE CATEGORIES OF POLICE SHOOTINGS

A simple classification system for OISs is that they are lawful, lawful but awful, and unlawful. A lawful shooting is simply defined as a shooting that meets the legal standard of fear for an officer's life, to protect a citizen, and/or stopping a threat. An unlawful shooting is shooting and killing someone who does not pose a threat to the officer or citizen.

"Lawful but awful" is a classification that does not appear in any court ruling but is so defined by police investigators. Lawful but awful is based on two possible courses of action. The first course of action is when an officer(s) makes a tactical error, where the error could have been avoided, and the error caused serious injury and/or death, as illustrated in Case Study I. The second course of action is where an officer(s) makes a decision to engage in an activity that is not supported by a series of articulable facts, which are needed to meet the standard of reasonable suspicion, nor does the decision rise to the level of probable cause, which is the standard needed to make an arrest without a warrant, as illustrated in Case Study II.

CASE STUDY I

Man with a Gun

Cleveland police officers Timothy Loehmann and Frank Garmback received a call of a Black male repeatedly pulling a gun from his pants and pointing it at people. The caller made two statements, saying that the gun is probably a fake and that the suspect is probably a juvenile. However, that information was not initially relayed to the officers. As the officers arrived on scene, Officer Garmback was driving and stopped the patrol car, so the passenger side of the patrol car was directly adjacent to the suspect, placing Officer Loehmann in an undefendable position, sitting in a patrol car facing an armed suspect. As Officer Loehmann exited the vehicle, the suspect drew the firearm from his waistband; Officer Loehmann fired twice, striking the suspect once in the abdomen, killing him. The suspect was later identified as Tamir Rice, 12 years old, carrying a toy airsoft gun, which is an exact replica of a real firearm.

Could this have been prevented? Yes, possibly—tactics, tactics, and tactics. If Officer Garmback had stopped 10 to 15 feet away, and both officers opened their patrol car doors to use the car doors as cover and challenged Tamir from a protected position, more than likely this shooting could have been avoided. Once Officer Garmback placed Officer Loehmann directly in front of Tamir Rice, Officer Loehmann had no choice but to respond to the threat. Officer Loehmann believed Tamir Rice was armed with a real firearm, coupled with the fact that Tamir Rice was in the process of drawing the firearm from his waistband (Cleveland Police Department, 2014; Danlyko, 2014).

CASE STUDY II

Citizen's Contact

It is 8 P.M. on a Friday. Officer Smith observes a Black male whom he does not know standing in a corner in front of a local convenience store. There are no complaints regarding the person, and Officer Smith does not see the man speak to anyone, nor does he acknowledge anyone. Officer Smith decides to approach the man, and the guy runs away. Officer Smith requests backup, advising other units that the suspect is running. The man runs into an alley, and Officer Smith follows. Once in the alley, Officer Smith catches up to the suspect, and they begin to fight. Officer Smith is losing control and becomes afraid that the suspect is going to seriously injure or kill him. Officer Smith draws his firearm, shoots, and kills the suspect.

Officer Smith had a right to get out of the patrol car and approach the man and attempt to execute what is known as a citizen's contact. However, when the guy ran and there were no other indicators, Officer Smith had no right to chase him. An officer will argue that he can follow a suspect on foot, which is true. However, if the suspect does not discard contraband or weapons while being followed, the officer has no legal authority to physically engage, apprehend, or stop him. Once Officer Smith put his hands on the suspect and they began to struggle, creating a situation where Officer Smith feared that he was going to die, Officer Smith felt he had no other choice but to shoot and kill the person that he illegally stopped.

The citizen's contact is legal; following a suspect on foot is legal; however, placing hands on the suspect with no other facts is illegal. The question becomes, does the officer have a right to defend himself in this case, or is he guilty of a crime? In these situations, police and citizens alike need to understand: The most successful police actions are executed by those officers who pay particular attention to detail, use every resource at their disposal, and follow the law. In every police action, it is not the end result; it is the process that will be scrutinized (Thomas, 2011).

CASE STUDY III

Good Decision-Making Leads to Termination

Weirton, West Virginia, police officer Stephen Mader responded to a domestic incident on May 6, 2016. On his arrival, Officer Mader was confronted by an armed subject. Officer Mader used the suspect's vehicle as cover; the vehicle was between Officer Mader and the suspect. The suspect was armed with a gun, holding it in his right hand and pointing it at the ground. Officer Mader began to rely on his situational training from the academy and his marine terrorism training, where he was taught to assess and take the whole person into account as he was making his assessment. Officer Mader began talking to the suspect in a calm voice, asking the suspect to put the gun down. This is contrary to traditional police training where officers are trained to repeatedly yell in loud verbal commands. The suspect stated, "Just shoot me." Officer Mader assured the suspect that he was not going to shoot him and figured it was an attempt at suicide by cop. Two other officers arrived on scene, and the suspect began waving the firearm. One of the officers shot the suspect in the head, killing him. After the shooting, it was determined that Officer Mader was correct; the suspect was attempting suicide by cop. Yet, a month later, Officer Mader was terminated because he did not use deadly force. The officer involved in the shooting was cleared. Officer Mader sued the city and received a settlement of $175,000 (Hamill, 2016).

1. What do you think about Officer Mader's decision? What would you do?
2. Was Officer Mader fired for officer safety reasons, or was he fired because he did not fit in with the agency's culture?
3. Was the other officer justified in shooting the suspect?
4. Can you see that the use of deadly force is very individualized and depends on one's perception and assessment of an encounter?

The questions that I receive most often in public regarding OISs are the following: Why did the officers kill the man? Why can't officers just shoot the suspect in the leg or hand? Are officers trained to shoot to kill? Let's begin by answering the last question first: Are officers trained to shoot to kill? The correct answer is "no." Police are trained to stop the threat (Hatch, 2002; Holbrook, 2004). Police deadly force training encompasses shooting at the largest part of the human anatomy, the torso.

Unfortunately, aiming for the suspect's torso is an attack on the suspect's vital organs; the goal is to stop the threat as quickly as possible and render first aid once the threat no longer exists or control has been established. The reasoning for such training is that under stressful situations it would be difficult to focus on an arm or a leg in an attempt to shoot it (Fyfe, 1996; Klinger, 2004; Waddington, 1991). Physiologically, the officer's body is in a fight or flight situation, which limits the officer's ability to utilize fine motor skills and drastically impairs the officer's ability to focus on smaller body parts such as an arm, leg, or shoulder (Dutton, 1985; Murray, 2004). In addition to the physiological response, most deadly force encounters involve the subject who is moving, which makes the smaller targets even more difficult to acquire. OIS data indicates that most deadly force encounters occur at a distance of less than 10 feet and, many times, the officers are exposed with no cover for protection. The immediacy of such an encounter will further limit an officer's ability to focus on smaller targets (Federal Bureau of Investigation, 2017b; Sweeney & Ferguson, 2004).

I WAS IN FEAR FOR MY LIFE

In almost every OIS, the officer utters the following statement: "I was in fear for my life." The phrase has been used so much that the public, specifically the minority community, has a difficult time believing that the officer was actually in danger, especially if the victim is unarmed, running away, driving away, or in a physical struggle with the officer. The rule of law is simple: The only time officers can use deadly force is to defend themselves or others. Deadly force is defined as any attack that can cause great bodily harm and/or death. Great bodily harm is defined vaguely in statutes but is usually associated with the minimum legal requirement of aggravated battery. Florida State Statute 784.045 defines aggravated battery as follows:

> 1 (a) A person commits aggravated battery who, in committing battery: 1. Intentionally or knowingly causes great bodily harm, permanent disability, or permanent disfigurement; or 2. Uses a deadly weapon. (b) A person commits aggravated battery if the person who was the victim of the battery was pregnant

at the time of the offense and the offender knew or should have known that the victim was pregnant. (2) Whoever commits aggravated battery shall be guilty of a felony of the second degree. (Florida State Legislature, 2017)

What the Florida statute fails to explain or specify is what is meant by great bodily harm. Is it a broken bone, a laceration to the face, a concussion, a broken jaw, or paralysis caused by an attack? The fact is that it is all of the aforementioned. And the method can be a weapon, hands, fists, or feet, as described in the following examples: shooting someone with a firearm causing injury less than death; using a firearm as a bludgeon to beat someone; using a knife to cut or stab; using a bottle to strike or breaking the bottle and using it to cut or stab; using a baseball bat, pipe, or tool to strike or bludgeon. All are considered weapons that fall under the aggravated battery statutes of almost every state in the United States.

The public downplays attacks on police that don't involve a firearm, because the public believes that a gun is the only real deadly weapon. This is never more evident than when I am training police recruits, and many are skeptical of the aforementioned weapons' ability to injure or kill an officer. It is not until I am able to demonstrate the lethality of the weapons that the recruits begin to understand the threat that these implements pose, and the limitations of an officer's respective skill sets and/or equipment. I often ask the question, "If you are being attacked by a subject with a weapon, what is the attacker's intention?" Most recruits respond with the following statement: "The attacker wants to injure or kill me." I follow with a second question: "What happens to you if you become incapacitated in some way?" Most, if not all, understand that if they become disabled due to an attack, they can become disarmed and/or killed.

The following are three case studies of OISs, with a series of reflective questions after each. After reading the case study, reflect on the scenario, consider what you might have done in that situation, answer the questions, and finally make a determination if the standard of "fear of death or great bodily harm to the officer" was met.

CASE STUDY IV

Traffic Stop

It is 2 A.M. and Officer Jimmy D'Angelo observes a car speeding on Main Street, and the vehicle runs a red light at Main and NW 13th

Street. Officer D'Angelo gets behind the suspect vehicle and activates his overhead lights. The suspect vehicle slows to 30 miles per hour but does not stop. Officer D'Angelo activates his siren and advises dispatch that the suspect vehicle is refusing to stop. Just as Officer D'Angelo contacts dispatch, the suspect vehicle turns onto a residential street and stops. Officer D'Angelo exits his vehicle, approaches the driver's side of the suspect vehicle, and orders the driver out at gunpoint. The driver refuses to exit his vehicle, ignoring Officer D'Angelo's repeated verbal commands. Officer D'Angelo briefly goes to the front of the suspect vehicle and continues to order the suspect out of the car and then returns to the driver's side window. Once at the driver's window, Officer D'Angelo begins beating on the driver's window with his firearm and continues to order the suspect out of the car. The suspect puts the car in drive, begins driving away while Officer D'Angelo is standing next to the vehicle. The suspect drives away in a straight pattern and does not swerve or angle his car in an attempt to hit Officer D'Angelo. As the suspect begins pulling away, Officer D'Angelo starts shooting at the suspect, firing six shots at the side of the suspect vehicle and a seventh shot into the rear window of the vehicle. The seventh shot strikes the suspect in the back of the head, killing him. On the video, the seventh shot is seen as delayed and not fired in the same succession as the first six shots.

1. Did Officer D'Angelo have the legal authority to stop the suspect vehicle?

2. What would you do, approach the vehicle once the suspect stopped, or would you have used your car for cover and ordered the suspect out of the vehicle?

3. It is 2 A.M.; what do you think was wrong with the driver? Why wouldn't he comply with Officer D'Angelo's verbal commands?

4. Do you believe that Officer D'Angelo had reason to believe the suspect was armed when Officer D'Angelo approached the suspect vehicle with his firearm drawn?

5. Why do you believe that Officer D'Angelo fired at the suspect vehicle as it drove away?

6. Did this incident meet the standard of "fear of death and/or great bodily harm to the officer"?

7. How would you classify this OIS?

CASE STUDY V

Assist a Citizen

It is 10 P.M. and Officer Mark Watson was dispatched to an "assist a citizen" call. Dispatch was unable to provide any other information except the caller was an elderly woman who needed some assistance with her son. Officer Watson arrived on the scene, and the caller advised Officer Watson that her son was in the bathroom and needed some help. The caller was not specific in her son's needs. Officer Watson walked down the hall, knocked on the closed bathroom door, and the son/suspect opened the door. After opening the door, the son/suspect engaged in a conversation with Officer Watson. Officer Watson noted that the suspect was delusional in his thoughts and the suspect's speech pattern was erratic. When Officer Watson asked the suspect to step out of the bathroom, the suspect turned and grabbed Officer Watson by the throat, and they began fighting. The suspect wrestled Officer Watson to the floor, straddled Officer Watson, and continued to choke Officer Watson. As the two fought, the bathroom door slammed shut, further isolating Officer Watson. The struggle was so intense that Officer Watson was unable to get to his radio or yell for assistance. Officer Watson could not stop the attack and, in response, pulled his firearm and fired three shots, killing the suspect. After hearing the shots, the suspect's mother called police dispatch and advised dispatch the officer was in trouble. The suspect's mother never came into the bathroom to check on the status of the officer or her son.

1. Did Officer Watson have legal authority to be in the caller's house?
2. Do you believe dispatch should have obtained more information or sent two officers until the nature of the problem was determined?
3. Once at the scene, do you believe that Officer Watson should have asked the suspect's mother more questions before moving down the hall to the bathroom?
4. Once at the bathroom door, as soon as Officer Watson noted that the suspect had mental health issues should he have immediately called for backup?
5. If backup had been called or two officers sent initially, would this have prevented the shooting?
6. Did this incident meet the standard of "fear of death and/or great bodily harm to the officer"?
7. How would you classify this OIS?

CASE STUDY VI

Traffic Stop and Foot Chase

At 9 A.M., Officer Michael Slager stopped driver Walter Scott for a brake light that was not working. Officer Slager approached Scott's vehicle, obtaining Mr. Scott's driver's license, registration, and proof of insurance. Officer Slager returned to his patrol car to check for warrants and if Mr. Scott had a valid driver's license. Once Officer Slager was in his patrol car, Scott exited his vehicle. Officer Slager ordered Scott back into his vehicle. Scott complied with the order. Shortly after getting back into his vehicle, Scott exited his vehicle a second time and fled the scene of the traffic stop on foot. Officer Slager advised dispatch that Scott was fleeing on foot and Officer Slager gave chase. After a brief foot chase, Officer Slager caught Scott, and there was a brief struggle over Officer Slager's Taser. Scott dropped the Taser at Officer Slager's feet, turned with his back to Officer Slager, and began running away. Officer Slager drew his firearm and fired five shots at Scott. Scott was struck four times in the back and once in the ear. Officer Slager advised dispatch of the shooting, ran back to where the Taser had been dropped, and carried the Taser closer to Scott's body. Officer Slager dropped the Taser near Scott's corpse as other officers were arriving on the scene to assist.

1. Did Officer Slager have the legal authority to make the traffic stop?
2. Was there anything improperly done by Officer Slager during the traffic stop?
3. Once Officer Slager caught Mr. Scott, was it proper police procedure to deploy a Taser to stop Mr. Scott from resisting?
4. When Mr. Scott briefly obtained control of Officer Slager's Taser, was Officer Slager in fear for his life?
5. Since Mr. Scott immediately dropped Officer Slager's Taser, was it Mr. Scott's intent to attack Officer Slager or use the Taser against Officer Slager?
6. Was Mr. Scott a threat to Officer Slager or anyone else, as Mr. Scott was running away from Officer Slager?
7. Did this incident meet the standard of "fear of death and/or great bodily harm to the officer"?
8. How would you classify this OIS?

POLICE PRIVILEGE

Attached to the title of law enforcement officer is a privilege that is not extended to every citizen. There is an inherent belief that officers possess and will display honesty, truthfulness in report writing, truthfulness in courtroom proceedings, and ethical conduct in the handling and processing of evidence. In essence, there is a belief that police will conduct themselves ethically, and if there is a question as to who is more truthful, the officer or the citizen, the tie usually goes to the officer. From a police perspective, this leads to what is described as "destructive entitlement." The following are several cases where officers or an agency received the benefit of the doubt because they were in law enforcement.

- A deputy sheriff attempts a traffic stop on a major street. The driver sees the deputy behind her but doesn't stop until she turns into the mall parking lot. The driver made the decision for her safety as well as the deputies. The driver immediately stopped once in the mall parking lot. The deputy exited his vehicle, drew his firearm, and ordered the female driver from the vehicle. When the driver did not move fast enough, the deputy opened the driver's door, pulled her out of the car, and arrested the driver for resisting arrest and issued her a citation for speeding. The driver attempted to file a complaint against the deputy, but the agency refused to consider the complaint. The evidence was available because it was captured by the deputy's dashboard camera. However, the agency stood by the deputy's report, which was falsified. It wasn't until a witness stepped forward and complained that the agency considered the complaint valid. The agency pulled the video of the traffic stop and, on completion of the investigation, the deputy was terminated. There were no criminal charges sought, and the deputy was allowed to keep his law enforcement standards, which meant he could be hired by another agency.

- A police officer is dating a local prostitute. The prostitute is arrested and receives a sentence of 60 days in the county jail. The officer (her boyfriend) advises jail personnel that the prostitute is his informant and that he needs to meet with the prostitute in a private secure room. Jail personnel provide the officer with the room. The officer visits the prostitute twice weekly in uniform. The jail provides the officer with the secure room to protect the identity of the prostitute, who is supposed to be an informant. The officer supplies the prostitute with crack cocaine on each of his visits and has sex with her during each visit. The officer used his position to gain entry into the jail with contraband. Although the officer violated state statute, he was neither charged nor prosecuted. The only punishment he received was termination from the department. The officer was allowed to keep his law enforcement standards, which meant that he could be hired by another agency. The prostitute received a sentence of one year for possession of contraband in a correctional facility.

- A police officer makes a traffic stop, and the driver is a Black male. During the traffic stop, the driver admits that he does not have a driver's license. Rather than be arrested, the driver flees in the vehicle, the officer chases the car on foot, and the driver stops. The officer approaches the vehicle and shoots the driver three times. The officer makes the statement: "I was in fear for my life." The entire incident is captured on the officer's body camera. The officer was arrested and charged with murder. He has been tried five times and was found not guilty, or there was a hung jury.

- A county-wide drug task force had several warrants for a number of drug dealers in its community. As the task force executed the arrest warrants, one suspect fled on foot. The chase and subsequent arrest was captured on local business videos. During the arrest, the suspect was knocked to the ground, and five officers are seen punching and kicking the suspect. The suspect offered no resistance. The leader of the assault on the suspect was the task force sergeant. Four of the officers plead guilty in federal court to a violation of the suspect's civil rights and received varying sentences, which ranged from six months to two years in prison. The fifth officer—the supervisor—plead not guilty, and the case went to trial. Despite the evidence that was recorded by an HD camera and clear as day, the jury found the sergeant not guilty. The sergeant was terminated, but the jury supported the officer's actions.

In each of the aforementioned cases, the officers, agency, and/or both received the benefit of the doubt because of their professional affiliation. If a civilian had acted in a similar fashion, what would be the outcome of such a case? Would there be criminal charges? How is it that officers can commit murder or a brutal assault and keep their standards to be hired by another agency to perpetrate the same or worse crimes? Associated with all but one of these incidents is a term rarely discussed, known as "officer-initiated violence."

Officer-initiated violence is violence that is perpetrated by officers when officers become impatient because the suspect is not complying with what the officer believes are lawful orders. Because the suspect is not moving fast enough or does not respond, it is often seen as a form of disrespect. Officers are taught to yell loud verbal repetitive commands, such as "stop resisting," "get on the ground," or "put your hands behind your back." When a suspect fails to comply with these orders immediately, as noted earlier, some officers become angry and view the suspect's noncompliance as a form of disrespect, even when the officer has a tactical advantage, through numbers, or the officer has the suspect at gunpoint. What the officer rarely thinks of is if the subject is deaf; if the subject is processing the officer's loud verbal commands coupled with the fact that the officer is pointing a gun in the subject's face; or if the subject is simply frozen out of fear. Officer-initiated violence should be seen as a form of destructive entitlement—you obey my command or else.

Police privilege damages police–community relationships. In the mind of minority community members, there is a perception and belief that there is one standard for police and one for minority community members. This is seen as nothing more than a form of destructive entitlement, which damages the credibility of police and the criminal justice system as a whole.

Damaging the Law Enforcement Brand

All organizations and institutions have a brand that is associated with the organizations' credibility. An organization or business brand is a promise of quality to the community or population that it serves. When an organization fails, there are several possibilities: The CEO is fired, and a new face is hired to rebrand the company and to regain confidence of its customers; the CEO opens the doors for all to see and admits where the organization has failed and makes a promise to do better, oftentimes inviting citizen/customer input; the CEO disciplines and/or terminates those responsible for the problem, discusses policy implications, and provides a road map for change. Examples of damaging the brand can be found in the war of words between former San Francisco 49er quarterback Colin Kaepernick and San Francisco Police Officers Association. Kaepernick's protest began in response to officers shooting and killing unarmed Black men. Kaepernick's protest was simple and quiet; he refused to stand but chose to kneel on one knee during the pregame playing of the national anthem. When asked by the media why he refused to stand during the playing of the national anthem, Kaepernick responded with the following statement, printed here in part:

> When there's significant change and I feel that flag represents what it's supposed to represent, and this country is representing people the way that it's supposed to, I'll stand.
>
> This is because I'm seeing things happen to people that don't have a voice, people that don't have a platform to talk and have their voices heard, and effect change. So I'm in the position where I can do that and I'm going to do that for people that can't.
>
> I've seen videos, I've seen circumstances where men and women that have been in the military have come back and been treated unjustly by the country they have fought for, and have been murdered by the country they fought for, on our land. That's not right. (Sandritter, 2016)

In response to Kaepernick's statements, the San Francisco Police Officers Union sent a response, including the following statements to NFL commissioner Roger Goodell:

> While we certainly acknowledge Mr. Kaepernick's first amendment right to remain seated during the National Anthem, as inappropriate as that may be,

we will not stand by while he attacks police officers in this country with such statements as, "People are on paid leave while people of color are killed."

Not only does he show an incredible lack of knowledge regarding our profession and "officer involved" shootings, but also shows a naivety and total lack of sensitivity towards police officers. Ironically it is those officers who have on numerous occasions protected Mr. Kaepernick and have ensured that the venues where the NFL holds its events are fully protected. (Halloran, 2016)

After the aforementioned war of words in August 2016, in October 2016 the president of the International Association of Chiefs of Police (IACP) made a public apology for the historical mistreatment of minorities. IACP president Terrence Cunningham stated:

Today's officers are not to blame for past injustices . . . said events over the past several years have undermined public trust. While we obviously cannot change the past, it is clear that we must change the future. We must forge a path that allows us to move beyond our history and identify common solutions to better protect our communities. For our part, the first step in this process is for law enforcement and the (International Association of Chiefs of Police) to acknowledge and apologize for the actions of the past and the role that our profession has played in society's historical mistreatment of communities of color. (Cunningham, 2016)

However, it is as if the apology fell on deaf ears, because in September 2017 Michigan State Police Colonel Kristie Kibbey Etue posted her personal views regarding the NFL players taking a knee and showing solidarity:

Dear NFL:
We will not support millionaire ingrates who hate America and disrespect our Armed Forces and Veterans. Who wins a Football game has ZERO impact on our lives. Who fights for and defends our nation has EVERY impact on our lives. We stand with the HEROES, not a bunch of rich, entitled, arrogant, ungrateful, anti-American degenerates. Signed, We the People. (Einenkel, 2017)

BLACK HYSTERIA

The term "Black hysteria" means that because of the abuses of the past, the Black community fails to accept any explanation for police and/or government behavior and views any of their actions as a form of racism or attacks on the community itself. No explanation is good enough; there will always be doubt and skepticism, which will be tainted with the belief that there is some form of conspiracy, and true transparency will never exist. It is due to this that the government's (police) explanations have no validity and White America devalues the Black community's responses. Everyone is yelling and no one is listening. It is important to note that the Black community's belief system is not without merit:

- It begins with slavery, which current White America has argued that it had nothing to do with, and it's time to move on.
- Consider the Tuskegee Experiment conducted from 1932 to 1972. The purpose of the experiment was to study the health effects of untreated syphilis on rural Black males when there was already a cure. It was offered in the guise of free medical treatment (Gray, 2013). This study was funded by the U.S. government and was no different than the atrocities that Nazi Germany and Dr. Josef Mengele performed on the Jews in the concentration camps under the guise of science.
- Examine the series of social problems hitting minority communities—segregation, poverty, poor educational systems, movement from an industrial society to a prison-industrial complex, illegal narcotics, drug wars, the war on drugs, police brutality, and mass incarceration.
- Go back and reexamine each of the cases presented in police privilege. Those are just a tiny fraction, the tip of the iceberg, that the minority community sees and experiences every day.

This was summed up by a Wilmington, Delaware, community member in a community meeting during an investigation into police community relationships. During that investigation, Black community members argued that they had no value and that the police department was not addressing their needs. This statement supports the community's perception:

I want the police to value our murdered children the same as they value the murder of one of their own. When our children are killed we rarely if at all hear anything from the police. When we call detectives, they will not return phone calls, we have so many unsolved murders and the bodies just keep piling up. However, when one of theirs is killed or injured, the police shut down the community, knock on every door, and question all of the possible suspects until they get their man. Don't our children deserve the same treatment? (Anonymous, personal communication, February 5, 2015)

The Unexpected Outcome: Black Lives Matter

What is Black Lives Matter (BLM) and why now? BLM is a community-based organization that was started in response to the murder of Trayvon Martin and the acquittal of George Zimmerman.

CASE STUDY VII

Trayvon Martin: The Birth of a Movement

Trayvon Martin was an unarmed 17-year-old, Black male, wearing a hoody, returning home from the local 7-Eleven after purchasing a can of iced tea and some candy. George Zimmerman was the Neighborhood Watch Block captain and observed Trayvon Martin walking through the Retreat at Twin Lakes neighborhood. Zimmerman called police dispatch, advising that he observed a suspicious person walking back and forth through the neighborhood. Police dispatch advised Zimmerman not to engage Trayvon Martin; in fact, Zimmerman was advised to stay in his vehicle and be a witness. Instead, Zimmerman engaged Trayvon Martin, attempting to stop and detain Trayvon Martin until police arrived. In response, Martin refused to cooperate and be detained. Martin and Zimmerman fought, and when Martin was winning the fight, Zimmerman pulled his firearm, shooting and killing Martin.

Zimmerman was charged with second-degree murder (Bloom, 2014). Zimmerman was found not guilty. The logic behind the jury's decision was the jury felt that Zimmerman met the burden of proof: in fear for his life or becoming the victim of great bodily harm. This case and the jury decision is classified as lawful but awful.

BLM describes itself as an ideological and political intervention organization in a world where Black lives are systematically and intentionally targeted for demise (Garza, 2016). BLM does not mean that other lives are not important; the movement emphasizes that Black people have no value in American society, and it is important to stand up and fight against injustices perpetrated and supported by the government's action or inaction. Since its inception BLM has been vilified by national organizations. The counterpart of the BLM movement is the Blue Lives Matter movement. All of the fighting and posturing has done nothing but continue to sever the relationships between law enforcement and the minority communities. This reached a crescendo with the assassination of unsuspecting New York City police officers as they sat in their patrol car; the sniper attacks in Dallas, Texas, and Baton Rouge, Louisiana; and the number of unsuspecting officers who have been viciously attacked or ambushed when responding to calls.

This war of words and war in the streets has become so divisive that an organization that calls itself "We the People" posted an online petition, requesting that the White House officially recognize and label BLM as a terrorist organization. Although BLM was not singled out, the FBI has labeled Black Identity Extremists Groups as potential domestic terrorists groups who target law enforcement, which serves the same purpose without specifically singling out BLM (Federal Bureau of Investigation, 2017a).

Damaging the BLM Brand

The ideology behind the BLM movement is a vision for social justice and equality, and the group mobilizes every time police have been involved in the shooting of an unarmed Black male. However, where the brand fails, even in the BLM demands that include end the war on Black people, reparations, invest-divest, economic justice, community control, and political power, they offer no solutions to addressing the gun violence in the Black community. BLM does not march when there is gang violence or a homicide in the Black community (Black on Black crime). Chicago has been the center of horrific gun violence during the summer holidays, and the data reflects an untold number of victims: July 4, 2014—70 shot, 13 killed; July 4, 2015—82 shot, 16 killed; July 4, 2016—66 shot, 4 killed; and July 4, 2017—100 shot, 12 killed. The pundits continue to ask, where is BLM? Or does BLM condone gun violence in the Black community and only find it offensive when police are involved? The failure to address the issue of gun violence in the Black community will always tarnish the brand of BLM and will remain central to a lack of credibility from mainstream America.

Interpreting Data from OISs

Today, the only data captured in regard to OISs is the *Guardian* and *Washington Post* newspapers. Each provides the reader with an opportunity to search their databases with specific parameters: race, gender, armed/unarmed, age, and/or classification—how the person died. When querying the database, you must be cognizant of what unarmed means and must identify the circumstances in which the person died. For example, a suspect's behavior is erratic and police are called to intervene. On arrival, the police determine that the subject is suffering from some form of psychosis, or the subject's behavior is erratic due to substance abuse. The officers attempt to take the suspect into custody for treatment and there is an intense, brief altercation, and the subject goes into cardiac arrest and dies. This is a set of unfortunate circumstances, but it is far from murder. Some subjects have gone into cardiac arrest when officers deploy a Taser or pepper spray. These cases are unusual, yet there is no intent to kill; the intent is to establish control.

The aforementioned scenario does happen; however, it is not limited to police. These kinds of deaths occur in psychiatric units, hospital emergency rooms, and jails/prisons, and are an issue that is often wrongly associated with police brutality. This type of death is known as police custody death syndrome or in-custody death syndrome. There are several underlying factors associated with this type of death, which include excited delirium, restraint asphyxia, positional asphyxia, or sudden custody death. Excited delirium is associated with drug abuse and/or mental illness. Tennant (1985) has termed this phenomena "post drug impairment syndrome" and cites many of the same characteristics identified by Wetli in his 1999 research. Di Maio and Di Maio (2005) describe the symptoms of excited delirium as extreme agitation and restlessness, incoherent and rambling speech, hallucinations, delusions with paranoid features, disorganized thought content, bizarre behavior, and combativeness (p. 103).

"Positional asphyxia" and "positional restraint asphyxia" are closely related terms. Reay, Fligner, Stilwell, and Arnold (1992) define positional asphyxia as the position of the body interferes with breathing. They further assert that in all cases of positional asphyxia, one or more contributory factors provide an explanation of the victim's inability to breathe and include alcohol/drug intoxication, concussive head injury, entrapment, restraint, or some form of physical disability (p. 94). Positional asphyxia is often associated with officers who wrestle with a combative subject using their body weight to control the subject by pressing a knee into the subject's back, and restricting the subject's ability to breathe, or several officers apply their body weight on the back of a subject to establish control and restrict the subject's airway.

Violently combative subjects have often been placed in a position that is known as the hogtie position. Hogtying occurs when a subject's feet are restrained by handcuffs, flex cuffs, or a hobble restraint and the subject's hands are handcuffed behind his or her back. The subject's feet are pulled to the center of the subject's back, and the subject's hands are connected to the feet restraints. The subject is then placed on his or her stomach on the ground and later in the patrol car for transport (Di Maio & Di Maio, 2005; Dolinak, Matshes, & Lew, 2005; Hatch 2002; Reay et al., 1992; Shepherd, 2005).

The hogtie position is used to keep the subjects from kicking officers, kicking out patrol car windows, or hurting themselves by slamming their head into the windows, doors, or cages which separate the subjects from the officer. Hogtying and placing the subject on the stomach, the subject is now in a position known as positional restraint asphyxia. The primary difference between positional asphyxia and positional restraint asphyxia is the application of restraints in the hogtie position.

Di Maio and Dana (1998) define sudden custody death as deaths that occur immediately after an arrest in which there is a violent struggle. Di Maio and Dana note that as long as there is a struggle and contact between the officer and the deceased, no matter what the cause of death, even a heart attack, it will most likely be ruled a homicide. They have concluded that most deaths occurring during the arrest occur after the struggle and are a combination of the physiological effects of the stress of the struggle and the action of drugs (pp. 499–506).

A word of caution for anyone who reviews data; be mindful of the circumstances of the incident and have a thorough understanding of agency policy and state statutes during your assessment. I randomly chose several incidents where unarmed Black males died while interacting with police: Akai Gurley was shot by police while walking down a dark stairway. Eric Garner resisted arrest; he was choked by New York City police and died. Jordan Baker allegedly fit the description of a robbery suspect; off-duty police chased Baker, and a struggle ensued and Baker was shot and killed; Baker was unarmed and was not the suspect. Kajuan Raye was shot in the back while running from Chicago police; Raye was unarmed. Terrence Crutcher parked his vehicle in the middle of the road; he did not respond to officer's instructions or attempts at communication; Crutcher walked away, and when he reached into his vehicle through an open window, he was shot and killed; police followed Crutcher to his car; officers exposed themselves to an unnecessary threat and could have used their cars for cover; Crutcher was not armed.

In 2015, *Guardian* data reports that 1,146 died at the hands of police in the United States.

- Of those 1,146 killed in 2015 by police, 307 were Black.
- 79 of the 307 Blacks killed by police were unarmed.
- 40 of the 79 unarmed Blacks were shot and killed by police.
- Other classifications/methods by which the remaining 39 unarmed Blacks were killed by police were as follows: 17 killed by Taser; 5 killed by vehicle; 16 died in custody; 1 method of death unknown.

As noted earlier, it is important to understand the classifications/methods of death as well as the circumstances by which each individual died. This argument is supported in a study conducted by Harvard researchers, which noted that there is no consistency in the recording of deaths caused in police-related incidents; some were classified incorrectly or underreported:

- Misclassification rates for police-related deaths topped 60 percent among several groups: people under age 18, Blacks, people killed by something other than a firearm (particularly Tasers, which accounted for 46 deaths), and people killed in low-income counties (Feldman, Gruskin, Coull, & Krieger, 2017, para. 26).

- Undercounting of police-related deaths varied widely across states. For instance, nearly all of the 17 police-related deaths in Oregon were counted, but none of the 36 such deaths in Oklahoma were (Feldman et al., 2017, para. 26).

BLACK AND POLICE = ANTI-AMERICAN

All of the divineness has created a new agenda. As noted earlier in this text, White America argues that Black Americans are malcontents and hate this country. On October 19, 2017, Richard Spencer, president of the National Policy Institute, a White nationalist organization, delivered a message at the University of Florida, which was a call for White America to rise saying that if Whites are not careful they will not have a place in the United States. Spencer uses the setting of flagship state universities to prove his hateful point. Spencer understands that many of these campuses embrace diversity and that his message will be met with disdain and he will be shouted down. Spencer streams his speeches worldwide on the Internet so that his followers can see how the educated elite act by refusing to hear his message. Through all of this, local law enforcement is responsible for protecting Spencer from protestors and violence. The take-away lessons from Spencer are these:

1. He picks university campuses strategically based on status, location, and/or demographics. The reason for the university setting is that it is a liberal place with liberal ideas on inclusiveness and diversity.

2. He controls the tickets and does so because he wants Antifa and those who oppose his views to get in. By allowing the opposition in, he sets the stage for antagonism. Antifa (Anti-Fascist Action group) opposes everything that Spencer and the White nationalist groups espouse. Antifa has no problem with violence and attacking Spencer, his membership, and any group that gets in the way of such attacks, including police.

3. Selecting universities and stacking the crowd with the opposition is a great marketing tool. The crowd will never let Spencer get his message out. The crowd yells, screams, and interrupts Spencer and his cadre from beginning to end.

4. Spencer takes the stance that he has a message for White people, and this privileged group of educated snobs, who have been poisoned by their professors and the institution, refuse to allow him and his people to speak. He argues that this is a sign that the privileged educated few in this country will control the destiny of White people, and he has videos of the events to "prove" it.

Therefore, White people, he implores, need to fight back, mobilize, and create a state that is all White.

5. Since Antifa has become so violent, it does nothing more than prove a point and create the great divide. Spencer can take the stand that he and his followers are nonviolent, and it is Antifa that is keeping Whites down.

6. When the crowd had well-worded, legitimate questions and criticisms of White supremacist notions, Spencer does not answer; he just responds by questioning the question.

7. Spencer picks and chooses historical facts and in so doing skips major facts in history, failing to acknowledge such things as slavery or the slaughter of the American Indian, both trigger points.

8. The tactics are very similar to those of President Trump, whom Spencer adores and has said as much. The underlying message to both of "making America great again" is actually "making America White again."

In the middle of all of this, some of the White nationalists have hijacked the version of the American police flag, which signifies Blue Lives Matter, and used it at their rallies. It was carried in Charlottesville, Virginia, next to the Confederate flag (Matsumoto, 2017). The Black community interprets the Charlottesville violence as follows: (1) Police are a racist organization and have been responsible for beating and killing unarmed Black men for years; (2) the Blue Lives Matter flag was carried alongside the Confederate flag in Charlottesville, Virginia, where violence erupted and one person was killed who was marching for justice; (3) had there been sufficient numbers of police, they could have prevented the violence in Charlottesville; (4) police wanted the protestors to be injured just like the old South.

The questions that have risen from the Blue Lives Matter flag/movement are as follows: What gave police the right to hijack the American flag and create a symbol of their own? By creating the Blue Lives Matter flag, did police understand that it would be seen as a symbol of hatred and bigotry? Do police understand that there is only one flag in this country, the American flag, and why aren't they using that as their symbol? Finally, do police understand that the impact that spinoff paraphernalia such as the Blue Lives Matter punisher flags, t-shirts, and vehicle stickers send is a message of systemic oppression?

Spencer and some police organizations have questioned the patriotism of Black Americans with the BLM protests and sports figures kneeling to protest inequality and unity in the United States. The best response in regard to the patriotism of Blacks in the United States ever made was by actor Anthony Anderson on the television show *Blackish*:

BLACK AMERICANS AND PATRIOTISM

Actor Anthony Anderson

Blackish Monologue January 11, 2017

I love this country even though at times it doesn't love me back. For my whole life my parents, my grandparents, me, for most black people, this system has never worked for us. But we still play ball, tried to do our best to live by the rules even though we knew they would never work out in our favor, had to live in neighborhoods that you wouldn't drive through, send our kids to schools with books so beat up you couldn't read them, work jobs that you wouldn't consider in your nightmares.

Black people wake up everyday believing our lives are gonna change even though everything around us says it's not. Truth be told, you ask most black people and they tell you no matter who won the election, they don't expect the hood to get better. But they still voted because that's what you're supposed to do.

You think I'm not sad that Hillary didn't win? That I'm not terrified about what Trump's about to do? I'm used to things not going my way. I'm sorry that you're not and it's blowing your mind, so excuse me if I get a little offended because I didn't see all of this outrage when everything was happening to all of my people since we were stuffed on boats in chains. I love this country as much—if not more—than you do. And don't you ever forget that.

I've been lucky enough to raise four beautiful children in a world that showed them Jay Z and Beyoncé as king and queen, a black family in the White House, and a woman run and almost win the presidency of the United States. So if you ask me if I love America, the answer is yes. Warts and all. Can it be better? I hope so. And I hope that we as a people have it in us to come together and make lemonade out of our lemons. (Anderson, Barris, Dobbins, Fishburne, & Groff, 2017)

CONCLUSION

It is easy to say that an unarmed Black man died at the hands of police and demand justice in every case where a person of color dies during the course of police action. The greater injustice to all is for police to expect that communities will accept any explanation because the police are the police and communities will continue to fault police for every action, even those that are legal. Government, no matter how well intentioned, needs to remember that "police are the people and work for the people." More important, every effort needs to be made to be transparent. To protect police from public scrutiny does nothing more than further destroy confidence in a system that is failing the people. There is no better example than the passage of North Carolina's state statute 132.-14A Law Enforcement Agency Recordings in 2015, which blocks the release of police body cam and dashboard camera footage (North Carolina State Legislature, 2015).

Are police so sensitive that they cannot tolerate criticism? If this is the case, then those who feel that way should not be police. As a reminder, look at the response from the San Francisco Police Officers Union in regard to Colin Kaepernick's protest. The great divide has easily turned into a war, which continues to be driven by mistrust and hatred. The reality is that no one wins. Police privilege and Black hysteria should be recognized for what they are, defensive postures where each group feels that it has some sort of right or sense of entitlement. There should be no greater cause than to find a common ground.

REFERENCES

Anderson, A., Barris, K., Dobbins, E. B., Fishburne, L., & Groff, J. (Executive Producers). (2017, January 11). *Blackish: Lemons* (television broadcast). Los Angeles, CA: ABC TV.

Bloom, L. (2014). *Suspicion nation: The inside story of the Trayvon Martin injustice and why we continue to repeat it.* Berkley, CA: Counterpoint Publishing.

Cleveland Police Department. (2014). *Tamir Rice video.* Cleveland, OH. Author.

Cunningham, Terrence. (2016, October 29). *Head of police chiefs group apologizes for "historical mistreatment" of communities of color.* San Diego: IACP.

Danlyko, R. (2014, December 2). Are police trained to shoot to kill? *Cleveland Plain Dealer*, p. A1.

Di Maio, T., & Di Maio, V.J.M. (2005). *Excited delirium syndrome: Cause of death and prevention.* Boca Raton, FL: CRC Press.

Di Maio, V.J.M., & Dana, S. E. (1998). *Handbook of forensic pathology.* Georgetown, TX: Landes Bioscience.

Dolinak, D., Matshes, E. W., & Lew, E. O. (2005). *Forensic pathology: Principles and practice.* Burlington, MA: Elsevier Academic Press.

Dutton, D. G. (1985). The public and the police: Training implications of the demand for a new model police officer. In J. C. Yuille (Ed.), *Police selection and training: The role of police psychology*, pp. 141–158. New York, NY: Springer Publications.

Einenkel, W. (2017, September 28). *MI State police colonel who called football players ingrates and degenerates won't resign.* Retrieved from https://www.dailykos.com/

stories/2017/9/28/1702398/-MI-State-Police-Col-who-called-football-players-rich-ingrates-and-degenerates-won-t-resign.

Federal Bureau of Investigation. (2017a). *Black identity extremists likely motivated to target law enforcement officers.* Washington, DC: Author.

Federal Bureau of Investigation. (2017b). *2017 Law enforcement officers killed and assaulted.* Washington, DC: Department of Justice.

Feldman, J. M., Gruskin, S., Coull, B. A., & Krieger, N. (2017). Quantifying under-reporting of law-enforcement-related deaths in United States vital statistics and news-media-based data sources: A capture–recapture analysis. *PLoS Medicine, 14* (10). Retrieved February 27, 2018 from https://doi.org/10.1371/journal.pmed.1002399

Florida State Legislature. (2017). *Florida State Statute, 784.045 Aggravated Battery.* Tallahassee, FL. Author.

Fyfe, J. J. (1996). Police use of deadly force. In G. S. Bridges, J. G. Weis, & R. D. Crutchfield (Eds.), *Criminal justice: Readings,* pp. 187–194. Thousand Oaks, CA: Pine Forge Press.

Garza, A. (2016). A herstory #BlackLivesMatter movement. In J. Hobson (Ed.), *Are all the women still white? Rethinking race, expanding feminisms.* Albany, NY: State University of New York Press.

Gray, F. D. (2013). *The Tuskegee syphilis study: The real story and beyond.* Montgomery, AL: New South Books.

Halloran, M. (2016, August). *Response to Colin Kaepernick's statements* (letter to Jed York, president of San Francisco 49ers, and Roget Goodell, commissioner, National Football League). San Francisco, CA: San Francisco Police Officers Association.

Hamill, S. D. (2016, September 11). Weirton terminates officer who did not fire at man with gun. *Pittsburgh Post Gazette.* Retrieved February 15, 2017, from http://www.post-gazette.com/local/region/2016/09/11/Weirton-fired-officer-who-did-not-fire-at-man-with-gun/stories/201609090080.

Hatch, D. E. (2002). *Officer involved shooting and use of force: Practical investigative techniques.* Boca Raton, FL: CRC Press.

Holbrook, R. M. (2004). *Political sabotage: The LAPD experience, attitudes towards understanding police use of force.* Victoria, BC: Trafford Publishing.

Kleinig, J. (2008). *Ethics and criminal justice: An introduction.* New York, NY: Cambridge University Press.

Klinger, D. (2004). *Into the kill zone: A cop's eye view of deadly force.* San Francisco, CA: Jossey-Bass.

Lippmann, M. R. (2007). *Contemporary criminal law: Concepts, cases, and controversies.* Thousand Oaks, CA: Sage Publications.

Matsumoto, S. (2017, August 24). *Multnomah County sheriff removes "Thin Blue Line" flag from courthouse break room.* Retrieved http://www.oregonlive.com/portland/index.ssf/2017/08/multnomah_county_sheriff_remov.html.

Michigan State Legislature. (1931). *MCL 750.360 Larceny; places of abode, work, storage, conveyance, worship and other places.* Lansing, MI: Author.

Murray, K. R. (2004). *Training at the speed of life, volume one: The definitive textbook for military and law enforcement reality-based training.* Gotha, FL: Armiger Publications.

North Carolina State Legislature. (2015). *State statute: 132.-14A law enforcement agency recordings.* Raleigh, NC: Author.

Reay, D. T., Flinger, C. L., Stilwell, A. D., & Arnold, J. (1992). Positional asphyxia during law enforcement transport. *The American Journal of Forensic Medicine and Pathology, 13* (2), 90–97.

Sandritter, M. (2016, September 25). *A timeline of Colin Kaepernick's national anthem protest and the athletes who joined him.* Retrieved from https://www.sbnation.com/2016/9/11/12869726/colin-kaepernick-national-anthem-protest-seahawks-brandon-marshall-nfl.

Shepherd, R. (2005). Deaths in custody. In M. Stark (Ed.), *Clinical forensic medicine: A physicians guide,* 2nd ed., pp. 327–350. Totowa, NJ: Humana Press.

Sweeney, P., & Ferguson, T. (2004). *Modern law enforcement: Weapons and tactics,* 3rd ed. Iola, WI: Krause Publications.

Tennant, F. (1985). Clinical diagnosis and treatment of post drug impairment syndrome. *American Journal of Psychiatry, 142,* 1251.

Tennessee v. Garner, 471 U.S. 1 (1985).

Thomas, D. J. (2011). *Professionalism in policing: An introduction.* Clifton Park, NY: Cengage Publishing.

Waddington, P.A.J. (1991). *The strong arm of the law: Armed and public order policing.* New York, NY: Oxford University Press.

Walker, S., Spohn, C., & DeLone, M. (2007). *The color of justice: Race, ethnicity, and crime in America,* 4th ed. Belmont, CA: Thomson/Wadsworth.

Wetli, C. V. (1999, May). The pathology of drug abuse: Discussions of case histories. In C. Wetli (chair), *Current topics in forensic pathology.* Symposium conducted at the meeting of the American Society of Clinical Pathologists, New Orleans, LA.

6

Psychological Mind-Set and Militarization of American Police

Since the shooting of Michael Brown and the subsequent riots in Ferguson, Missouri, some media has argued that American police have become a military force, often portraying them as an occupying army. The media argues that American police are civilian and question why American police need military-style weapons, armored vehicles, tactical body armor, and helmets and are dressed in military-style fatigues. This is America, not Russia; we are a free society.

At law enforcement conferences, several civilian attendees have debated with law enforcement professionals as to why local law enforcement needs military-style vehicles and equipment. Their response and subsequent questions are always the same: "An officer was ambushed, how is that equipment going to help him? Or you are turning our streets into a war zone. This isn't Afghanistan or Iraq but America. This scares me, when will it stop, more police more guns, we have to do something."

It would be nice to go back to the good old days when American policing was simple beat officers; facing limited access to illegal narcotics; limited access to firearms with high-capacity magazines; and policies that declared wars on drugs and crimes; those were truly the good old days. It is also important to note that American law enforcement has always been two steps behind the changing landscape of crime in this country. As a profession, policing is slow to change, and most of the changes have been the result of some tragedy that law enforcement has endured, usually the death(s) of an officer(s).

Here we examine the police mission and the ever-changing landscapes that police face. The reader will examine police department transition from a civilian force paramilitary organization to what has been described today as occupying armies. The reader will have an opportunity to examine police SWAT, the good and bad; the psychology of survival; violence and the police response to violence (sniper attacks, school shootings, police gun battles, and the lessons learned from each), local law enforcements' acquisition of military equipment; and the need for officers to learn how to return to psychological homeostasis after critical incidents. We review three case studies, and through the case studies answer the ever-pressing question: Is militarization a necessary move by agencies? Or is it as the ACLU describes it: a war on the streets of America, excessive militarization of American policing (American Civil Liberties Union, 2014)?

TRADITIONAL POLICING

It appears that Americans remember the good old days of policing, and that is what they want to see again. The roots were set by Sir Robert Peel and the reforms he instituted in England in 1829. The Peelian Reforms' most note-worthy contributions were to modernize policing in the form of preventative foot patrols where police worked closely with the residents. The second goal of Peelian Reform was crime prevention (Lentz & Chaires, 2007; Peak, 2006; Walker & Katz, 2005). The Peelian Reforms are similar to policing today, with several differences: population growth, the needs of the individual communities, the proliferation of violence, substance abuse, and the demands for police services.

What Is the Role of the American Law Enforcement Officer?

The most common answer is "to protect and serve the citizens." For the purpose of this exercise, take a moment and jot down some ideas. I believe that you will find the police task is much more complex than originally thought. In 1972, the American Bar Association attempted to describe the police role in America by outlining the following police responsibilities: identify and apprehend criminal offenders; preventive patrol; aid individuals who are in danger; protect constitutional guarantees; traffic direction enforcement; conflict resolution; identify problems that impact police and government; create a feeling of security in the community; order of maintenance; and provide services on an emergency basis (p. 9).

When I look back over the 40 years and my involvement with police, I have a difficult time identifying their role in American society. The simple truth of the matter is police have no definitive role here. In fact, law enforcement's role is one that is defined by law, politics, economics, and the needs of the community in which they serve. In essence, the role is ever-changing because of the evolving demands of American society and the needs of their individual communities (Waddington, 1999; White, 2004). Some examples of that ever-changing role are to administer Narcan to those who have overdosed on opioids; assess and transport the mentally ill in crisis to a mental health facility; act as the first line of defense against terrorism; investigate acts of human trafficking; investigate computer crimes and child pornography; and respond to active shooter incidents. I chose these incidents because these responsibilities indicate that the era of the traditional beat cop is a creature of the past. The substitute has been community policing, which is an excellent tool, yet community policing has its limitations because it is personnel-intensive and police are moving at the speed of light to keep up with the demands of their communities.

Prior to the events of 9/11, policing had embraced the concepts of community policing. Cronkhite (2007) notes that pre-9/11 law enforcement had strong community ties and was successful in crime reduction, and public trust was strong (p. 327). After 9/11, the police mission changed and was so identified in the Post 9-11 Project. The Post 9-11 Project was convened in 2004 and attended by the International Association of Chiefs of Police, the National Sheriff's Association, the National Organization of Black Law Enforcement Executives, and the Police Foundation with a goal of assisting state and local law enforcement in the management of an ever-changing police environment (pp. i–ii).

The conference members identified and developed a host of objectives and goals for post-9/11 law enforcement. One idea that stands out in regard to combining traditional police operations with post-9/11 responsibilities is shifting eras and mission reconfiguration. Mission reconfiguration recognizes that the police mission changed after 9/11, yet the traditional policing models of crime control and community policing could not be ignored. It offered that American policing should transition from the community policing model to a domestic security model (p. ii).

Mass murder, school shootings, and terrorism are the latest national crises that have had an impact on the police role in American society. Historically, American policing has had its role defined by landmark court decisions, which outline or place limits on police behavior such as *Miranda* or *Tennessee v. Garner*; the civil rights movement; the inner-city riots of the 1960s; the National Organization of Women and their push for protection in cases of domestic violence; the closing of mental hospitals in the 1960s and the release of mental health patients to community mental health; Mothers against

Drunk Driving and their campaign for greater enforcement; the proliferation of gang violence; the introduction of cocaine, then crack cocaine, and now methamphetamine; HIV/AIDS; technology; and police misconduct and brutality cases. Each of the aforementioned issues has had, and will continue to, impact the identity and mission of American law enforcement. The questions should be the following: What else will local law enforcement be required to add to its already full plate? Can you think of a job other than policing that has had so many demands placed on it?

The debate regarding police role in a particular community is closely associated with the agencies' style of policing: Does the agency employ a crime fighter/maintenance of order strategy, a peacekeepers' strategy, or a community policing strategy? What I have learned over the years is that oftentimes the organization cannot identify its style of policing, and many are quick to say community policing and they aren't even close.

CHANGING TIMES: FROM OFFICER FRIENDLY TO A WARRIOR

The 1960s and 1970s was a time of social discourse, which demanded change by local law enforcement. In fact, there were a number of threats to the American way of life, on all fronts, and law enforcement found itself ill-prepared to respond to some threats. The need for specially trained police units was in response to a number of sniper attacks in the 1960s and 1970s, hostage takers and barricaded gunmen, and the rise of domestic terror organizations, with the violence each of these groups perpetrated against government and citizens espousing their respective agendas.

The Turning Tide: Sniper Attacks That Set the Stage

There were a number of sniper attacks and ambush incidents against police during the inner-city riots of the 1960s.

CASE STUDY I

Reflections from the 1967 Detroit Riots

I was an 11-year-old boy growing up in Detroit during the 1967 riots. The 10th precinct was two blocks from my house. I would sleep on the floor as snipers attacked the police station. In response to the attacks on the police station, the Detroit police and National Guard would unleash a barrage of bullets. I could hear the 50-caliber machine guns fire over and over. The gunfire would last for 15 to 20 minutes each night.

In the morning, my friends and I would walk past the police station and observe the bullet holes in that building and the hundreds of bullet holes in the storefront buildings across the street from the station (Anonymous, personal communication, March 1, 2018).

- 1966, University of Texas, Austin—Charles Whitman stockpiled a cache of weapons on the top of the 300-foot tower located at the center of the University of Texas campus. Whitman, an ex-marine, went on a shooting rampage, murdering 14 people and wounding 31 others. Police had no specialized response, such as counter-snipers or SWAT.
- 1973, New Orleans, Louisiana—At a Howard Johnsons motel, Mark Essex murdered a number of people and then went to the roof and began shooting at police. Essex murdered seven people, three of them police officers, and wounded eight others. Police had no specialized response such as counter-snipers or SWAT. The marines offered the police a helicopter mounted with a 50-caliber machine gun. After firing several hundred rounds from the 50-caliber machine gun mounted in the helicopter, police shot and killed Essex.

The formal militarization of police began with the Los Angeles Police Department's Special Weapons and Tactics Unit (SWAT) and the New York City Police Department's Emergency Services Unit, both established in 1967. Just as police in Austin, Texas, and New Orleans, Louisiana, were unprepared, the cities of Los Angeles and New York had been experiencing a number of incidents that demanded a specialized response.

- 1969, Los Angeles Police Department—SWAT attempted to serve a search warrant for weapons at the Black Panther Party headquarters. While attempting to serve the warrant, Black Panthers resisted, and there was a four-hour siege and gun battle between the Los Angeles Police Department SWAT team and the Black Panther Party. Thousands of rounds were exchanged, wounding three Black Panther members and three Los Angeles police officers (Balko, 2013).
- 1973, Los Angeles Police Department—SWAT raided the headquarters of the Symbionese Liberation Army (SLA). LAPD received a tip that SLA members were in a house. Some 400 LAPD officers responded with LAPD SWAT. LAPD SWAT had semiautomatic weapons, and SLA members returned fire with fully automatic weapons. During the shootout, 9,000 rounds were

exchanged. No officers were injured. Three SLA members were shot and killed by LAPD SWAT, and six others died huddled in a crawl space under the house. LAPD SWAT fired an incendiary tear gas canister into the SLA, house and it is believed that the canister started the fire, which killed the six SLA members found in the crawl space under the house (Balko, 2013).

Police SWAT Disasters

SWAT teams are a necessary evil in the United States. However, as with anything dealing with organizations, the organizations are measured only by their failures, not their many successes, which are rarely made public. The failures have become examples used by anti-government groups as a rallying cry of government interference and control. The following four incidents went wrong and have become the call to arms against the government and police.

- December 28, 2017, Wichita, Kansas—After an argument over a *Call of Duty* video game, suspect Tyler Barris, who lived in Los Angeles, made a fake 911 call to Wichita police. Barris did not provide his name and advised police dispatch that he was at a home in Wichita, had shot his father in the head, and was holding his mother and a sibling at gunpoint. Barris also advised police that he poured gasoline inside the home and might just set the house on fire (Wichita Police Department, 2017). Police surrounded the house and using a loud speaker called for the suspect to come out. Andrew Finch, a real resident of the house in Kansas, responded to the loud speaker and was ordered to place his hands on his head as he exited the house. Finch dropped his arm toward his waistband while exiting and was shot and killed by police (Manna, 2017). Although Finch did make a "furtive movement" toward his waistband, no one was in danger. The officers were behind cover, protected, and there were no civilians outside. Police dispatch could have searched for a number and called the house to see if this was in fact a legitimate call. This incident is called swatting. "Swatting" is defined as making a false call to police and describing horrific crime scenes, and police respond with all of the necessary resources. The question is, police were safe, so why did they shoot?
- February–April 1993, Waco, Texas—The Bureau of Alcohol, Tobacco, Firearms and Explosives (ATF) went to execute a search warrant for illegal guns at the Branch Davidian Compound. Once on the property, it is not clear what caused the gun battle, but an intense gun battle erupted between members of the Branch Davidians and ATF agents. Four ATF agents and six Branch Davidian members were killed. The Branch Davidians refused to surrender, and the incident was turned over to the FBI. The standoff lasted for 51 days. In the end, the FBI assaulted the Branch Davidian Compound with tear gas. A few hours afterward, the Branch Davidian building caught fire. Surviving

Branch Davidians stated that the FBI started the fire through the insertion of the tear gas. The FBI claims the Branch Davidians started the fires. A total of 76 Branch Davidians died, 71 as a result of the FBI tear gas assault. Nine Branch Davidian members survived (Department of Treasury, 1993; Federal Bureau of Investigation, 1993).

• August 1992, Naples, Idaho—Bureau of Alcohol, Tobacco, Firearms and Explosives (ATF) arrested Randy Weaver on weapons charges. Weaver was released on bond and, through a series of mistakes, he was never notified of his court date. On April 21, 1992, U.S. marshals set up surveillance on the Weaver Cabin at Ruby Ridge. The marshals threw rocks at the Weaver Cabin to test the response of Weaver's dogs. The dogs responded, and after a short chase the marshals shot Weaver's dogs. Sammy Weaver, Randy Weaver's son, fired at the marshals, and the marshals returned fire, killing Sammy. A deputy U.S. marshal was killed by Kevin Harris, a friend who was accompanying Weaver. After the death of Weaver's son, the FBI Hostage Rescue Team (HRT) took responsibility for the standoff. On August 22, the second day of the standoff, an HRT sniper shot Randy Weaver as he and several other family members were entering a shed to look at his dead son's body. As Weaver and family members ran back to their cabin, Weaver's wife was shot and killed by an HRT sniper. Civilian negotiators (friends) assisted in ending the standoff on August 30, 1992, five days after it began. Since Weaver and his wife were both unarmed, the HRT sniper did not justifiably shoot either under the color of law, because neither posed a threat (Department of Justice, 1994; U.S. Senate, 1996).

• May 1985, Philadelphia, Pennsylvania—Police had received numerous calls regarding MOVE's use of a bullhorn at its compound at all hours of the day and night. The MOVE organization was an anti-government group aiming to preserve African heritage. Three weeks later, police obtained a number of arrest warrants. Police arrived in force and attempted to clear the building to no avail. The Philadelphia Fire Department blasted the roof of the house with fire hoses in an attempt to force MOVE members from the house. It is uncertain who fired the first shot, but a gun battle ensued. MOVE members refused to exit the house, and in response the Philadelphia Police Department dropped a bomb on the roof of the house. The MOVE home was at the center of a number of row homes. The building caught fire, the fire spread, and 65 homes were destroyed. Firefighters who were on standby were ordered not to fight the fire for fear that police could not protect them. Eleven MOVE members died, six adults and five children (Philadelphia Special Investigations Commission, 1985).

Changing Patrol Officers' Mentality: The Will to Survive

From the beginning, there has been a different mind-set for patrol officers and those assigned to SWAT. SWAT received all of the specialized training, and patrol officers received very little. SWAT trained weekly/daily, and patrol officers received training annually or semiannually. As the war on drugs began, violent attacks on police occurred more frequently. Patrol officers began to encounter violent, heavily armed subjects during routine patrol. The traditional tactics and mentality that had served police well for years had to change to meet this new threat and new forms of aggression.

The first major transition for police departments was to move from the traditional, 6-shot revolver to semiautomatic pistols, which held 15 rounds. This change was necessary to give police a fighting chance against suspects who were carrying fully automatic assault weapons and semiautomatic pistols that carried as many as 30 rounds of ammunition. Unfortunately, the transition to new weapons did not happen until a number of officers were killed; many were killed while reloading their empty 6-shot revolvers.

In response to the violent attacks, updated weaponry, and the increase in line-of-duty police deaths, law enforcement trainers began to evaluate the quality of police training, and from that evaluation emerged a new way of thinking known as officer survival and/or officer safety. Soon to follow was a training series known as street survival. The program was designed for patrol officers with the understanding that criminals had become much more sophisticated and violent. Street survival made it clear that suspects were routinely practicing countermeasures to traditional police tactics. The suspects' practice had been captured during police interviews of inmates and video clips of inmates practicing in the prison yard.

- 1980, Street survival seminars by Calibre Press—A civilian-owned company, Calibre Press was the first to introduce the topic of street survival to law enforcement officers in the United States. It was a two-day seminar and provided examples of officer fatalities, mental preparation, the importance of tactics, and developing a survival attitude. It was a step above any training received at the local police academy. Although the information was much needed and highly useful, the seminar sensationalized officer deaths. There was no balance to the training; it was about winning and winning at all costs. The seminar included Hollywood movies, discussions, and examples, all designed to encourage officers to develop a survival attitude. The real problem with Calibre Press was that it was owned and operated by civilians. Although much needed, Calibre Press creators had no real idea of the importance of returning officers to mental homeostasis after each encounter and providing examples of that balance in the context of training.

- With the street survival seminar, Calibre Press published its first book titled *Street Survival: Tactics for Armed Encounters* and in 1986 published a second book titled *The Tactical Edge: Surviving High Risk Patrol*. Even today, both of these books are bibles for patrol tactics and remain a mainstay in police libraries. The training was/is offered in a seminar format; there is no hands-on training. Today, the *Street Survival* franchise is owned by a retired law enforcement officer, who recognizes the value of balance in training and understanding the complete picture.

- The need for maintaining an officer survival edge is supported by researchers in a 2018 study. Tiesman, Gwilliam, Rojek, and Marsh (2018) completed a meta-analysis of data concerning nonfatal injuries to law enforcement officers from 2003 through 2014, utilizing the National Electronic Injury Surveillance System–Occupational Supplement to estimate the average number of nonfatal law enforcement officers' injuries that officers sustain in the United States annually. The data reflects the following:

  a. Between 2003 and 2014, an estimated 669,100 law enforcement officers were treated in U.S. emergency rooms for nonfatal injuries.

  b. The overall rate of 635 per 10,000 full-time equivalents was three times higher than all other U.S. workers' rate (213 per 10,000 full-time equivalents).

  c. The three leading injury events were (1) assaults and violent acts (35%), (2) bodily reactions and exertion (15%), and (3) transportation incidents (14%).

PSYCHOLOGY OF SURVIVAL

Patrol officers were introduced to the concept of survival psychology, mental conditioning, and tactical thinking in the street survival seminars. Adams, McTernan, and Remsberg (1980) offered the survival triangle, which offered the following in regard to surviving armed encounter: Officers must have prepared themselves mentally, have rehearsed the tactics, and have good shooting skills. The officer must also be able to integrate each of these in a crisis situation. In addition, Remsberg (1986) explains, for those officers who are unprepared, to rely on luck. He offers four interrelated weighted variables: 5 percent is mental skill, 3 percent is physical skill, 15 percent is shooting skill, and 75 percent is luck (p. 16).

Surviving is more than just a skill set. It is a belief system, and there is a clear difference between the statements "I want to live" and "I will live." The will to live is generated from the personality (Myss & Shealy, 1993). In policing, a survival state of mind is tied to a series of physical skills that are perishable and require practice:

1. Firearms is a skill set that is learned in the police academy where officers are trained in basic firearms handling skills, in which they must qualify by attaining a minimum of 80 percent on the states' qualification course, night shooting

qualification, decision shooting, and long gun qualification. Depending on the state, basic firearms training in the police academy is on average 80 hours. If a new officer does not go to the range on his or her own time, firearms proficiency will diminish over time. Firearms is a perishable skill set.

2. Defensive tactics is a series of empty hand control skills. This skill set is designed to teach officers how to establish control of a subject through the use of empty hand skills or deployment of intermediate weapons. Again, this is taught in 80 hours and may never be revisited after graduation from the police academy. Defensive tactics is a perishable skill. As with firearms, the only time that it may be revisited is because the manufacturer who certifies the training, or the state licensing board of police officers, may mandate recertification once a year.

3. Physical fitness—In many agencies there is no fitness requirement, nor is it regulated by the state licensing board. Officers graduate from the academy in excellent physical condition. Without a mandate from the agency, many let their fitness levels decline. Fitness is a perishable skill.

Officers recognize the danger of the profession; however, as with any profession, as officers grow older, their confidence may well get the best of them. Many senior officers believe they have mastered the profession and understand human behavior and, better yet, the behavior of most criminals. What the officers don't take into consideration is that as they become more involved in their personal lives and their profession takes a back seat to the needs and challenges of their families, the skills that are needed most languish. To make up for the missing skill set, some officers become abusive and threaten subjects to establish and maintain control of a situation. The quiet calm that the officer once exhibited is no longer there. In a 10-year analysis of the FBI's Officer's Killed and Assaulted Report between the years 2006–2016, a profile emerges of the officers who are most likely to be feloniously killed: White male, average age 38.6 years old; the average number of years of service is 11.6 years, and the weapon most often used to kill these officers is a firearm (Federal Bureau of Investigation, 1996–2016). Adams et al. (1980) describes this as the Superman complex and overconfidence in a waning skill set.

To obtain a better understanding of how officers were killed due to training failures, poor tactics or no tactics, and/or insufficient equipment, several famous police shootings are presented and have become the rallying cry to mandate change. It is important to note these incidents have occurred before and after 1980 when street survival was first introduced:

- *Sniper attacks*—December 2017, Las Vegas, Nevada, sniper attack on concert goers; July 2016, Dallas, Texas, sniper attack on police; and in Baton

Rouge, Louisiana; July 2016 sniper attack on police. All three incidents have changed the mentality of police. Rarely have police had to prepare for a threat from above except in dignitary protection, large outside gatherings such as New Year's Eve celebrations, and in cases where subversive groups have marched. Without preparation, these become target-rich environments as shown in the catastrophic loss of life in each of the aforementioned incidents.

Lessons learned: Every time that there is a large gathering of people, even either a march or outdoor concert, police and/or security must evaluate the location as if they were preparing for a dignitary. Countermeasures must be in place to defend the attendees and those on the ground. However, for patrol officers who are responding to a call for service, there is usually nothing that can be done, especially if an ambush is planned. The patrol officer is an easy target. The best tactics in the world cannot thwart an ambush.

• *School shootings*—February 2018, Parkland, Florida, Parkland High School; December 2012, Newtown, Connecticut, Sandy Hook Elementary School; April 2007, Blacksburg, Virginia, Virginia Tech; April 1999, Littleton, Colorado, Columbine High School. In all but one of these school shootings, the suspect was a student. There are many reasons that students make the decision to take revenge on their fellow students. Law enforcement's role has changed from waiting for SWAT to respond to the threat to a new form of response known as active shooter. Officers can intervene with as few as one officer, usually the school resource officer, or three or more officers based on their time of arrival on the scene.

Lessons learned: Officers who are on the scene must respond immediately to the threat, be it one officer or three or more to stop the loss of life. This did not happen in Parkland, Florida. School resource officers should have the proper equipment to address such threats. Since the Virginia Tech shooting, colleges and universities have responded with the development of behavioral assessment and consultation teams. The goal of the team is to identify, assess, intervene, and prevent school shootings and suicides before they occur. Most of these teams have similar responsibilities and assess behaviors associated with intimidation; threats to harm self or others; disruptiveness; out-of-ordinary behavior; reaction to the death of a family member; and evidence of depression or suicidal thoughts/plans. The team members include representatives from the university police, counseling center, housing, dean of students, and a number of other participants. This system works only if faculty and students report unusual behavior, social media postings, and any other information that may assist in identifying a potential threat to the campus community or the individual. Public schools should create a system with the understanding that prior to most attacks students post on social media, discuss their feelings with fellow students, or express acts of violence in written assignments (Vossekuil, Fein, Reddy, Borum, & Modzeleski., 2004).

- *Police gun battles*—February 1997, North Hollywood, California, North Hollywood shootout; April 1986, Miami, Florida, FBI shootout; April 1970, Newhall, California, Newhall incident.

    In each of these gun battles the police were outgunned, outmanned, tactically inferior, or deficient in training, or the officer underestimated the suspect's abilities.

    Lessons learned: After the Newhall incident, officers' firearms training changed from bull's-eye one-handed shooting to combat-style shooting and has evolved to include decision shooting, nighttime shooting, tactical movement, and shooting from different positions. The traditional 12-gauge shotgun has been replaced by AR-15 assault-type weapons. After the FBI shootout, police learned never to underestimate their opponents and to share information with other jurisdictions.

Use of Military-Style Vehicles by American Police

There are a series of questions that the public should try to answer as they attempt to assess the need for military equipment and vehicles acquired by their local law enforcement agencies:

1. What is the daily mission of law enforcement in your community?
2. What are the tools needed to accomplish that mission?
3. Does your community have violent gangs, and what is the violence like in your community?
4. Do you have drug houses in your community, and are those drug houses fortified with steel-reinforced doors and bars over the windows?
5. What are the most common weapons used to commit homicide in your community? Are they assault-type weapons, are they fully automatic, and/or do they use handguns with large-capacity magazines?
6. How many schools do you have in your community? Do you have school resource officers? Do the resource officers have the proper equipment to respond to an active shooter incident?
7. Have the officers in your agency been taught the importance of balance, meaning they treat citizens with respect but have the ability to transition into survival mode to respond to threats when necessary?

These questions were asked as a point of reflection and to serve as a reminder that the challenges and demands of local law enforcement have changed. The need for the equipment is lost every time a law enforcement officer is seen abusing a person for no apparent reason. Such is the case with Johnnie Rush, who was beaten and arrested by Asheville, North Carolina, police for jaywalking (see Case Study II). The decisions that officers make during the arrest and beating of one person tarnish the image of the profession and have the public asking the question: What purpose does military equipment serve in a civilian police organization? After viewing such videos, the minority community's belief is that military-styled weapons, armored vehicles, and military-style clothes are signs that the police are at war with them; they are using the instruments of war as tools of oppression and to control them through fear and intimidation. After each of these incidents, it is hard to separate the real needs of the police from the abuses.

CASE STUDY II

Jaywalking

A Black Man's Felony

Johnnie Rush, a 33-year-old Black male, was stopped by Asheville, North Carolina, police officers for jaywalking. During the stop, an argument ensued. When officers ordered Rush to put his hands behind his back, to arrest him, Rush ran. As the officers chased Rush, one officer said: "Black male, white tank top thinks it's funny. You know what's funny is that you are going to get fucked up hard core." The officers caught Rush, smashed his head into the pavement, shot him with a Taser, and arrested him. Rush said: "You didn't have to punch me in the face." The officer replied: "You didn't have to make me" (Asheville, North Carolina Police Department, 2017).

This incident occurred in August 2017 and was released to the public on February 2, 2018.

Reflective Questions

1. What message does this send to the minority community?
2. Why the delay in the release of the video?
3. Is there one standard for police and another for citizens?
4. From a minority perspective, how would you view the acquisition of military-style equipment? Is it needed, or is the military-styled equipment another form of police and government oppression?

CASE STUDY III

Military Vehicles

Sniper Rifle Deployment

During the Ferguson, Missouri, riots, SWAT officers were perched on top of their military-style vehicles, pointing their sniper rifles at the protestors and rioters. The explanation police offered was that the snipers were looking for armed subjects in the crowd. The role of a sniper is to deploy and remain unseen by using the highest point at or near a location, usually on the top of a building. The sniper can be as far away as 800 yards or more depending on the sniper's ability. With the sniper is a second person, who is called a spotter. The spotter is the observer who has the job of observing the crowd, locating potential threats, and assisting the sniper with gauging distance and wind so that the sniper's shot will be accurate. Essentially, you have two people observing the crowd, the sniper through his or her rifle scope and the spotter through his or her spotting scopes. Their role is to identify armed threats with the goal of protecting the people and police on the ground. A sniper should be out of sight, utilizing high ground for a tactical advantage and obtaining a complete picture of the area observed.

Reflective Questions

1. You are a protestor; you see a sniper perched on top of a military vehicle, pointing a sniper rifle at you; what message is the police department sending?

2. Why would the police violate sniper protocols and use the top of military vehicles as opposed to the highest point in the city?

3. If the police were truly looking for armed protestors in the crowd, why didn't they assign a spotter with the sniper and have two sets of eyes with high-powered scopes working the crowd?

4. The media reported this abuse, which began a campaign regarding local law enforcement and the acquisition of military equipment; do you believe their concerns were justified?

5. How would you address the issue of law enforcement obtaining military equipment? Would you abolish the program or introduce criteria and/or standards that agencies would have to meet before obtaining the equipment?

6. When an agency violates a standard protocol, how would you hold that agency accountable?

7. Should all agencies be impacted because one or two agencies violate the law or protocol?

8. From a police department standpoint, if you needed the equipment, how would you introduce the equipment to the citizens in our community? Or would you keep the acquisition of the equipment a secret?

PRESIDENTIAL ORDER 13688—LAW ENFORCEMENT ACQUIRES MILITARY EQUIPMENT

In response to the media observations and stories concerning law enforcement's use of military vehicles and the deployment of SWAT snipers during the Ferguson, Missouri, protests and riots, President Obama changed the policy, limiting acquisition of military equipment to local law enforcement by establishing a series of guidelines. The rules mandated training when agencies acquire controlled equipment, including mandates for adoption of general policing standards, including community policing training, constitutional policing, and community input and impact principles. In addition, the agencies must adopt standards that address the evaluation, use, and supervision and offer transparency in regard to the equipment acquired (Law Enforcement Equipment Working Group, 2015, pp. 4–5). When you read the guidelines, it is clear that the Working Group and President Obama recognized that law enforcement has a need for the equipment. They also recognized that there needs to be oversight and training with the acquired equipment. Although not mentioned, the objective of the training and oversight is designed as tools to address the warrior mentality and provide the much-needed insight and balance of the officer's treatment of the citizens they police. The restrictions that President Obama imposed concerning the sale of military equipment to local law enforcement have been reversed by President Trump. Prior to President Trump's reversal, the Department of Defense had recalled 126 armored vehicles, 138 grenade launchers, and more than 1,600 bayonets (Noble, 2017).

Returning to Homeostasis after the Chaos Ends

For American police to be successful in their communities, the officers must understand and be able to change the channels of their personality repeatedly to be effective. On one call, officers may need to be aggressive to establish control of a subject. On a call with a suicidal subject, the officer's personality will have to be one that displays calm, patience, and resolve to prevent the suicide. Finally, on another call the officer will have to display empathy and compassion when informing a family of a loved one's death.

The personality is dynamic and allows one to make adjustments to the ever-changing environment (Allport, 1937; Cloninger & Cloninger, 2011; Rogers, 1995). However, what happens to police is officers refuse to show emotion and they create a number of personality barriers, refusing to allow anyone in. Psychologically, officers dissociate themselves from the citizens. The citizens are no longer seen as people in need of police services. The citizens become *them* or *those people*. This disconnect is a form of emotional survival for officers and can become the source of a collective consciousness which is usually subconscious and rarely expressed except to those the officers trust. This process is known as "enmification," identifying the citizens of a community as the enemy (Rieber & Kelly, 1991).

Finally, finding that psychological sweet spot, where officers can return to homeostasis, a middle ground, is very difficult because of the emotional tug-of-war officers experience daily. The sad part is that this emotional purgatory that officers use as a means of survival impacts their professional and personal lives.

CONCLUSION

The militarization of police is more than the equipment that agencies acquire from the federal government. It is associated with a policing strategy known as crime fighter/maintenance of order style of policing, officer safety/street survival, and the ever-changing police mission.

Maintenance of order policing is driven by large numbers of arrests usually associated with quality of life and zero tolerance policing: possession of marijuana, open container, loitering, disorderly conduct, jaywalking, riding a bicycle without a light, parking tickets, and moving citations for anything. When an agency employs this type of policing, the officers are conditioned to believe that their value is based on productivity, not the quality of their work, or the community's needs. In this type of agency, each month an officer's productivity is posted in the squad room for everyone to see. In addition, supervisors push officers to be proactive, make arrests, write tickets, because supervisors don't want to be labeled as ineffective. If a supervisor is labeled as ineffective, it may well impact future opportunities within the organization.

In this type of organization, there is no community involvement; police dictate to the community. What police and trainers have failed to understand is that officers need to find the psychological middle ground or mental homeostasis to avoid the dissociation, which is associated with maintenance of order policing. The dissociation separates the officers from the community and creates an atmosphere of us versus them. Minority communities are most often victimized by this type of policing, leaving minority community members feeling oppressed and disenfranchised (Schuck & Rabe-Hemp, 2017).

In the end, minority community members refuse to accept explanations of police even when the officers' actions are just. Minority communities and police become locked in an epic accusatory battle, akin to two rams that butt heads continuously until one dies. The community responds through acts of violence, property damage, protests, and ultimately riots. Police respond with more aggressive forms of policing and more arrests, deploying military vehicles, riot gear, and tear gas. This epic standoff continues to create a divide that has yet to find a common ground, which fosters an atmosphere of trust. Who will end the standoff?

REFERENCES

Adams, R. J., McTernan, T. M., & Remsberg, C. (1980). *Street survival: Tactics for armed encounters*. Northbrook, IL: Calibre Press.

Allport, G. W. (1937). *Personality: A psychosocial interpretation*. New York, NY: Holt, Rinehart & Winston.

American Civil Liberties Union. (2014). *The war comes home: The excessive militarization of American policing*. New York, NY: Author.

Asheville, North Carolina Police Department. (2017, August 24). *Body camera footage of the beating of Johnnie Rush*. Asheville, NC: Author.

Balko, R. (2013). *Rise of the warrior cop: The militarization of America's police forces*. Philadelphia, PA: Public Affairs Publishing.

Cloninger, C. R., & Cloninger, K. M. (2011). Person centered therapeutics. *International Journal of Person Centered-Medicine, 1* (1), 43–52.

Cronkhite, C. L. (2007). *Criminal justice administration: Strategies for the 21st century*. Sudbury, MA: Jones & Bartlett Publishing.

Department of Justice. (1994). *Report of the Ruby Ridge task force to the office of professional responsibility of investigation of allegations of improper governmental conduct in the investigation, apprehension, and prosecution of Randall C. Weaver and Kevin Harris*. Washington, DC: Author.

Department of Treasury. (1993). *Investigation of Vernon Wayne Howell also known as David Koresh*. Washington, DC: Author.

Federal Bureau of Investigation. (1993). *United States Department of Justice: Report on the events at Waco, Texas*. Washington, DC: Author.

Federal Bureau of Investigation. (1996–2016). *1996–2016 Law enforcement officers killed and assaulted*. Washington, DC: Department of Justice.

Law Enforcement Equipment Working Group. (2015). *Recommendations pursuant to Executive Order 13688: Federal support for local law enforcement equipment acquisition*. Washington, DC: Author.

Lentz, S. A., & Chaires, R. H. (2007). The invention of Peel's principles: A study of policing "textbook" history. *Journal of Criminal Justice, 25*(1), 69–79.

Manna, N. (2017, December 29). *Family says son killed by police in "swatting" was unarmed, didn't play video games*. Retrieved from http://www.kansas.com/news/local/crime/article192147194.html.

Myss, C., & Shealy, C. N. (1993). *The creation of health: The emotional, psychological, and spiritual responses that promote healing*. New York, NY: Three Rivers Press.

Noble, A. (2017, August 28). *Trump reverses Obama, reinstates program sending military surplus to local police*. Retrieved from https://www.washingtontimes.com/news/2017/aug/28/trump-reinstate-military-surplus-local-police/.

Peak, K. J. (2006). *Policing America: Methods, issues, challenges,* 5th ed. Upper Saddle River, NJ: Pearson/Prentice Hall.

Philadelphia Special Investigations Commission. (1985). *Philadelphia Special Investigation Commission (MOVE) Records*. Philadelphia, PA: Author.

Remsberg, C. (1986). *The tactical edge: Surviving high-risk patrol*. Northbrook, IL: Calibre Press.

Rieber, R. W., & Kelly, R. J. (1991). Substance and shadow: Images of the enemy. In R. Rieber (Ed.), *The psychology of war and peace: The image of the enemy*. New York, NY: Plenum Press.

Rogers, C. R. (1995). *On becoming a person: A therapist view of psychotherapy*. Boston, MA: Houghton Mifflin.

Schuck, A. M., & Rabe-Hemp, C. (2017). Inequalities regimes in policing: Examining the connection between social exclusion and order maintenance strategies. *Race and Justice*. Retrieved March 15, 2018, from http://journals.sagepub.com/doi/10.1177/2153368716689491.

Tiesman, H. M., Gwilliam, M., Rojek, J., & Marsh, S. (2018). Nonfatal injuries to law enforcement officers: A rise in assaults. Retrieved from http://www.ajpmonline.org/article/S0749-3797(17)30716-X/fulltext.

U.S. Senate. (1996). *Ruby Ridge: Report of the subcommittee on terrorism, technology and government information of the Senate Committee on the Judiciary*. Darby, PA: Diane Publishing.

Vossekuil, B., Fein, R. A., Reddy, M., Borum, R., & Modzeleski, W. (2004). *The final report and findings of the safe school initiative: Implications for the prevention of school attacks in the United States*. Washington, DC: United States Secret Service and United States Board of Education.

Waddington, P.A.J. (1999). *Liberty and order: Public order policing in a capital city*. London, UK: UCL Press.

Walker, S., & Katz, C. M. (2005). *The police in America and introduction,* 5th ed. New York, NY: McGraw Hill.

White, J. R. (2004). *Defending the homeland: Domestic intelligence, law enforcement and security*. Belmont, CA: Wadsworth Publishing.

Wichita Police Department. (2017). *911 Audiotape, SWATTING incident*. Wichita, KA: Author.

7

Twenty-First-Century Policing, Crime Control, or Quality Assurance

Policing is a profession that has continually searched for its identity and the answers to address society's many problems. In the past, agencies have instituted such tools as community policing, diversity/implicit bias training, procedural justice, equity in policing, and leadership training, yet none of the programs have really had a long-term impact. Some agencies have begun to implement President Obama's, six pillars from the President's Task Force on 21st-Century Policing, with a focus on policing through innovation.

Throughout this book there are a number of discussions concerning police practices and the tools used to remedy the issues, such as consent decrees. The findings of consent decrees offered several consistent themes: the use of excessive force; unconstitutional stops, searches, arrests, biased policing; ineffective/no tracking system of officer behavior and performance; poor/no systems of complaint intake against officers, investigation of officers, and adjudication of the cases; and a failure to engage in community-oriented policing (T. E. Perez, personal communication, March 16, 2011, pp. 2–3). To address these issues, agencies have begun to look at different management systems that are all-inclusive, and a new term has begun to gain some traction—"quality assurance."

Quality assurance is nothing new and has been used by the military, the field of medicine, and industry in the manufacturing process. Depending on the industry, the goals are simple, eliminate mistakes, or develop the best possible product for consumers. This chapter provides the reader with insight into 21st-century policing, the Violent Crime Act of 1994, Commission on Accreditation for Law Enforcement Agencies (CALEA) and the accreditation process, the psychology of emotion and disconnect, and case studies of the Wilmington, Delaware, and Ft. Myers police departments. The reader will also have an opportunity to compare the programs and attempt to determine which is best. Is it one size fits all, or will agency size, budget, and mission determine what will be the best for that agency?

TWENTY-FIRST-CENTURY POLICING TASK FORCE

Change in law enforcement is usually slow and very painful; as I noted in Chapter 6, most of the changes that have been made in policing were due to the death of an officer. Farmer (1984) states the following: "A tragedy of policing, despite gains realized in recent years, is the proclivity to circle the wagons against change" (p. 8). Society is moving at the speed of light with technology and communications systems, and law enforcement is still struggling with something as simple as the interoperability of communication systems. The ability of officers to communicate from different agencies during a critical incident is essential and was identified after 9-11. Yet many agencies can't agree on a system that is interoperable with adjoining jurisdictions. This is one example of policing being slow to change, and as much as American policing moves forward, it seems to revert to the old or remain stuck in time.

Twenty-First-Century Policing: New and Innovative or New Packaging Old Concepts

When President Obama convened the Task Force on 21st-Century Policing, it was in response to officer-involved shootings of unarmed Black men, the minority community's response to the shootings, and the civil unrest that followed. President Obama's executive order stipulated that the task force develop strategies that were "consistent with applicable law, identify best practices and otherwise make recommendations to the President on how policing practices can promote effective crime reduction while building public trust" (Office of Community Oriented Policing Services,

2015, p. 1). The subsequent investigation and information gathered was categorized into what the task force final report identifies as six underlying themes which are directly associated with the six pillars of 21st-century policing:

- *Change the culture of policing*—Guardians versus warriors: The final report calls for law enforcement to protect the dignity and human rights of all, to be the protectors and champions of the Constitution. This rethinking of the role of police in a democracy requires leadership and commitment across law enforcement organizations to ensure internal and external policies, practices, and procedures that guide individual officers and make organizations more accountable to the communities they serve.

- *Embrace community policing*—Community policing is a philosophy as well as a way of doing business. The commitment to work with communities to tackle the immediate and longer-term causes of crime through joint problem-solving reduces crime and improves quality of life. It also enhances officer safety and increases the likelihood of individuals to abide by the law.

- *Ensure fair and impartial policing*—Procedural justice is based on four principles: (1) treating people with dignity and respect, (2) giving individuals "voice" during encounters, (3) being neutral and transparent in decision-making, and (4) conveying trustworthy motives. In addition to practicing procedural justice, understanding the negative impact of explicit and implicit bias on police-community relations and taking constructive actions to train officers and the community on how to recognize and mitigate key factors.

- *Build community capital trust and legitimacy*—Grow from positive interactions based on more than just enforcement interactions. Law enforcement agencies can achieve trust and legitimacy by establishing a positive presence at community activities and events, participating in proactive problem-solving, and ensuring that communities have a voice and seat at the table when working with officers.

- *Paying attention to officer wellness and safety*—Law enforcement officers face all kinds of threats and stressors that have a direct impact on their safety and well-being. Ensure that officers have access to the tools that will keep them safe, such as bulletproof vests, tactical first aid kits, and training. Promote officer wellness through physical, social, and mental health support.

- *Technology*—New and emerging technology is changing the way we police. It improves efficiency and transparency but also raises privacy concerns and has a significant price tag. Body-worn cameras, less-than-lethal use-of-force technologies, communication, and social media all require a legal and pragmatic review of policies, practices, and procedures. These policies, practices, and procedures should be developed with input from the community and constitutional scholars (Office of Community Oriented Policing Services, 2015, p. 1).

Before you move on, take a moment and reflect; do any of the aforementioned six pillars sound like something that was presented before by different presidents and/or crime control policies or initiatives?

Although not exactly the same, similar issues were detailed in Chapter 1 discussion of the 1967 Kerner Commission Report. In the investigation of the causes of the 1967 riots, the number one complaint that Black citizens expressed was police practices. The commission noted: "The abrasive relationship between the police and the minority communities has been a major—and explosive—source of grievance, tension and disorder. The blame must be shared by the total society" (Kerner Commission, 1968, p. 14). The commission's findings included a detailed review of police operations; recommendations to eliminate a sense of insecurity within minority communities; institution of a series of mechanisms for community members to air their grievances against local police; development of policies to assist in decision-making; recruitment of more Negro officers and promote them accordingly; and development of a "Community Service Officer Program" to attract Negroes to the profession of policing (Kerner Commission, 1968, p. 15).

Violent Crime Control and Law Enforcement Act of 1994

In 1994 President Bill Clinton signed the Violent Crime Control and Law Enforcement Act of 1994. The legislation appropriated $9 billion for state and local law enforcement to hire 100,000 community-oriented police officers (U.S. Congress, 1995). The money was made available through a competitive grant process. In the grant the agency had to show a need and how the officers would be utilized. Some agencies created what are known as community-oriented police teams (COP teams). If an agency received the grant, the position(s) were federally funded for three years, and there was a stipulation that the agency would have to keep the officers after the grant expired. Most, if not all, agencies had the ability to comply with this portion of the grant because of the rate of attrition in policing—retirement, termination, or resignation. Over the years, I have been involved in a number of law enforcement agency assessments, and each agency has had a different definition of community policing and, in many instances, it was business as usual.

CASE STUDY I

Community-Oriented Police Team

I was part of a three-person COPS team, which included a supervisor and two officers. We were assigned to a geographic area that was one square mile in the city's historic district. It was run down and drug infested, with crack dealers on every other corner; the acts of violent crime were associated with the crack cocaine trade and local gangs. The team's responsibility was two-fold: First was enforcement, impact drug and violent crime in the assigned area. Our second area of responsibility, which in many ways was the most important, was to engage the community, often becoming a conduit/facilitator with other local government departments. The community felt that it had been abandoned when it came to city services; when the residents called for something as simple as a street light out or abandoned vehicles, city government was unresponsive and ignored the request.

The team was responsible only for that geographic area; we did not take calls for service except for those calls that occurred in our assigned area. We were afforded an opportunity to patrol on foot, use bicycles, scooters, and patrol cars and set our work schedule to address the changing crime pattern. We were allowed to use whatever resources needed to address the neighborhood's problems. We took all calls for service that occurred in our assigned area, and if patrol beat us to a call, because we were tied up, we would relieve the units in our area and take the call as soon as we could respond.

Developing a working relationship with the community began while on foot patrol and knocking on doors, meeting members of the community, and asking for their input as far as problems. We organized neighborhood cleanup projects and developed a partnership with Code Enforcement to address the abandoned homes which had become havens for prostitution and crack use. We initiated graffiti removal and got to know the drug dealers/gang members on a first-name basis. We learned the drug trade, when drugs were delivered, when they would be on the corner; shut down drug houses; and developed strategies to make arrests. The most disgusting thing I observed as an officer was a five-year-old boy acting as a runner in a drug deal for his mother, accepting money from the user, taking the money to his mother, and taking a vile containing $10 worth of crack to the user.

Our Accomplishments

- In six months we made over 300 arrests for the *sale and possession of crack cocaine.*

- We created a three-on-three basketball program called COPS & Kids every summer for the kids in each of the COPS team locations in the city. Local businesses donated money, paying for uniforms, lunch, and drinks. At the end of the summer, we held a three-on-three championship for each of the age groups and had a banquet and handed out trophies. We did this as part of our duty, every Tuesday and Thursday for four hours.

- We followed our neighborhood kids to their local school and taught a program called Too Good for Drugs to the sixth graders. The program was similar to Drug Abuse Resistance Education Program (DARE), adopted by the local school board, and designed by teachers for teachers.

- Crime analysis revealed that we had an impact on violent crime and drug activity; crime was displaced or moved to another area of the city.

- We arrested a number of drug dealers and were able to get them to become our informants to avoid being classified as habitual offenders to avoid receiving life in prison.

- We asked and received assistance from the local university to bring its free dental clinic to our neighborhood for community members.

- We partnered with the local university and ran a tutoring program. The education majors from the university were the tutors and received college credit for their role in the tutoring program, which lasted a full 16 weeks. Computers were donated by local businesses, and we set up tutoring sights in each of the COPS team areas and provided support to the program as needed.

Is this traditional policing? No, far from it. Some officers would and have called this social work. All I can say is the impact was huge. I have retired; even today adults who were kids at the time approach and thank me for making a difference and showing them something other than drugs.

Although effective, community policing is personnel intensive and difficult to sustain, with constant cutbacks and limited budgets. Communities and agencies must understand that if the entire agency does not adopt the community policing philosophy, develop strategies for all officers to be involved, the program will have limited success.

In addition to community policing, the Violent Crime Control and Law Enforcement Act of 1994 provided a number of other initiatives: establishing a police corps similar to the Community Service Officer Program; law enforcement family support designed to study the effects of stress on law enforcement officers and disseminate the findings to law enforcement—the funds could be used to pay for counseling services; police pattern and practice making it unlawful to deprive a person of his or her civil rights; collect data on the excessive use of force; and provide greater access to technology and training. When it comes to initiatives in policing, the 1994 Crime Control Act is identical to the findings of President Obama's Task Force on 21st-Century Policing. From a community's viewpoint, I would ask the question: Why can't our law enforcement agencies move forward?

Although there have been a number of advances in policing, one of the greatest failures of policing as a profession has been its inability to establish a universal set of standards or guidelines. It is a profession where an individual can still be hired with a high school diploma or GED; no standardized physical fitness requirements are needed; each state has a different set of training standards to become certified/licensed; some states don't require mandatory training or updates; and some officer's mental health and backgrounds are questionable when hired. There are many different definitions and standards of professionalism, which is central to damaging the profession as a whole. Baker (1995) supports this assertion and argues that officer skills differ radically from state to state, and often between adjoining jurisdictions within the same state, because there is no universal standard (p. 1).

PROFESSIONALISM THROUGH ACCREDITATION

In 1979, this lack of consistency was addressed when four law enforcement associations decided to meet and develop a process to professionalize policing. The participants were the International Association of Chiefs of Police, the Police Executive Research Forum, the National Organization of Black Law Enforcement Executives, and the National Sheriffs Association. The end result of this collaboration was CALEA, with the sole purpose of credentialing law enforcement agencies that met CALEA's established series of professional standards (Baker, 1995; Medeiros, 1987). Even though CALEA was established in 1979, it still has its detractors. McAllister (1987) observed that the most common argument against accreditation is the standards mean nothing and they represent the lowest common denominator in policing.

CALEA is a nonprofit private organization, which has created 924 standards for an agency to become accredited (Baker, 1995; Commission on Accreditation for Law Enforcement Agencies, 2018). The goals of CALEA are to strengthen crime prevention and control capabilities; formalize essential management procedures; establish fair and nondiscriminatory personnel practices; improve service delivery; solidify interagency cooperation and coordination; and increase community and staff confidence in the agency (Commission on Accreditation for Law Enforcement Agencies, 2018).

The concept of CALEA is an excellent idea, but it has its limitations. CALEA is unable to hand down meaningful sanctions against an officer or the organization because it doesn't have the power to do so. If an agency lost its accreditation, it would still be a police department and provide service to the community. There are only two bodies that have the ability to provide such sanctions: The first is the Justice Department by suing the police department and/or through consent decrees. Both of these practices have been suspended under Attorney General Jeff Sessions. The other agency is usually the governing criminal justice body or attorney general of the state in which the agency is located. These bodies can strip an officer of his or her standards for unethical or illegal behavior. This argument is supported by Kultgen (1988), who outlines five responsibilities of a professional corporation. The two that impact CALEA and its lack of enforcement ability are described:

- Standards of competence: These would include education, tests for admission to practice, and reviews to ensure that practitioners maintain expertise. A licensing agency would need the power to censure, penalize, fine, suspend, or revoke services, none of which CALEA has.
- Standards of conduct: These include a code of professional behavior, rules, laws, and their enforcement. The organization would have to support ethical practitioners against pressures to violate standards through sanctions against clients and employers who exert pressure, none of which CALEA has.

With what I view as negatives or limitations to accreditation, I interviewed the manager of a local police department's communications center. She is in the process of preparing her communications center for a CALEA accreditation assessment, and she advised the following:

I admit that there are limitations to accreditation. However, when a police department or communications center seeks accreditation, the standards that CALEA mandates, mean that my people will have access to some much-needed resources and services that have been ignored up until now. From my perspective, it puts the governmental entity who employs us on notice of our needs and forces it to address them. Often, administrators and government will ignore the obvious, believing that things are just fine. Our goal is to become better and provide our people with the necessary resources and tools to better serve our community. It's no longer us telling our bosses that there needs to be change, the assessment makes it clear, we either meet standards or we don't. The accreditation process, the assessment, and the findings, are usually the catalyst for change and a move toward professionalism and an improved level of service. (P. Ford-Thomas, personal communication, March 23, 2018)

CASE STUDY II

Wilmington Delaware Police Department: An Agency That Lost Its Way

In 2014, *Newsweek* magazine published an article titled "Murder Town USA (aka Wilmington, Delaware)." The article revealed the following synopsis of violent crime in Wilmington:

> This year, there have been 27 homicides in Wilmington, tying its record 27 murders in 2010, and 135 people have been shot. Twenty-two of them died. With a population of just over 71,000, Wilmington had a violent-crime rate of 1,625 per 100,000 people last year, according to the FBI's 2013 Uniform Crime Report (that crime rate measures murder and nonnegligent manslaughter, rape, robbery and aggravated assault). The national average was 368 per 100,000 people. Wilmington ranks third for violence among 450 cities of comparable size, behind the Michigan towns of Saginaw and Flint, according to a Wilmington News Journal report. For a city mired in violence, the most stunning fact of all may be that Wilmington just got its first homicide unit. (Jones, 2014, para. 3)

After the *Newsweek* article appeared, the Delaware State legislature passed House Joint Resolution 2, which established *The Wilmington Public Safety Strategies Commission*. The commission was intended "to conduct a rapid, intensive, and comprehensive examination of public safety strategies in the City of Wilmington" (p. 6). The Police Foundation from Washington, D.C., was hired to assess several areas of the Wilmington Police Department's (WPD) performance in the areas of community policing, legitimacy, complaints and professional responsibility, supporting crime victims, sustaining evidence-based–community-based violence prevention programs, TAPS and CompStat, crime analysis, technology, information sharing, real-time crime center processes, coordination with other law enforcement agencies and task forces, cameras (downtown visions), warrant service and equipment.

Each of the aforementioned issues was assessed and considered contributing factors to WPD's poor performance and inability to solve homicides and violent crime. However, the major impediment to WPD's success in crime reduction was the poor relationship that WPD had with the Black community. In meetings, the Black community repeatedly expressed: "The police just don't care, they act as if they are an island and refuse to work with us—they are a castle protected by a moat and a wall keeping the community out" (Police Foundation, 2015, pp. 1–2).

The Black community advised that the culture of WPD changed 15 years ago and has created a void of mistrust, anger, and apathy. In essence, the Black community has adopted a code of silence, refusing to assist WPD in any way. The Black community is infested with gangs, drugs, and violence and plagued by a number of unsolved homicides, robberies, and rapes.

Lesson learned: Even with the addition of all the technology in the world, improved training, and evidence collection processes, WPD is learning that without community support, there is no trust; without trust, there is no information exchange; without information, violent crime will remain unchecked. WPD's culture has to change before partnerships between the community and police can be established.

CASE STUDY III

Ft. Myers Police Department: Another Agency That Lost Its Way

In July 2016, the Ft. Myers News Press in Florida began an investigation of the Ft. Myers Police Department (FMPD) after reporters began uncovering problems with a Violent Crimes Joint Task Force. The investigation lasted several months and culminated in a damaging investigative report, with the headline reading "Many Cases Not Prosecuted Due to Incompetent Police Work" (Dulaney, 2016).

The city of Ft. Myers had been plagued by gang violence and an annually increasing murder rate (Freeh Group, 2017). The police administration refused to acknowledge that there was a gang problem. Yet the Medical Examiner's Office could identify the gangs based on its investigations of homicides, noting the location of the shootings (identifying territory) and the tattoos that the gang members had, revealing their affiliation. The gangs had recorded and posted videos on YouTube, walking down the street and firing AK47s in the air and terrorizing residents of the neighborhood.

In response to the violence, the FMPD and the Lee County Sheriff's Office created a Violent Crime Task Force. The task force had two goals:

reduce gun violence and take violent offenders off the street. The Black community complained that the task force was profiling them and stopping members of the community for no reason at all. One resident noted that she had been stopped 10 times having done nothing wrong except driving a Cadillac Escalade; it was a classic case of driving while Black. In another case, the task force executed a traffic stop on a vehicle driven by a Black male. The officers advised the driver that he was stopped because the tint on his window was too dark. During the stop, officers advised the driver they smelled marijuana in the car and arrested him. In a search incident to the arrest, the officers recovered a firearm from the vehicle. The driver was a convicted felon and in the state of Florida, which enhances the penalty if convicted on firearms charge. The case was submitted to the State Attorney's Office, and the State Attorney's Office refused to press charges. The driver was on parole, and the Department of Corrections violated the driver's parole, sentencing the driver to 90 days in jail. Shortly after being released from jail, the driver murdered a man. The suspect was arrested and subsequently charged with murder.

The News Press investigation uncovered the following: In the first 112 closed cases, no charges were filed 41 percent of the time; 71 percent of arrests dealt with drugs, violation of probation, or driving with a suspended license; more than half of the people arrested by the task force had no record of violent crime; and 10 cases involved the possession of guns, but charges were never filed in eight of them (Dulaney, 2016).

The News Press investigation resulted in the city of Ft. Myers hiring the Freeh Group to complete an independent audit of the FMPD and their practices.

The Freeh Group uncovered the following during its audit: The agency was driven by quantity, not quality; the agency was disconnected from the Black community and minority citizens; some officers were corrupt, notifying drug dealers before search warrants were to be executed; promoting corrupt officers to supervisory ranks; because of the corruption, the Black community refused to provide information on homicides and drugs for fear of retaliation, and discipline was inconsistent; and the leadership rejected new and innovative ideas.

Lessons learned: FMPD found itself in the same position as WPD, wherein it had become disconnected from the Black community.

The culture and police practices were detrimental to the much-needed police community partnerships. FMPD needed training in the area of homicide investigation, data collection, and intelligence gathering. Finally, FMPD needed to address its corruption and discipline problem to regain credibility in the community and within the station.

QUALITY ASSURANCE IN POLICING

Quality assurance in policing has been touted by some agencies as the answer for agencies that have lost their credibility, or to prevent the loss of credibility, as was the case in Wilmington and Ft. Myers. Prior to completing the research on the topic of quality assurance, several law enforcement administrators were asked what they thought the term "quality assurance" meant when applied to law enforcement. One administrator believed that quality assurance provided a way of measuring an agency's effectiveness when it comes to arrests and the successful prosecution of cases. Another offered that it was not quantifiable, but he thought quality assurance could best be measured by the community's view of the organization. Another noted it is the quality of the officer's overall work performance and that quality of policing translates into good report writing, closing cases, and making arrests. The reality is that they are all correct. In regard to law enforcement, quality assurance goes by many names; however, the quality of police work is rarely assessed. When each administrator was asked how he or she would measure quality, after some considerable thought, the most common response was through some form of community survey. In addition, when each administrator was asked how he or she would assess improvement of each officer's performance in report writing, quality of arrests, closing cases, and the successful prosecution of those arrested, each felt that this task would be too difficult to achieve.

Quality assurance is a process that begins with changing the culture of an organization through such processes as team building. Peters (1987) notes that there are seven demands facing organizations and these demands impact an organization's environment. In evaluating the seven demands, only three apply to law enforcement: technology, public demands, and labor force demands (pp. 3–34). Commercial enterprise/industry was the first to embrace quality assurance, and industry's research dates as far back as the 1940s, with social scientists Kurt Lewin, John Collier, and William Whyte and later Rensis Likert. Their collective body of work is titled *Productivity and Quality of Worklife*, which details that in order for quality assurance to be meaningful (culture change) it must include input and views of line employees, first-line supervisors, and input from higher levels of management/command staff (Cummings & Worley 1993).

Quality Assurance Models

There are two models of quality assurance—total quality management (TQM) and Sigma Six, which offer different methods for achieving the same goal. The sole purpose of TQM is to focus all of the organization's resources and activities on the concept of quality (Cummings & Worley, 1993). Cummings and Worley (1993) note that TQM is typically implemented in five stages: senior management's buy-in and commitment; training all employees in the implementation and principles of the quality assurance program; quality improvement projects utilizing working groups or individuals to improve processes within the organization; measure progress through the agreed-upon benchmarks; determine if the organization has achieved the benchmarks—if the benchmarks have not been met, assess why and modify the program as needed, and if the benchmarks have been met, reward the accomplishments (pp. 328–330).

Six Sigma seeks to create error-free business performance by measuring variability in any process (Pyzdek & Keller, 2014). Unlike TQM, Six Sigma trains a small number of in-house leaders, known as Sigma Black Belts, to a high level of proficiency in the application of quality assurance principles and techniques. As much as Six Sigma attempts to differentiate itself from TQM, the reality is that it recognizes the need for involvement from all levels of an organization through working groups. The outcome and assessment of quality assurance measures is the same as TQM.

Quality Assurance Models in Medicine and the Military

Beyond industry, the principles of quality assurance were applied to the medical profession in 2001. The implementation of quality assurance in the medical profession was an attempt to reduce the number of mistakes in patient treatment. A report authored by the National Committee for Quality Assurance (n.d.) noted that the health care system had many flaws, which were categorized in the following manner: (1) *underuse*—patients did not receive medically necessary attention; (2) *misuse*—each year more than 100,000 patients had received the wrong care and injured—in addition, there were more than 1.5 million medication errors each year; and (3) *overuse*—patients in this category received unnecessary treatment, and/or there were alternatives that were cheaper and as effective (p. 6). The long-term goal quality assurance in the medical profession is to improve a patient's quality of life. This system of quality assurance is the internal processes of checks and balances associated with the system, which were developed and implemented by employees. Although medicine has adopted quality assurance, medical errors remain the third leading cause of death in the United States, totaling more than 250,000 per year (Makary & Daniel, 2016).

Another industry that utilizes quality assurance is the military. The military's use of quality assurance is twofold: (1) to ensure the products purchased and used by branches of the military are safe and (2) to ensure that a product does not negatively impact the performance of the end user or the mission. In the military, quality assurance is used to increase safety, minimize accidents, and, finally, minimize human error. To minimize human error, the military has implemented a system of checklists for almost everything. The checklists are most often associated with equipment use to verify that the end user has not missed or forgotten something. If it is a mission, that mission will have a number of goals and objectives. On completion of the mission, there is an assessment to determine what, if anything, could have been done differently (U.S. Army, 2014).

Quality Assurance in Policing: Is It the Answer?

Quality assurance in law enforcement is a rare animal and is often limited to bureaus or divisions within a law enforcement agency, such as the crime lab and/or police dispatch. The crime laboratories are unique, in that the employees who are assigned to the crime lab must be credentialed through a professional organization. The professional organizations have developed standards of quality assurance that their credentialed members adhere to. Some examples are fingerprint identification, firearms examiner, and questioned document examiners. From the crime lab to the examiners, each has its unique set of quality assurance standards. The goal in setting such standards is to eliminate the introduction of junk science and mandate ethical behavior based on a rule of law and performance.

However, when it comes to law enforcement agencies as a whole, quality assurance has been elusive at best. Some agencies use it as a form of checks and balances to ensure that officers are performing their jobs as they should. The New York City Police Department (NYPD) has a complex system of audits, which begins at the precinct level and extends to special units whose sole purpose is to audit reports and investigate officer misconduct. The system is designed to perform random weekly, monthly, and biannual reviews of reports and complaints (Kelley & McCarthy, 2013).

The problem with the law enforcement model is that it is far from quality assurance. Quality assurance begins with foundational data, which identifies a problem, or a series of problems, with performance or the quality of a product. The organization identifies the source of the problem and, after developing and implementing a corrective strategy, assesses the outcome with that employee—a week, a month, six months, and a year later to gauge improvement. As noted earlier, this is not the quality assurance model that law enforcement has adopted.

Missing in the law enforcement model is the lack of line officer involvement in the development and implementation of the program, nor are the officers trained in the model. They are usually briefed only on the implementation of the model. In law enforcement, the implementation of these programs has been from the top down. Other examples in the United States are the Tampa Police Department in Tampa, Florida, and the Minneapolis Police Department in Minneapolis, Minnesota. In examining the programs in Tampa and Minneapolis, each has modeled its program after the NYPD model, which is nothing more than a system of audits.

When examining quality assurance, it appears that agencies are more concerned about the internal checks and balances with no, or very little, input from the community. Crime does have a monetary value, yet the personal losses are unlike any business, and victims should not be considered as profits and losses. This argument is supported by Eterno and Silverman (2012), where they state that police are responsible for upholding/protecting the constitutional rights of U.S. citizenry. They also argue that law enforcement officials hold the key to data and how it is presented to the public (pp. 13–14). When examining quality assurance, the questions that comes to mind is: What does an organization value—data/numbers or the citizens that it serves, or both? How does an agency measure the quality of its work and its officers?

It is important to note that quality assurance is closely associated with rebranding, and both concepts are not stand-alone. Rebranding and/or changing the culture of any organization is triggered when the organization has lost the public's trust. Principles that must be associated with quality assurance are ethics, trust, organizational values, and integrity (Goestsch & Davis, 2016). Since policing involves public trust and partnerships, agencies are judged on their response to a violation of the organization's rules, law, unethical conduct, and the agency's interaction and response to the community they serve.

The challenge that law enforcement faces in instituting such a process is the limited vision of many administrators. This is especially true if agencies promote their chiefs from within. In many cases, the chief who is promoted from within is blinded by tradition. Administrators must understand that instituting a program such as quality assurance on its own does nothing, unless the administration institutes a process designed to change the culture. Changing an organization's culture requires progressive thinking, inclusion of working groups from different divisions, and community input. Anything short will be characterized as status quo, and to do so without input places the chief in a precarious position—all alone. In today's climate, minority citizens ask: Why should we believe anything that you say, when the law enforcement profession as a whole is a tarnished brand?

THE PSYCHOLOGY OF SURVIVAL AND DISCONNECT

When you characterize the police personality, it is one that is developed over time, incorporates a number of defense mechanisms, as a form of protection against the constant bombardment of human suffering. Chapter 6 describes the police personality in the following terms: Law enforcement officers refuse to show emotion, and they create a number of personality barriers, refusing to allow anyone in. Psychologically, officers dissociate themselves from the citizens. The citizens are no longer seen as people in need of police services. The citizens become *them* or *those people*. This disconnect is a form of emotional survival for officers and can become the source of a collective consciousness, which is usually subconscious and rarely expressed except to those the officers trust.

The process of survival psychology has been described as a mind-body disconnect, also known as dissociation. In forensic psychology and criminal behavior, Yochelson and Samenow (1976) attribute one's ability to adjust to threats, danger, and acts of violence to the officer, victim, or criminal having developed a shut-off mechanism, which insulates them from the act of violence. This mechanism allows officers, victims, and/or offenders to push fears away from conscious consideration, and it is a critical psychological defense. This mechanism has been discussed by the likes of Freud, Egger, and Lifton, all describing what appears to be some out-of-body experience or dissociative state. The state of mind is not dissimilar to that which is described by victims of traumatic experiences.

Finally, in regard to the police personality, there is one additional theory that provides insight into an officer's need to emotionally disconnect from the community; the theory is known as adult attachment theory. Gillath, Karantzas, and Fraley (2016) offer two major categories of adult attachment theory—attachment anxiety and attachment avoidance. Attachment anxiety can best be described as low self-worth and fear of abandonment. Attachment avoidance is described as being uncomfortable in close relationships, having excessive self-reliance, refusing to depend on others, ignoring emotions, and suppressing feelings related to love and relationships (pp. 10–22). Finally, when coping with fears and threats, they have learned to disassociate their feelings and emotions from the threatening party. Attachment avoidance characterizes the police personality, which many have described as cold and noncaring.

CONCLUSION

Law enforcement has attempted to regain the minority community's trust by implementing different models and/or style of policing, which have been instituted to manage officers' performance or deliver law enforcement services. Many agencies use their web pages to describe a host of services that they provide to the public and declare a commitment to community policing. The WPD espoused a number of programs. One program that WPD touted was its Victim Advocate Program. During the Police Foundation assessment, it was discovered that WPD had a horrible track record of assisting victims. The foundation interviewed surviving family members of homicide, and they had never spoken to a Victim Advocate. Some of the homicide victims were killed five years prior to the foundation interviews; other surviving family members had lost a child within 30 days prior to the foundation's arrival.

The foundation also discovered that WPD homicide detectives would not return phone calls to family members of homicide victims or contact family members with updates. In Wilmington, Delaware, the Black community became angry and disenfranchised by the neglect that they received from WPD. The foundation found the problems were systemic, such as the suspension of Black students at a rate which was twice that of their White counterparts with identical backgrounds and/or past criminal activity and the lack of an alternative school system for juveniles who had been suspended, which lends itself to indoctrination into gangs since there is no school requirement; the justice system offered no alternatives to incarceration for juveniles who committed simple misdemeanors, through the use of civil citations; and finally, there were no partnerships between the schools, police, juvenile justice, and the courts to offer prevention or intervention programs to assist juveniles in decision-making, resisting gangs, and/or employment training.

The same or similar actions were noted in the assessment of the FMPD by the Freeh Group. The FMPD, much like WPD, denied the existence of gangs in the community, yet all of the evidence was present. If asked, both chiefs and the administrators would look confused and respond: "We don't have a gang problem." The officers would acknowledge that there was a problem, noting the unchecked violence on the streets. FMPD's style of policing was aggressive, and officers found value in numbers, and FMPD touted statistics as an effective measure of crime fighting.

In an annual report, FMPD offered an expansive list of programs, all designed to give an appearance of a positive working relationship with the Black community, ongoing community partnerships, and credited solving a number of homicides to old-fashioned police work. Even worse is the crime fighting model of policing that FMPD employed, far from collaborative, and furthering a deep divide between the community and FMPD. Finally, for several years FMPD advertised that it was an accredited law enforcement agency receiving accreditation from CALEA, the national accrediting body discussed earlier, and the Commission of Florida Law Enforcement Accreditation. Dulaney (2017) noted that FMPD misled accreditation assessors, had no strategy for fighting violent crime, had allegations of corruption, and had rampant discrimination within the department and in the community, yet FMPD was still able to receive accreditation.

Historically, if you examine law enforcement as a whole, the only time that change occurs is if an organization has been forced to do so. As discussed in Chapter 2, the public lost its guardian when the Department of Justice opted out of consent decrees and Attorney General Jeff Sessions outlined a new direction for the Justice Department. In essence, the Department of Justice would no longer provide oversight and intervene on the public's behalf when police violate a citizen's civil rights or when citizens are denied due process. Attorney General Sessions closed his memo with the following statement:

> The Deputy Attorney General and the Associate Attorney General are hereby directed to immediately review all Department activities including collaborative investigations and prosecutions, grant making, technical assistance and training, compliance reviews, existing or contemplated consent decrees, and task force participation in order to ensure that they fully and effectively promote the principles outlined above. Nothing in this Memorandum, however, should be construed to delay or impede any pending criminal or national security investigation or program. (J. B. Sessions, personal communication, March 31, 2017)

If the culture of policing never changes, then the organization will never change. The research shows that police need to change their mentality from crime fighters to guardians. I will argue that police without oversight or threat of intervention from a higher power policing is dangerous. It allows officers to act with impunity. The mission statement of the Department of Justice states: "to ensure fair and impartial administration of justice for all Americans." By leaving local law enforcement agencies and local governments to their own devices, the fundamental protections granted by the U.S. Constitution have been abandoned by the very agency whose purpose is to protect the rights of Americans.

For any of this to be done correctly—agencies rebranding themselves and developing an identity that is designed to be inclusive—there needs to be a willingness to change the culture and a willingness to stay the course. The style of policing that local law enforcement implements must be one that has a solid track record, with definitions that cannot be bastardized, and it must incorporate the six pillar– of 21st-century policing, because the 21st-century policing report draws from years of research, and there is data to support the outcomes.

Finally, the concept of collaboration has always been discussed in the context of police community relations. However, it should and must go a step further and include the courts, business/industry, schools, police, and community. The public and politicians need to recognize that law enforcement has limited resources, is stretched to the limit, is driven by crises, and can only do so much. There's no doubt that law enforcement needs to rebrand its image and change its culture; the questions that the profession must answer are: How does American policing want to be defined? And considering the current climate, what must law enforcement do to gain the trust of the communities that it serves?

REFERENCES

Baker, S. A. (1995). *Effects of law enforcement accreditation: Officer selection, promotion, and education*. Westport, CT: Praeger Publications.

Commission on Accreditation for Law Enforcement Agencies. (2018). *The commission: CALEA's goals*. Retri eved from http://www.calea.org/content/commission.

Cummings, T. G., & Worley, C. G. (1993). *Organizational development and change*, 5th ed. New York, NY: West Publishing.

Dulaney, C. (2016, November 28). Analysis: Fort Myers violence task force crackdown fell short. *News-Press*. Retrieved March 1, 2018, from https://www.news-press.com/story/news/2016/11/28/news-press-analysis-fort-myers-violence-task-force-crackdown-fell-short/91941960/.

Dulaney, C. (2017, August 10). Ft. Myers police kept accreditation despite misleading reports. *News-Press*. Retrieved March 1, 2018, from https://www.news-press.com/story/news/2017/08/10/fort-myers-police-kept-accreditation-despite-misleading-annual-reports/474371001/.

Eterno, J. A., & Silverman, E. B. (2012). *The crime numbers game: Management by manipulation*. Boca Raton, FL: CRC Press.

Farmer, D. J. (1984). *Crime control: The use and misuse of police resources*. New York, NY: Plenum Press.

Freeh Group. (2017). *Fort Myers Police Department: Needs assessment*. Wilmington, DE: Author.

Gillath, O., Karantzas, G. C., & Fraley, R. C. (2016). *Adult attachment: A concise introduction to theory and research*. San Diego, CA: Elsevier Publishing.

Goestsch, D. L., & Davis, S. B. (2016). *Quality management for organizational excellence: Introduction to total quality*. Hoboken, NJ: Pearson Education.

Jones, A. (2014, December 9). Murder town USA (aka Wilmington, Delaware). *Newsweek*. Retrieved March 3, 2018, from https://www.delawareonline.com/story/news/crime/2014/12/09/newsweek-magazine-wilmington-murder-town-usa/20141081/.

Kelley, D. N., & McCarthy, S. L. (2013). *The report of the crime reporting review committee to Commissioner Raymond W. Kelly concerning COMPSTAT auditing*. New York, NY: New York City Police Department.

Kerner Commission. (1968). *Report of the National Advisory Commission on Civil Disorders: Summary of report*. Washington, DC: Author.

Kultgen, J. (1988). *Ethics and professionalism*. Philadelphia: University of Pennsylvania Press.

Makary, M. A., & Daniel, M. (2016). Medical error: The third leading cause of death in the US. *British Medical Journal, 353*, i2139–2143.

McAllister, B. (1987, March 17). Spurred by dramatic rise in lawsuits, police agencies warm to accreditation. *Washington Post*, p. A7.

Medeiros, K. H. (1987). Accreditation: Expectations met. *Police Chief, 54*, 14.

National Committee for Quality Assurance. (n.d.). *The essential guide to health care quality*. Washington, DC: Author.

Office of Community Oriented Policing Services. (2015). *The President's Task Force on 21st century policing implementation guide: Moving from recommendations to action*. Washington, DC: Author.

Peters, T. (1987). *Thriving on chaos: Handbook for management revolution*. New York, NY: HarperCollins Publishing.

Police Foundation. (2015). *A report of community input on public safety strategies in the city of Wilmington*. Washington, DC: Author.

Pyzdek, T., & Keller, P. (2014). *The sigma six handbook*, 4th ed. Columbus, OH: McGraw Hill Publishers.

U.S. Army. (2014). *Product assurance: Army quality program*. Washington, DC: Author.

U.S. Congress. (1995). *Violent Crime Control and Law Enforcement Act 1994, Title I: Public safety and policing*. Washington, DC: Author.

Yochelson, S., & Samenow, S. (1976). *The criminal personality: A profile of change*. Northvale, NJ: Jason Aronson, Inc.

8

The Future and
Recommendations for Change

Every chapter of this book is an exploration of American law enforcement and its failure to adapt to change. This failure illustrates that policing as an institution that is in conflict with the people that it serves. As noted, there have been numerous attempts to force change at a national level from the Kerner Commission, 1967; the establishment of the Law Enforcement Assistance Administration, 1968; President Bill Clinton's signing of the Violent Crime Control and Law Enforcement Act, 1994; and, finally, President Obama's 21st-Century Policing Task Force, 2015, but none seem to have a lasting impact or the ability to facilitate change. As stated in previous chapters, change in law enforcement is usually slow, very painful, and usually due to the death of an officer(s). Farmer (1984) made it clear: "A tragedy of policing, despite gains realized in recent years, is the proclivity to circle the wagons against change" (p. 8).

After dedicating 20 years of my life on the front lines of policing—being a street officer, working for five different agencies, and training thousands of officers in every subject matter imaginable—I have always wondered why the profession has been so slow to accept change. Why has the profession circled its wagons and fought against change? I remember teaching my first class of veteran officers, and one sergeant asked: "Why can't things stay the same? Why can't we concentrate on just our city, our community? The rest of the world doesn't matter." Yet officers were dying all over the country, and my agency was stuck in the 19th century when it came to policing, training, and the psychological skills necessary to survive an encounter.

In each attempt to force change in policing through a national initiative, if not directly stated, the underlying goal was an attempt to change the culture of policing, to force the institution of policing to acknowledge the community and form partnerships. There is an old adage in policing: "WE BE." Translated, that means: "We will be here when the new Chief arrives and we will be here when the Chief leaves." The job of executive leadership is both difficult and demanding. The average tenure of a metropolitan police chief fell from 5.5 years to between 3.5 years and 4.5 years (Peak & Glesnor, 2002; Rainguet & Dodge, 2001). This chapter provides the reader with insight into the impediments of cultural change in policing, an example of missed opportunities, police community partnerships, and their limitations. The reader also has an opportunity to examine comprehensive programs, which are interrelated, are resources for intervention and prevention, and can be sustained with the understanding that police resources are limited due to budgetary constraints, personnel, and impending crises.

RESISTANCE TO CHANGE

I have acted in the capacity of consultant to one law enforcement agency in the southeastern United States since 2008. The agency has had two police chiefs since that time, and both have provided me with unfettered access to the department. In 2008 the first chief contacted me after six months in office, stating: "This agency needs to move from the dark ages to the 21st century."

Inherited Problems

This organization had always promoted the chief from within and, as a result, the culture of the agency was stagnant and remained unchanged for years. To outsiders and city fathers, it appeared the organization had been managed properly and was successfully meeting its objectives and promoting its value system. The agency did not collaborate with other agencies and had practiced a self-imposed form of isolationism. After an in-depth examination, here is what was discovered behind the smoke and mirrors:

- The agency had a poor communication system, which was not compatible with adjoining jurisdictions. Not only was the communication system incompatible, but it provided poor or no radio reception at one end of the city because of antenna placement. In addition, the laptops had no Internet capability, and officers could not communicate with dispatch via their laptops.

- The department participates in a Take Home Car Plan and had a fleet of 30 vehicles. Most of the patrol vehicles had driven more than 100,000 miles driven and were in constant need of repair. There had been funding in the police department budget each of the previous five years for the purchase of two new vehicles. However, money was returned to the general fund as unspent capital.

- The agency's firearms were 15 years old, and some were inoperable. Some officers have been forced to purchase weapons for duty use.

- The agency policies were outdated and need to be rewritten.

- Officers and investigators were not allowed to go to training unless it was radar certification, breath test operator's course, or a Taser instructor's course. There were investigators who had never attended an investigator's course, field training officers (FTO) who had never been to FTO training, and supervisors who had never been to a first-line supervisor's course. If training was conducted, it was to meet state standards, and the trainer was brought to the organization. The agency maintained an annual training budget of $15,000, not to mention second dollar funding received from the state. In fact, training monies were returned to the city's general fund and the state as unused each year.

- All intermediate weapons (batons and pepper spray) were taken away from the officers except the Taser. The philosophy was the Taser was to replace all intermediate weapons. The agency's use-of-force options are empty hand control, Taser, and lethal force.

- The two midnight sergeants who were assigned to night shift did not work an entire shift with their assigned squads. Patrol shifts were 12-hour shifts, which ran from 7 A.M. to 7 P.M. and 7 P.M. to 7 A.M. The two night-shift supervisors began their shift at 2 P.M. and ended at 2 A.M., leaving no supervisory coverage between the 2 A.M. and 7 A.M.

- During approved overtime details, officers were paid cash. Their earnings were never channeled through the city finance office, and officers did not pay taxes or Social Security on the income they earned.

- During Christmas for the past 20 years, a local wrecker company took orders for alcohol and gave each employee a fifth of liquor. A sergeant would go to each employee and take their order. Orders were taken for everyone in the department, including the retired chief and his deputy chief.

- The agency had a history of hiring officers who had been terminated by other agencies for some form of misconduct. These officers had to meet one requirement, that they had not been stripped of their standards by the Police Officer Standards and Training supervisory body. The hiring of these officers was ordered by the manager.

- It was common knowledge to everyone except the new chief that one veteran officer was addicted to amphetamines and came to work impaired daily. The officer's addiction was discovered after being involved in a car accident. Policy dictated a drug test post-accident. An internal investigation uncovered who had knowledge of the officer's amphetamine problem.

- The agency was not in tune with the Black community. In fact, the only time the officers were seen in the Black community was when they responded to calls for service. The officers were not noted for being active when it comes to drug activity, proactive policing, or problem-solving. The officers spent most, if not all, of their time making traffic stops and writing citations.

Missed Opportunities: Community/Business Surveys and Training

To obtain a better understanding of police community relationships, the new chief developed two surveys, one for community members and one for businesses. The surveys were designed as a tool for the officers to break the ice and get to know the community and business members. The chief envisioned this as the first step in establishing community policing.

Each patrol officer was asked to interview 10 residents in one of 13 subdivisions. This was not put out as an order to the officers, but the officers were asked to participate, in a letter written by the chief (see Appendix A). The surveys were limited to 10 questions and designed to break the ice with introductions. Excluding the supervisors, there were 15 officers, and 15 officers × 10 surveys each = 150 surveys. The officers completed 60 surveys. The supervisors were to oversee this task and report to the chief weekly; this did not happen.

The patrol supervisors were tasked with contacting local business owners and setting up meetings with industry leaders to complete surveys specifically designed for business and industry. There were three supervisors, and 3 supervisors × 10 surveys each = 30 surveys. One supervisor completed 20 surveys of the local businesses. However, not one survey was completed of the city's 30 multimillion-dollar industrial partners.

The lack of participation sent a clear message to the new chief that few, if any, members were interested in changing the culture of the organization. The officers were satisfied with the status quo and saw no need for change. Ultimately, less than 50 percent of the officers and one supervisor participated in this survey event. Missed was a golden opportunity for the agency to begin forging partnerships with the community and industry partners, who are vital to the city's tax base. During his tenure, the chief promoted and fired a deputy chief; fired two patrol officers, a sergeant, and a detective;

and replaced them with new officers. Prior to his retirement in 2015, the old culture had negatively impacted and continues to negatively impact the new hires, dragging them down.

In 2017, the city manager was concerned about the Black Lives Matter movement and the shooting of unarmed Black men and the protests that followed; and she wanted to make sure if the agency did not have a relationship with the Black community, they would receive the training and begin to make inroads. In aiming to avert a catastrophe, the city manager stated: "I don't want this to happen in our city." The agency contracted the services of Police Counseling Services, LLC, to develop and present a program. The program was titled Professionalism in Policing. The focus of the program was to provide a training forum for officers, which allowed them to explore such topics as race, ethics, police decision-making, understanding the law enforcement role in the 21st century, and how these issues impact police relationships with their respective communities.

The topics have been hot-button issues for the past 50 years. The goal of the series was to challenge widespread beliefs and to remind officers of their role in society as well as their respective communities. The training series was interactive, consisting of lecture, group assignments, class discussions, and relevant video.

Consequences

The city had experienced one homicide and two shootings from January 1, 2005, through December 31, 2017. However, in January 2018 the city experienced its first homicide in more than 12 years. A day later, five people were shot, three adults and two children ages two and three. The police department determined that the homicide was gang related and the gangs were fighting over drug territory. The second shooting was retaliation for the homicide committed the day prior. The police department and local churches held a community meeting, asking the Black community for help in locating the suspects, two juveniles wanted for murder. The Black community closed ranks and offered no assistance. In fact, both suspects were hiding in the community. One 15-year-old Black male has been arrested and the second 15-year-old has an active murder warrant but is still not in custody. The police department openly admits that there is a gang problem. However, the agency has no ties to the Black community, and the Black community refuses to share information with police. Even with a reward, no one has come forward.

Clueless Yet Entitled: How Can We Combat Crime and Meet Community Needs?

The agency received its final installment of training April 5, 2018. The subject matter was *21st-century policing*. In one of the group exercises, they were asked a series of thought-provoking questions designed to identify problems and challenge officers to come up with solutions:

- What are the three top challenges your agency faces today? The responses were consistent: a new report writing system; more personnel; and new equipment, specifically cars. Not one group or officer mentioned the "gang problem" or "shootings."
- Pick a neighborhood in your city and identify the problems. Again, not one officer mentioned or addressed the problem of gangs or any policing issue that the city has today. The officer's responses were about traffic enforcement.
- Name the person(s) other than pastors and churches that you would collaborate with to address the problems in the community. The officers could not identify one person by name; they could only categorize them, such as business leaders and teachers.
- Does your agency use data to assist in identifying problems and design patrol strategies for patrol officers? The answer was "no," yet the data is available to community members and those seeking to move to the city.
- What are the agency's goals and objectives? There were none stated.
- The chief has tried to work in collaboration with the supervisors/officers to no avail. The solution is holding supervisors accountable and, if necessary, demote those in charge.

PSYCHOLOGY OF CULTURAL CHANGE

Twenty-first-century policing is a proposal to change the institution. However, it can be argued that it is nothing new, just the repackaging of old material with some additions. There is a clear understanding by outsiders that the institution needs change, yet police are digging in their heels and resisting change. Lewis (2016) argues that we experience change without resistance as we move through life, and in fact we embrace many of the changes: jobs/promotions, family/children, new cars, hairstyles, and/or clothes (p. 54). Resistance is experienced when change is imposed by one or more parties. Police and police unions will question the validity of any research and findings of any commission by asking: "What does the president and his commission of eggheads know about policing? They have never been in our shoes or spent one day on the street." As one senior sergeant stated when asked about a new administrator: "Different clown, same circus" (D. Parker, personal communication, n.d.).

With an agency being subject to administrative change on average every five years, there are several constants: policing is policing, crime doesn't stop, and the agency will still be there long after this new chief has come and gone. What this means to a new chief is he or she will inherit the old command staff, an organizational culture that is deeply entrenched with an old set of values, which makes the concept of change very difficult. Alvesson (2002) notes organizational culture should not always be seen as something that has consensus and harmony, but it should be viewed as dynamic in terms of contradiction, hidden agendas, and conflict (p. 121). Schein (2017) argues we cannot see the forces that cause certain types of organizational behaviors and offers three different types of cultures that are inherent in every organization:

a. *Artifacts* are the leftovers that a new chief inherits. In the case of policing, it is personnel, operational procedures, policies, structure, behavior, and attitudes. The new chief has the difficult task of sorting through the malaise in an attempt to change the culture of the organization. In addition to the organization, the chief must address the demands of the city/county officials, the union, and the community, each with different demands (pp. 25–26).

b. *Espoused beliefs and values* are strategies, goals, shared perceptions, norms, and beliefs that have been instilled by the leaders. In response to officer misconduct and/or officer apathy, a new chief may determine that the problem lies in the new employee selection process and the standards need to be more stringent standards, or the issue may be associated with supervision or the lack thereof. The answer for many of the problems can be found in the history and past practices of an organization. Oftentimes history is dismissed for a quick fix, to show the public and governmental officials that the new chief is in charge and making changes.

c. *Assumptions* that one brings to the table are usually associated with past experiences and are often relied on to provide solutions to problems. The problem with such assumptions is they are not based on research and fact-finding and may or may not work (p. 30).

Within one police organization there are multiple organizational cultures, which are defined by rank, specialization, even division/bureau, and each of these will have an impact on an officer's performance because they define norms for individual organizational performance, as well as operational norms and standards. Organizational culture affects how people think and feel, but more important, it defines identification, loyalty, commitment, and the concepts of value and self-worth within an organization (Cameron & Quinn, 2011; Druckman, Singer, & Van Cott, 1997; Schein, 2017). Harigopal

(2006) argues change creates stress and challenges the organizational value system as well as its effectiveness (p. 274). The success or failure of an organization hinges on management and employees having their needs met or at least finding a healthy compromise (Gilley, Quatro, Hoekstra, Whittle, & Maycunich, 2001; Kurke, 1995). Kurke (1995) outlines the needs of both the management and employees:

- Management's needs include operations, administrative, performance, costs containment, political pressures, and interagency cooperation.
- On the other hand, employees' needs include self-esteem, personal performance record, compensations, job security, opportunities for advancement, personal time/family, and the intangible benefit of membership in a police organization (p. 395).

In the assessment of the Wilmington, Delaware, Police Department (WPD) and in interviewing several officers from the Ft. Myers Police Department (FMPD) there was one common thread, the culture of the agency had changed. Some have described the culture change as an agency losing its way. In the case of WPD, outsiders and senior officers advised that there had been a new chief approximately 10–12 years prior to the 2015 assessment. The retirees, senior officers, and community members as well as the Attorney General's Office all advised that for some unknown reason the chief lost the respect of the officers and the officers disconnected. Thus, the quality of the work product as well as the department's interaction with the community eroded.

In the case of the FMPD during the mortgage crisis that began in 2001 and stopped in 2008, the city of Ft. Myers was financially devastated. The city of Ft. Myers was ranked fourth of the top 25 cities that had been adversely impacted by this financial crisis (Foreclosure-Response, 2014). In response to this financial hardship in 2008 the Ft. Myers city fathers offered an early retirement incentive for 42 officers. This buyout reduced the number of sworn officers from 215 to 173, and at its lowest point the number of sworn personnel in 2014 was 168 officers (Thomas, Staab, & Baer, 2015). The buyout left FMPD with young inexperienced officers and supervisors. FMPD became a breeding ground for a number of problems which were outlined in the Freeh Assessment, which highlighted acts of corruption, officer apathy, disconnect from the community, and poor police work.

SOCIAL WORK MENTALITY

Many officers argue that their job has nothing to do with the community and when asked to participate in anything other than responding to calls, preventative patrol, and making arrests, it changes the job from police officer to social worker. When describing a social work mentality, officers have offered this stereotype: a do-gooder; a caring liberal who is concerned for their fellow human being; and who does not believe in jail; social workers are associated with advocacy for the poor, mentally ill, and disenfranchised. The stereotype that police have of social workers and social work is not far from the actual description provided by Berg-Weger. Berg-Weger (2016) posit that social work is different from all of the other helping professions, yet it is eerily similar to the police stereotype:

> Social workers consider their clients' social environments—their families, homes, places of work, states of physical and mental health, and communities and their clients' interaction within those environments. In addition, social works emphasis is on advocacy, social justice, and stresses influencing policy makers to address human conditions homelessness, hunger, teen pregnancy, poverty, health and economic disparities, and discrimination. (p. 5)

The same clientele that social workers have sworn to assist and support are the population that law enforcement interacts with on a daily basis. As I reflect on the populations, both professions serve one of the most common questions asked of entry-level police recruits: Why do you want to be a police officer? The most common response to this question is: "Because I want to help people." What happens to the new police candidate who enters the profession with a desire to help people? Why have the new officer candidates abandoned their initial objective?

BUILDING BLOCKS FOR SUCCESS—TRUST AND COMMUNICATION

Officers have argued and will argue that the most significant obstacle to organizational change within a law enforcement agency are the organizational stressors, more specifically the lack of trust officers have in police administrators. Collins and Gibbs (2003) support this argument and note occupational stressors associated with policing were more closely associated with organizational stressors than with daily operational stressors (p. 265). Some of the organizational stressors in policing have been identified as poor policies and practices of the department, excessive paperwork, a lack of communication, organizational structure—a strict chain of command, lack of control over workload, agency politics, nonparticipation in decision-making, inadequate support, and lack of consultation (Bartol & Bartol, 2015; Brown & Campbell, 1994; Coman & Evans, 1991; Golembiewski & Kim, 1991; Reiser, 1974; Zhao, He, & Lovrich, 2002).

"Trust" is an interesting word because officers are truly paranoid of administrators and the administrators' intentions. To overcome the organizational barriers, it is important to establish an open line of communication. If a chief wants to effect change, it is incumbent of the chief to create a vehicle of open communication where ideas are shared at all levels of the organization. Collinson and Cook (2007) argue that leaders must overcome their own assumptions and present their subordinates with open meaningful forums for dialogue and an exchange of ideas. In fact, Collinson and Cook note that in order for an organization to renew itself, it must articulate its values through discussion, argument, and joint decision-making (p. 201).

Reale (2005) posits in order for change to be meaningful and effective, it must involve stakeholders, a guidance team(s), or committee(s) (p. 147). The stakeholders should come from every discipline within an organization; in policing it depends on the size of the organization, with each division having its own guidance team or representatives. The key to breaking down the barriers is the chief's interaction with the representatives/team members to establish trust and foster an open line of communication between all personnel and the chief. In some organizations this committee is ongoing and is known as the Chief's Council, which meets monthly and only with the chief. Some Chief's Council meet without supervision being present, as this provides a certain freedom without fear of retribution.

Researchers argue that before an agency can change that, there must be an assessment to determine if the agency is ready for change (Cohen, 2005). A readiness assessment should include an assessment of the following areas: the external environment, mission, policies and procedures, culture, structure, practices, leadership, and climate (Hitchcok & Willard, 2008; Proehl, 2001; Russell & Russell, 2006).

NOT A POLICE PROBLEM ALONE

The problem of drugs, gangs, and violence in the Black community is not a police problem alone. There is no doubt that police must intervene in the process and make arrests to have an impact on drugs and violence, but this cannot be accomplished without a comprehensive strategy. Parts of the comprehensive plan can be implemented immediately. Other components of the plan will take time: buy-in and the recruitment and investment from a number of community partners and institutions. A successful plan must include collaborative partnerships that are comprehensive:

- *Legal*—police, law enforcement task forces that incorporate local, state, and federal agencies; state/federal prosecutors, judges, parole/probation, and juvenile justice.

1. Local police—The efforts should begin with identifying the problems through crime analysis and data and develop a strategic plan to address the problems. Train officers in what to look for, criminal case development and management, and interaction with the community. Require that officers get out of the patrol car to talk with citizens and in the same vein encourage the officers to address problems and make arrests.

2. Initiate a task force—The goal is to focus on violent street crime: homicides, shooting, illegal firearms, and drugs. The task force should include local, state, and federal officers with the goal of investigating existing or new acts of violence tying them to gang activity and charging the gang members federally under the Racketeer Influenced and Corrupt Organizations Act (RICO). RICO is the same legal tool that has been used to break the back of the Mafia and gangs. The maximum penalties for racketeering includes fines of up to $25,000 and a maximum of 20 years in federal prison. In addition, RICO requires the forfeiture of all business interests and gains gleaned from the criminal activity (U.S. Congress, 1971).

3. The courts including state/federal prosecutors, judges, and probation/parole. The prosecutors must sign on and be willing to take chances on good cases that are circumstantial. The judges must be willing to give defendants high bonds when a defendant is identified as one of the targets in the violence and gang investigations as long as the judge finds that the arrests meet the standard of probable cause, in other words quality arrests. Parole/probation must be willing to work with law enforcement and be willing to violate those parolees/probationers who are found in violation of the terms and conditions of their parole/probation: failing urine or breath tests; in violation of curfew; and searching their houses for weapons or illegal narcotics.

4. Juvenile justice—Work with the local juvenile justice system to obtain gang intelligence. Usually gang activity and alliances begin in juvenile justice lockup and change from time to time. The gang members can easily be identified through tattoos and gang signs. All of this intelligence information is essential in combating gang violence and drugs in the community.

The legal component is very aggressive; it is one where the initiating agency must do its homework by identifying the suspects and the problems, developing strategies to combat the problem, training everyone so that the criminal cases can be developed, and recruiting the necessary partners to have an impact. This is not some random act enforcement; it should be done with precision to avoid the complaints that law enforcement is indiscriminate in its actions, harassing everyone from a neighborhood or a particular ethnic group. By targeting the individuals who are creating the problem, it prevents the good citizens who are caught in the crossfire from becoming collateral damage and antipolice.

- *School board* should adopt educational programs that assist children in making good decisions. These programs should begin in elementary school and continue through high school. These programs should be taught by teachers and integrated into the curriculum. In the past police have participated in the Drug Abuse Resistance Education (DARE) program and the Gang Resistance Education and Training Program (GREAT) program; both of these programs are excellent. However, DARE and GREAT are designed to be taught by law enforcement, which has limited resources, and there may be a time that an agency has to abandon the program because of a crisis. If a program or curriculum is designed to be taught by teachers and law enforcement officers are used to supplement the program from time to time, it minimizes the likelihood that there will an interruption of services due to a law enforcement.

  There are a number of excellent programs available to educators and should be selected by a committee, which should include representatives from school administrators, teachers, students, parents, law enforcement, and juvenile justice. Each representative has direct knowledge and offers a unique perspective of the decision-making challenges and negative influences that children in their respective community face on a daily basis.

- *Community violence prevention/reduction programs* such as Operation CeaseFire and Cure Violence: Both programs are very similar and designed to stop and/or intervene in gang violence and homicides using a public health model.

  1. Both models incorporate various tools to target this violence: Community mobilization; public education campaign; services offered, such as GED programs, anger-management counseling, and drug or alcohol treatment; and help find child care or look for a job that can improve the lives of at-risk youth, including gang members. The key component of both programs is the use of violence interrupters.

  2. Violence interrupters establish a rapport with gang leaders and other at-risk youth. Interrupters work alone or in pairs acting as mediators in gang conflicts. After a shooting, violence interrupters attempt to intervene by meeting with gang leaders and offer nonviolent alternatives to retaliatory violence. Violence interrupters are usually former gang members who have served time in prison, which gives them greater credibility among current gang members.

  3. Both models mobilize the community to change the accepted norms associated with violence by enlisting faith leaders, businesses, and community members/groups to advocate for change (Cure Violence, 2018; Ritter, 2009).

- *Business/industry*—Many cities have business and industry partners where the city fathers offer tax refunds, capital investment tax credit, and workforce training incentives. City fathers need to expand the partnership to include the training of future: IT and software developers, bank managers, researchers, engineers, and so on. These are excellent opportunities for those classified as at-risk youth. The positions could be offered as summer employment and, if successful, can be offered as after-school employment. Such programs are investments in the future and can act as an intervention/prevention program. There is an old adage in long-range shooting in regard to equipment which applies here: "Buy once cry once"; it has been modified to address the community: "Invest once or cry a lifetime."

CONCLUSION

When thinking of police involvement in anything, it must be addressed in a multidimensional format. Police do not have all the tools, nor are they the answer, for every social problem. Police have to be willing to open their doors and embrace partnerships. Police have to be willing to accept that they are human and will make mistakes and that their behavior should be scrutinized when it comes to excessive force and deadly force. The dialogue has to be open and honest. The community demands information, and law enforcement should be willing to offer the information.

Have you ever wondered why some cities have riots/marches while other communities don't when police are involved in a bad shooting? The key is being honest with the community, being up front, and establishing a rapport, so when mistakes are made, or police are involved in misconduct, the community is willing to allow the agency(s) to complete an investigation and trust the outcome. This takes work, up-front meeting with people, listening to what the community has to say, and being responsive to their concerns. Many officers view law enforcement administrators who are involved in such behavior as sellouts and not supportive of the officers. Some agencies do this well, and others have closed the door and refuse to acknowledge the community.

The one group that I know police officials refuse to have discussions with are gang members. If law enforcement never sits at the table with gang members in an attempt to understand their anger, fear, and frustration, then that door will always be closed and that portion of the community will remain disenfranchised. Gang members and police have one thing in common—neither likes or trusts the other. Khubchandani and Price (2018) note that poor performance in school is a predictor if an adolescent will be involved in gang activity, perpetrate acts of violence, and/or carry a weapon of violence. On the other hand, if a youth is an A/B student, actively involved in sports, and engages in sound life decisions, research indicates that the student will not be involved in gang activity, perpetrate acts of violence, and/or carry a weapon. Ultimately, lifestyle and environment (parental support) play a major role in the choices of juveniles.

REFERENCES

Alvesson, M. (2002). *Understanding organizational culture.* Thousand Oaks, CA: Sage Publications.

Bartol, C. R., & Bartol, A. M. (2015). *Introduction to forensic psychology: Research and application,* 4th ed. Thousand Oaks, CA: Sage Publications.

Berg-Weger. (2016). *Social work and social welfare: An invitation,* 4th ed. New York, NY: Routledge Publishing.

Brown, J. M., & Campbell, E. A. (1994). *Stress and policing: Sources and strategies.* New York, NY: John Wiley.

Cameron, K. S., & Quinn, R. E. (2011). *Diagnosing and changing organizational culture,* 3rd ed. San Francisco, CA: Jossey-Bass.

Cohen, D. S. (2005). *The heart of change field guide.* Boston, MA: Harvard Business School Publishing.

Collins, P. A., & Gibbs, A.C.C. (2003). Stress in police officers: A study of the origins, prevalence and severity of stress-related symptoms within a county police force. *Occupational Medicine, 53*(4), 256–264.

Collinson, V., & Cook, T. F. (2007). *Organizational learning: Improving teaching, learning, and leading in school systems.* Thousand Oaks, CA: Sage Publications.

Coman, G., & Evans, B. (1991). Stressors facing Australian police in the 1990s. *Police Studies, 14,* 153–165.

Cure Violence. (2018). *Cure Violence: The model.* Retrieved from http://cureviolence.org/the-model/.

Druckman, D. Singer, J. E.& Van Cott, H. P. (1997). *Enhancing organizational performance.* Washington, DC: National Academy of Science.

Farmer, D. J. (1984). *Crime control: The use and misuse of police resources.* New York, NY: Plenum Press.

Foreclosure-Response. (2014). *Resources for preventing foreclosures and stabilizing communities.* Retrieved March 30, 2018, from http://www.foreclosurereponse.org/index.html.

Gilley, J. W., Quatro, S. A., Hoekstra, E., Whittle, D. D., & Maycunich, A. (2001). *The manager as change agent: A practical guide to developing high performance people and organizations.* Jackson, TN: Perseus Publishing.

Golembiewski, R. T., & Kim, B. S. (1991). Burnout in police work: Stressors, strain, and the phase model. *Police Studies, 14,* 74–80.

Harigopal, K. (2006). *Management of organizational change: Leveraging transformation,* 2nd ed. Thousand Oaks, CA: Sage Publications.

Hitchcok, D., & Willard, M. (2008). *The step by step guide to sustainability planning: How to create and implement sustainability in any business or organization.* Sterling, VA: Earthscan.

Khubchandani, J., & Price, J. H. (2018). Violent behaviors, weapon carrying, and firearm homicide trends in African American adolescents, 2001–2015. *Journal of Community Health*. Retrieved April 10, 2018, from https://link.springer.com/article/10.1007/s10900-018-0510-4.

Kurke, M. I. (1995). Organizational management of stress and human reliability. In M. I. Kurke & E. M. Scrivner (Eds.), *Police psychology into the 21st century*, pp. 391–416. Hillsdale, NJ: Lawrence Erlbaum Associates.

Lewis, S. (2016). *Positive psychology and change: How leadership, collaboration, and appreciative inquiry create transformational results*. Malden, MA: John Wiley & Sons Publishers.

Peak, K. J., & Glensor, R. W. (2002). *Community policing and problem solving: Strategies and practices*, 3rd ed. Upper Saddle River, NJ: Prentice Hall.

Proehl, R. A. (2001). *Organizational change in the human services*. Thousand Oaks, CA: Sage Publications.

Rainguet, F. W., & Dodge, M. (2001). The problems of police chiefs: An examination of the issues in tenure and turnover. *Police Quarterly, 4*(3), 268–288.

Reale, R. C. (2005). *Making change stick: Twelve principles of transforming organizations*. Park Ridge, NJ: Positive Impact Associates.

Reiser, M. (1974). Some organizational stress on policemen. *Journal of Police Science and Administration, 2*, 156–159.

Ritter, N. (2009). *CeaseFire: A public health approach to reduce shootings and killings*. Retrieved from https://www.nij.gov/journals/264/Pages/ceasefire.aspx.

Russell, J., & Russell, L. (2006). *Change basics*. Alexandra, VA: American Society for Training and Development.

Schein, E. H. (2017). *Organizational culture and leadership*, 5th ed. San Francisco, CA: Jossey-Bass.

Thomas, D. J., Staab, B., & Baer, E. (2015). *Ft. Myers police department personnel study 2015*. Ft. Myers: Florida Gulf Coast University.

U.S. Congress. (1971). Racketeer Influenced and Corrupt Organizations Act, 18, U.S.C., Chapter 96. Washington, DC: Author.

Zhao, J. S., He, N., & Lovrich, N. (2002). Predicting five dimensions of police officer stress: Looking more deeply into organizational settings for sources of police stress. *Police Quarterly, 5*, 43–62.

9

Closing Commentary: Stop Shouting, Start Listening

On Wednesday, April 20, 2018, at 3 P.M., two Gilchrist County deputies, Sergeant Noel Ramírez and Deputy Taylor Lindsey, were assassinated while they sat in a restaurant to have lunch. Gilchrist is a small rural county located in North Central Florida, roughly 30 miles west of Gainesville, Florida.

The assassination of these two deputies hit close to home and breaks my heart. I have met their leader, Sheriff Robert Schultz, an outstanding sheriff. I listened intently to his message to the community and the country memorializing Sergeant Ramírez and Deputy Lindsey as heroes and describing the cowardly act that took their lives. Sheriff Schultz also asked the question: What did you think would happen when a group is constantly demonized in the media?

However, in that same newscast I watched about these two officers killed, the next story was about two Black men being arrested for trespass as they sat in a Starbucks waiting for a meeting. Before you go any further, I want to be clear that by no means am I equating the assassination of Sergeant Ramírez and Deputy Lindsey with the arrest of two innocent Black men.

I am asking readers to think about the rhetoric and agendas on both sides.

The Black community wants to be treated fairly, and police want to be respected and supported. Both sides are lost behind their words, and neither is listening to the other. As a retired police officer, I cry every time I read or see the news reporting that an officer was killed in the line of duty. As a 62-year-old Black man, I cry every time an unarmed Black man is killed under the color of law.

Therefore, I will ask the question: When will both sides be willing to place their agendas aside, come to the table, and create lasting, meaningful solutions to problems that have plagued police/community relations since slavery?

Appendix

Chief's Letter to Agency Officers Regarding Surveys

In Chapter 8, there is a discussion regarding a new chief who was aiming to implement community policing, and his officers collectively participated in a form of passive aggressiveness by refusing to assist the chief as requested in information gathering. The chief asked the officers to meet with community and business members and complete surveys. The following is the letter that the chief sent to his officers asking for their cooperation. Copies of the residential and business surveys follow the letter. The chief envisioned that the surveys would be the first step in establishing a dialogue with community members and business leaders. This was supposed to be the first step in instituting community policing but became a missed opportunity.

Dear Colleagues:

As you know I have a strong sense of community. A few weeks ago, I asked the supervisors in a staff meeting what the mission of the department was in relationship to the community. The only answer I would not accept was "Protect and Serve." Ironically, no one knew or had an answer. However, my inquiry was not limited to the supervisors and it seems that no one in the agency knew the answer.

I want each of you to understand that the Police Department is entering a new era, one that I will call professionalism. Not to say that you weren't professional before but the goal is to become more efficient, meet your needs in regards to training and supervision, and meet the needs of the community. Keep in mind that we are only an effective agency as long as the community supports us. Without their support we become an occupying army and everyone loses in the process.

Conducting this survey is the beginning of this new era. There will be three (3) different kinds of surveys: one for the residents, one for businesses, and one for industry. As an agency we need to find out what each of these community members thinks of us and how we can best serve them.

I have developed a new mission statement for the organization and this survey is the beginning of the first segment Partnerships. The term *Partnerships* is all inclusive meaning citizens, business, and industry. When we have successfully completed this task, I will unveil part two (2) our Values and Mission Statement.

Finally, I know that you think knocking on doors and meeting with the public is not your job. As police officers we often forget that our real job is customer service, failing to meet that need often creates a disconnect between us and the community. With that said, I am asking that each of you take this assignment seriously, knock on doors, and be cordial to our partners.

Respectfully,
Chief

POLICE DEPARTMENT
RESIDENTIAL SURVEY

Name of Resident _____ **Address**_____

Phone Number_____

A. Residency: ○ Own ○ Rent ○ Visitor

*B. How long have you lived in the city? ○ 1–5 years ○ 6–10 years

○ 11 yrs

C. Gender: ○ Male ○ Female

D. Ethnicity: ○ Caucasian ○ African American ○ Native American
○ Asian/Pacific Islander ○ Hispanic ○ Other

E. Age: ○ Under 20 ○ 20–24 ○ 25–34 ○ 35–44 ○ 45–54
○ 55–64 ○ 65+

F. Neighborhood affiliation: (Important to help target enforcement efforts)

___ The Hills	___ Merrywood	___ The Oaks
___ The Highlands	___ Turkey Creek	___ Williams Housing
___ Coconut Heights	___ Meadow Glenn	___ 23 Place Apartments
___ The Villas	___ Hillside Apartments	___ Sherman Oaks

*1. What is your opinion of the Police Department?

2. Have you ever had any contact with the police department? If so under what circumstances?

a. Traffic Enforcement

b. Investigation/Complaint

c. Community Event

2a. What was your opinion of the officer's conduct during this encounter?

3. How safe do you feel, for yourself, your family, and your property?

4. Currently, what would you like to see the police concentrate on in your area? Check all that apply

❏ Burglaries ❏ Traffic Violations ❏ Vandalism ❏ Loud Parties

❏ Auto Thefts ❏ Auto Burglaries ❏ Loitering ❏ Satisfied

4a. List any other concerns that you may have:

5. In your neighborhood, check the box that most applies to your level of concern for the following questions.

	Great	Some	None	Experienced in the last two years
a. Your house will be broken into	○	○	○	❏
b. You will be robbed, or stolen from	○	○	○	❏
c. You will be attacked on the street	○	○	○	❏
d. You will be attacked in your house	○	○	○	❏
e. Your car will be damaged or broken into	○	○	○	❏
f. Your car will be stolen	○	○	○	❏
g. You will be sexually attacked	○	○	○	❏

5a. How often do you walk, run, or bike in your neighborhood?

	Frequently	Infrequently	Not at all
5 A.M.–5 P.M.	○	○	○
5 P.M.–12 A.M.	○	○	○
12 A.M.–5 A.M.	○	○	○

6. Personal involvement: (check all that you would do)

❏ Report suspicious activity ❏ Report a crime ❏ Assist as a witness

❏ Assist a person in need of help ❏ Testify against a criminal ❏ Not get involved

7. **How would you like to see us better serve you in your neighborhood? Check all that apply**

   ❑ Cruiser Patrol   ❑ Foot Patrol   ❑ Bicycle Patrol   ❑ Acceptable as is

8. **Importance of existing Services? How important are the following services to you?**

	Very	Slightly	Not at all
Youth Programs	○	○	○
Crime Prevention Programs	○	○	○
Traffic Enforcement	○	○	○
Investigation by Detectives	○	○	○
Dare	○	○	○
After-School Programs	○	○	○
Citizen's Academy	○	○	○

9. **If you had contact with a Police dispatcher during the past year, how would you rate your experience?**

   ○ Excellent   ○ Good   ○ Fair   ○ Poor

10. **Additional comments and suggestions that you feel that will improve the services of the Police Department:**

POLICE DEPARTMENT
BUSINESS/INDUSTRY SURVEY

Business Name: _____

Business Address: _____

Person Interviewed: _____

Business Phone Number: _____

_____

1. What is the nature of your business?

2. Has your business been subject to any crimes or incidents in the last 12 months?

   _____ Yes _____ No

   If yes, what was the nature of the crime:

   _____ Robbery _____ Theft _____ Burglary _____ Criminal Mischief
   _____ Credit Card Fraud _____ Check Scams _____ Arson
   _____ Juvenile Problems _____ Employee Theft

3. Did you report all of these crimes or incidents to the Police?

   _____ Yes _____ No

   If you did not report a crime or incident, why was that?

   _____ No chance of catching criminals
   _____ Not important enough/police have better things to do
   _____ Feared unsympathetic response from the police
   _____ Sorted it out myself
   _____ The item stolen/damaged was not insured or not valuable
   _____ Don't like the police/don't trust the police

_____ Afraid of victimization by offender or their friends

_____ The matter was handled internally

_____ Other

4. How satisfied are you with the level of service that businesses are provided by the police?

___ Very Satisfied

___ Satisfied

___ Dissatisfied

___ Completely dissatisfied

5. What types of security systems do you use for your business/industry?

_____ Alarms   _____ Access Control

_____ Video Surveillance _____ Inventory Control Devices

6. What initiatives or services would you like to see us implement for the business/industry community?

7. From a business/industry perspective, what one issue do you think the police should be focusing on?

8. What type of partnerships would you like to see the police department form with business and industry of this community?

Index

Whyte, William, 164
Wichita Police Department, 138
Wildeman, C., 23, 24
Willard, M., 182
Williams, G. T., 82
Williams, H., 68
Wilmington Delaware Police Department
(WPD), 161–62
Wilmington Police Department (WPD),
161–62, 163, 169, 180
Wilmington Public Safety Strategies
Commission, The, 161–62
Wilson, Darren, 27–28
Wittenbrink, B., 65

Wolf, M., 24
Women in policing and implicit bias, 75–77
Wong, H. Z., 30
Woolworth sit-in, 1963, 4
Worley, C. G., 164, 165
Wright, R., 93
Wright, R. A., 57–58

Yearwood, D. L., 37
Yochelson, S., 168

Zeisel, H. Z., 91
Zhao, J. S., 181
Zimmerman, George, 122–23

About the Author

David J. Thomas, PhD, LMHC, is professor of forensic studies at Florida Gulf Coast University in Ft. Myers, Florida. He is the author of *Understanding Violent Criminals: Insight from the Front Lines of Law Enforcement*; *Police Psychology: A New Specialty and New Challenges for Men and Women in Blue*; and *Professionalism in Policing: An Introduction*. Thomas is senior research fellow with the Police Foundation in Washington, D.C., and is a recognized expert in in the use of force and police practices in the state of Florida and in the Federal Court System. In addition to his academic pursuits, Thomas is the CEO of Police Counseling Services, LLC, where he provides consulting and counseling services to several law enforcement agencies in North Florida.